Turtles in the Terrarium

Young Chicken Turtle, *Deirochelys reticularia*. Photo by M. Smith.

**Second, revised and expanded edition
Gerhard Mueller
Translator: William Charlton**

TFH

© **by T.F.H. Publications, Inc.**

Distributed in the UNITED STATES to the Pet Trade by T.F.H. Publications, Inc., One T.F.H. Plaza, Neptune City, NJ 07753; on the Internet at www.tfh.com; in CANADA Rolf C. Hagen Inc., 3225 Sartelon St. Laurent-Montreal Quebec H4R 1E8; Pet Trade by H & L Pet Supplies Inc., 27 Kingston Crescent, Kitchener, Ontario N2B 2T6; in ENGLAND by T.F.H. Publications, PO Box 15, Waterlooville PO7 6BQ; in AUSTRALIA AND THE SOUTH PACIFIC by T.F.H. (Australia), Pty. Ltd., Box 149, Brookvale 2100 N.S.W., Australia; in NEW ZEALAND by Brooklands Aquarium Ltd. 5 McGiven Drive, New Plymouth, RD1 New Zealand; in SOUTH AFRICA, Rolf C. Hagen S.A. (PTY.) LTD. P.O. Box 201199, Durban North 4016, South Africa; in Japan by T.F.H. Publications, Japan—Jiro Tsuda, 10-12-3 Ohjidai, Sakura, Chiba 285, Japan. Published by T.F.H. Publications, Inc.
MANUFACTURED IN THE
UNITED STATES OF AMERICA
BY T.F.H. PUBLICATIONS, INC.

Contents

The Central American Wood Turtle, *Geoemyda (Rhinoclemys) pulcherrima manni*, is found in wet, open woods in Nicaragua and Costa Rica and is sometimes exported by the former. Photo by K. T. Nemuras.

CELSIUS° = 5/9 (F° − 32°)   FAHRENHEIT° = 9/5 C° + 32°
METRIC MEASURES AND EQUIVALENTS
CUSTOMARY U.S. MEASURES AND EQUIVALENTS

1 inch (in)		= 2.54 cm
1 foot (ft)	= 12 in	= .3048 m
1 yard (yd)	= 3 ft	= .9144 m
1 mile (mi)	= 1760 yd	= 1.6093 km
1 nautical mile	= 1.152 mi	= 1.853 km
1 cubic inch (in³)		= 16.387 cm³
1 cubic foot (ft³)	= 1728 in³	= .028 m³
1 cubic yard (yd³)	= 27 ft³	= .7646 m³
1 fluid ounce (fl oz)		= 2.957 cl
1 liquid pint (pt)	= 16 fl oz	= .4732 l
1 liquid quart (qt)	= 2 pt	= .946 l
1 gallon (gal)	= 4 qt	= 3.7853 l
1 dry pint		= .5506 l
1 bushel (bu)	= 64 dry pt	= 35.2381 l
1 ounce (oz)	= 437.5 grains	= 28.35 g
1 pound (lb)	= 16 oz	= .4536 kg
1 short ton	= 2000 lb	= .9072 t
1 long ton	= 2240 lb	= 1.0161 t
1 square inch (in²)		= 6.4516 cm²
1 square foot (ft²)	= 144 in²	= .093 m²
1 square yard (yd²)	= 9 ft²	= .8361 m²
1 acre	= 4840 yd²	= 4046.86 m²
1 square mile(mi²)	= 640 acre	= 2.59 km²
1 millimeter (mm)		= .0394 in
1 centimeter (cm)	= 10 mm	= .3937 in
1 meter (m)	= 1000 mm	= 1.0936 yd
1 kilometer (km)	= 1000 m	= .6214 mi
1 sq centimeter (cm²)	= 100 mm²	= .155 in²
1 sq meter (m²)	= 10,000 cm²	= 1.196 yd²
1 hectare (ha)	= 10,000 m²	= 2.4711 acres
1 sq kilometer (km²)	= 100 ha	= .3861 mi²
1 milligram (mg)		= .0154 grain
1 gram (g)	= 1000 mg	= .0353 oz
1 kilogram (kg)	= 1000 g	= 2.2046 lb
1 tonne (t)	= 1000 kg	= 1.1023 short tons
1 tonne		= .9842 long ton
1 cubic centimeter (cm³)		= .061 in³
1 cubic decimeter (dm³)	= 1000 cm³	= .353 ft³
1 cubic meter (m³)	= 1000 dm³	= 1.3079 yd³
1 liter (l)	= 1 dm³	= .2642 gal
1 hectoliter (hl)	= 100 l	= 2.8378 bu

Preface

The purpose of this book is not to be an encyclopedia reflecting our current state of knowledge of the turtles, but rather a general introduction to turtle care for the hobbyist. This applies both to the systematics and nomenclature used here as well as the advice on the care of turtles.

The basis for the systematic classification of the families, genera, and species used in this book is the *Liste der rezenten Amphibien und Reptilien*, whose section on turtles appeared as number 100 in the series *Das Tierreich* (1977, Verlag Walter de Gruyter, Berlin). For the most part, the classification still is valid today, though there have been several taxonomic changes at all levels within the group. A discussion of the scientific questions raised by changes in taxonomy properly belongs in the specialist literature and cannot be the purpose of this book.

The same is true of the usage of the scientific names, particularly concerning the consequences that result when more recent publications divide previously valid, larger genera into several smaller, independent genera. On the other hand, you could continue to treat these groups as subgenera, thus retaining the common generic names. This is a question of personal opinion as well as practicality. For good and understandable reasons, the author has chosen the second way.

In the discussions of the habits and care of the turtles, the author largely relies on his own diverse and fundamental experiences of the last several decades. Other turtle keepers may have made other observations. The author urges the critical reader to go to the specialist literature to clarify contradictions or to compare their observations to a different set of experiences.

The author would welcome a discussion of these kinds of questions, because it would enliven the specialist literature. Furthermore, the exchange of diverse experiences brings us closer to the goal set by the author: To offer the turtles kept in captivity the highest possible standard of natural care and to keep the animals in the best of health.

Dr. Heinz Wermuth
Ludwigsburg

Southern Painted Turtle, *Chrysemys picta dorsalis.* This is one of the most popular of aquatic turtles. Photo by A. Norman.

Foreword

Most people are not fond of lizards, crocodiles, and especially snakes. Turtles, however, generally appeal to young and old. More than a few people kept a turtle of their own in childhood or bought one more recently as a pet for their children. Unfortunately, they often were slowly—or more quickly—"cared to death" (not without reason, experts say that turtles can be dying for years). This usually happens out of ignorance and without any bad intentions. In my opinion, we should only keep turtles in captivity when we are ready to make sacrifices for them (this, of course, applies to keeping any animal). We must be willing to offer them the best possible care, feed them a proper and varied diet, offer them appropriate quarters, and provide them with a compatible mate.

My first Painted Turtles, which I acquired as a school boy, were something special for me. All of my frogs, salamanders, lizards, and snakes quickly lost their appeal. In those days, however, we unfortunately knew little about keeping, diet, and habits. There was little literature, and it often contained information that did not correspond to reality. Thus, it happened that the turtles dried out and died during the—supposedly necessary—hibernation.

Because of war service, confinement as a prisoner of war, school, and establishing a career, for a long time I was unable to come back to the fancy of my youth. Not until I had more leisure time and a large enough apartment was I able to take up this hobby again. Later, in my own house, I finally was able to keep and breed turtles in suitably large terraria. It has now been well over 20 years since I started keeping turtles again.

The purpose of this book is to serve as a stimulus and guide for the serious hobbyist to keep the animals correctly. My main concern is to pass on my many years of experience and that of other experienced keepers, and in so doing to spare as many captive turtles as possible from unnecessary suffering. The listing and description of the species should be an aid in the identification of the turtles.

I would like to give my special thanks here to the Eugen Ulmer Verlag, who gave me the opportunity with this book to give a broad public access to my own practical experiences and the information collected from the literature on the subject of turtles. Best thanks also to Dr. Heinz Wermuth and his former collaborator Mrs. Ursel Friederich, who advised me in various specialist details.

Heartfelt thanks are also due to Hans Dieter Philippen. Special thanks go to Prof. Dr. Werner Frank, Hohenheim, for his expert support on the subject of "illnesses and their treatment," as well as to all the others who shared my vision and who gave me valuable tips along with their experiences.

Not least, I thank my beloved wife, who contributed immeasurably to the success of this work. She put up with flooded rooms, soaked carpets, escaped food animals (vermin?), and lost leisure time. Above all, she deciphered and transcribed the hieroglyphics that made up the manuscript.

Gerhard Mueller
Rudersberg

Indian Star Tortoise, *Testudo* (*Geochelone*) *elegans*. These are bred in small numbers by a few hobbyists. Photo by K. T. Nemuras.

Foreword to the Second Edition

I had not expected such a positive reaction to my book when it appeared in 1987. So many letters and calls, not just from Germany but from other European countries as well, have made me certain that I reached the goal I set of conveying my experiences and those of many other experienced turtle keepers to the turtle fancier. Of course, a few errors also crept in and I did not check closely enough some findings from other authors or hobbyists, but nothing is perfect.

Now I have had the opportunity to work on an expanded edition with even more color photographs and some new findings, in the hope that this book will find additional readers and will provide them with an aid in the correct keeping of turtles.

I have made a few changes to the nomenclature. In the new edition, I have deliberately referred to the currently authoritative *Liste der rezenten Amphibien and Reptilien*. The Verlag Walter de Gruyter in Berlin published its section on turtles in 1977 as issue 100 of the series *Das Tierreich*. The constant renamings only confuse the hobbyist and in my experience often are totally inappropriate. I would like to thank Ulmer Verlag, who made it possible for me to revise and expand the second edition. My heartfelt thanks go to Heinz Wermuth for his friendly support with many technical questions. The tips by Mr. Engert for the genus *Graptemys* also were very valuable to me.

Gerhard Mueller
Rudersberg

Preface to the English-language Edition

Books by German terrarium hobbyists long have been important to the American and English audience of reptile and amphibian fanciers. They are not without their problems, however, when trying to adapt them to an English-speaking audience. The language is not a problem, but often the taxonomy is a true nightmare. American and German herpetologists tend to use different names at almost all levels for some very familiar animals, and turtles are not exempt from controversies over names. In this book the author has followed, with some exceptions, a respected though generally quite outdated German list. American hobbyists instead tend to follow mostly the names in Iverson (*A Revised Checklist with Distribution Maps of the Turtles of the World*, 1992),

the most recent survey of the turtles. To an American hobbyist many of the names used in this book appear very old-fashioned, but they are no less correct than more familiar combinations in American pet books.

I have decided to leave the names as they were given by Mueller and insert modifications and differences of opinion about names in brackets: []. The common names used here, however, follow American usage throughout; no attempt was made to use translations of the German common names. Where information of interest to American hobbyists has been added, it is enclosed in brackets.

The original German edition contains short bibliographies after most species. These are unlikely to be of major use to American and English hobbyists who do not have access to the mostly German and Dutch sources listed, so they have been omitted from this edition. Additionally, most of the bibliographies are quite out of date and do not reference important papers, books, and articles that have appeared in the American and English literature in the last decade, so their use is quite limited.

In the chapter on diseases, the brand names of the recommended drugs generally have been left in the text, though I am fully aware that many of the chemicals mentioned are not available to hobbyists in the United States and probably England without a prescription from a veterinarian. When in doubt about a mentioned drug, please talk to your veterinarian.

This book has gained quite a following over the years because it recounts first-hand experiences by the author with a broad variety of turtles. The quality of these experiences never changes and they always are interesting to read, and sometimes are profitable to successfully keeping your turtles.

Jerry G. Walls

Evolutionary History and Structure of Turtles

FOSSIL HISTORY

The turtles belong to the reptilian subclass Anapsida, reptiles without openings on the sides of the skull behind the eyes, which contains the strictly fossil Cotylosauria (the so-called stem reptiles) and the turtles (order Testudines).

The living turtles, according to the ideas of Dr. O. Kuhn, a respected paleontologist, evolved from two suborders of fossil turtles, the Eunotosauria and the Amphichelydia. Paleontologists believe that the small and poorly known fossil *Eunotosaurus watsoni* is not an ancestral form of the turtles, but rather represents a parallel branch. Paleontologists have not yet found the skull of *Eunotosaurus*, and therefore they only suspect that it belongs to the Anapsida. For the most part, the ancestral turtles were unable to retract the head under the shell, but presumably they had already diverged into the two evolutionary paths that led to the suborders of the cryptodires or "neck concealers" and the pleurodires or "neck turners."

Nearly all the ancestral turtles had a highly arched carapace with many bony parts that turtles no longer have today. They also had more cranial bones. The vault of the cranium, because of grooves and ridges on the outside, was not smooth. No hole was present for the "third eye," the pituitary opening. The geologic age of the ancestral turtles extends back into the Lower Triassic, thus nearly 200 million years. In the Tertiary with its warm climate, many turtle species lived in central Europe, but later they dispersed or became extinct. Scientists have also found the fossils of large marine turtles in central Europe in places covered by the ocean in the Tertiary. The largest known fossils are of a giant marine turtle, *Archelon ischyros* (from the Upper Cretaceous of the United States), with a total length of 6 meters (19.7 feet), as well as *Meiolania* (a tortoise-like form from the Upper Cretaceous of northern Australia), more than 6 meters long and with a skull width of nearly 60 centimeters

(24 inches). The largest giant tortoise—*Colossochelys atlas*—also was at least 6 meters long and lived in the early Tertiary in India.

[All these supposedly gigantic turtles now are thought to be much smaller than given in older estimates. *Archelon*, for instance, had a carapace less than 2 meters long and a total length with extended neck of about 2.7 meters, 9 feet; *Meiolania* (and its relatives from Argentina and New Caledonia) was at most only 2 meters long, though the extremely broad head horns must have made it appear gigantic. *Colossochelys* now is treated as a species of *Geochelone* and thought to be considerably smaller than 6 meters, probably only 2 meters. The largest described turtle presently seems to be *Stupendemys geographicus* from South America, a fossil form with the carapace at least 2.3 meters, 7.5 feet, long. Earlier exaggerated shell lengths in fossil turtles are due to extrapolations from small fragments of the shell and a lot of bad science.]

Even today paleontologists do not agree about the true phylogeny of the turtles, although that is not a subject requiring further discussion here.

STRUCTURE

Because of their shell, the carapace, the turtles hold a special position within the reptiles. The shell provides protection from enemies, because they can retract their extremities into it when threatened. Many species also have thick horny scutes or scales on the exposed parts of the drawn-in limbs that help protect the soft parts.

In the box turtles and a variety of other turtles with a similar adaptation, the plastron or lower shell is movable in the middle because of the presence of a flexible transverse hinge; two such hinges are present in the mud turtles. When threatened, after the turtle retracts the extremities it closes the two halves of the plastron against the carapace, thus protecting the turtle on all sides. There are other species that can only close their shells partially, such as several

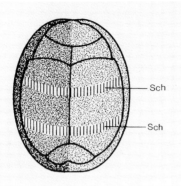

Plastron of a mud turtle. sch = hinges

Kinosternon species, and some, such as members of the genus *Kinixys*, that have a hinge in the carapace.

In contrast, the softshell turtles have a greatly reduced bony shell and completely lack the horny scales or scutes. A leathery skin, which naturally offers little protection, replaces the scales. These species, however, have the ability when threatened to bury themselves in sand or mud in seconds, thus making themselves invisible. I will discuss this in detail in the descriptions of the individual species.

The figures show the structure of the shell and skeleton of turtles, without touching on each special feature. Of particular note is that the corium forms broad plates of secondary bone that fuse with the ribs. They form a true shell and simultaneously serve as the substrate for the horny scutes.

Differences also exist in the growth of turtles. In some, such as the *Testudo* species, *Cuora*, and others, the new horny scute grows under the old (smaller) one, so that with continual repetition the dorsal scutes form concentric grooves in the manner of annual rings of tree trunks [though in turtles the rings represent seasonal growth and are not equivalent to years or any other regular calendar period]. Other turtles simply shed the old horny scutes after the new ones grow. The

Structure of the skeleton of a turtle with opened plastron. 1. skull; 2. cervical vertebrae; 3. forearm (radius and ulna); 4. upper arm; 5. shoulder; 6. ribs transformed into bony plates; 7. dorsal vertebrae; 8. vertebral plate; 9. pelvis; 10. femur; 11. lower leg (tibia, fibula); 12. caudal vertebrae; 13. plastron.

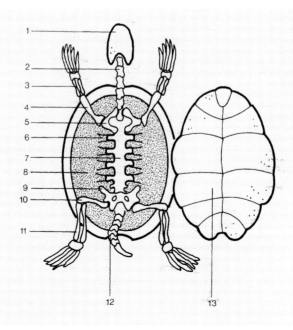

same is true of the ventral scutes. I regularly observed this process with *Emydura albertisi* and *Emydura macquarri*, *Elseya novaeguineae*, *Chelodina novaeguineae*, as well as with *Pseudemys* and *Chrysemys* species. The turtle may shed the old horny scutes over a period of three to four weeks. This often happens when we return the turtles to the indoor terrarium after an outdoor stay. The shedding process is particularly conspicuous when the turtle sheds the old scutes individually. The old scutes often have a thick covering of algae and contrast strongly with color of the underlying new scutes. This process continues until the turtle has shed all the old scutes.

Turtles also employ different strategies for retracting the head. Most turtles are able to retract the head; the remainder can only place it to the side. According to this criterion, we divide them into two large groups: the neck concealers (Cryptodira) and the neck turners or side-necks (Pleurodira). A small group of the Pleurodira, the Pelomedusidae, retracts the neck slightly first and then turns it to the side. The retracting mechanism, however, is only one of the characters used to distinguish the neck concealers and side-necks. In their anatomic characters, pelomedusids prove to be true side-necks.

Turtles have no teeth; instead, the margins of the jaws end in very sharp, horny cutting edges [tomia] that most adult turtles can use to inflict a painful bite. Larger specimens, such as the softshell turtles or snapping and alligator snapping turtles, can bite a person's finger off [though this is rare, with crushing and deep lacerating cuts more likely].

Scientists have found vestiges of teeth only in ancestral forms of the genera *Triassochelys* and *Proganochelys* from the late Triassic. [In these forms they were on the roof of the mouth and not on the jaws.]

As is true of most reptiles, turtles do not have cutaneous glands. The skin is smooth or rough and may have hard, horny plates, particularly on the parts of the limbs exposed in the retracted or bent state. Cutaneous appendages on the chin (barbels) often are important distinguishing characters. The Matamata (*Chelus fimbriatus*) has lobe-like cutaneous processes on the head that,

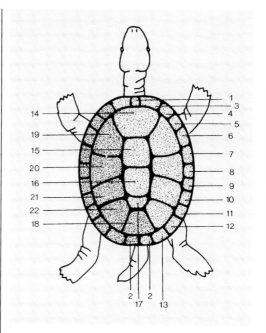

Carapace. 1. nuchal scute; 2. supracaudal scutes; 3-13. marginal scutes; 14-18. vertebral scutes; 19-22. costal scutes. Note: Supramarginal scutes (not shown here) are located between the costal and leading marginal scutes.

Plastron. 0. intergular scute; 1. gular scutes; 2. humeral scutes; 3. pectoral scutes; 4. abdominal scutes; 5. femoral scutes; 6. anal scutes. Note: Inframarginal scutes (not shown here) are located between the scutes of the plastron and the underside of the marginal scutes of the plastron.

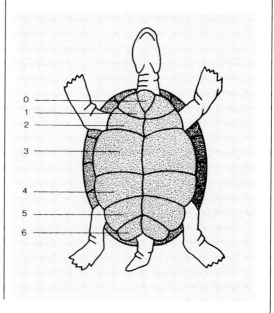

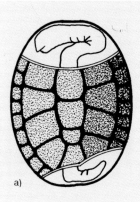 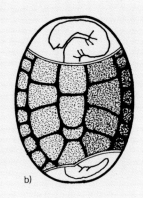 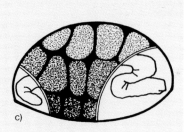

Behavioral differences in retracting the head into the shell: a) Pleurodira (neck turners); b) Pelomedusidae; c) Cryptodira (neck concealers).

in conjunction with the greatly flattened form, give the turtle its peculiar appearance.

SENSES

Turtles have a poorly developed sense of hearing, although scientists have not proved that they can hear nothing at all. We suspect that they are better able to detect low frequencies, and that they cannot detect high frequencies. Bellairs has remarked that the sense of hearing seems to be poorer in turtles than in crocodiles and lizards, particularly regarding frequencies above 1000 or 2000 hertz. For example, the Wood Turtle (*Clemmys insculpta*) proved to be very sensitive to frequencies up to 500 hertz, but displayed a rapid decrease in hearing ability at frequencies above 1000 hertz. Scientists have reported similar results with other species. Thus, sound apparently plays a minimal role in the life of the turtles, except during mating season, when some species (especially tortoises) often produce quite obvious sounds.

On the other hand, turtles have well-developed eyesight. They can detect an "enemy" at a surprising distance. If you carefully stalk a turtle pond, a slightly careless movement is sufficient to send all the basking turtles into the water.

Turtles also have a very good sense of smell. Even under water turtles can smell or, more precisely, sense scents. I was able to confirm this frequently with, among others, a softshell turtle. The turtle often lay hidden in the sand, with only the tip of its snorkle-like snout slightly exposed. If I tossed some fish or beef heart into the water

at a good distance from the turtle, after a short time first the head appeared, then the long neck. All the while the turtle scented keenly. Now it emerged completely, shook the last grains of sand from its body, and swam directly to the piece of food, even when its location was out of sight from the turtle's position.

Turtles also have a good sense of direction. If, for example, a turtle has discovered a place in the terrarium (this usually applies to the outdoor terrarium) where it can take shelter, then when reintroduced to the terrarium even after a long absence (for example, over winter) it hurries directly to this place to hide.

I do not believe, as some people claim, that turtles recognize their keeper. They beg for food from anyone who approaches their enclosure. They also exhibit behaviors, however, that are not just instinctive, but that draw on experience and learning ability as well.

GROWTH AND LONGEVITY

We have observed repeatedly in the terrarium that the growth of turtles conforms to the size of the enclosure, and after we transfer them to a larger terrarium they suddenly start to grow again. The literature often reports very inconsistent maximum sizes. I often have observed that the species I keep sometimes grow significantly larger than the literature reports. Growth depends primarily on diet and keeping conditions. Juveniles grow comparatively fast in the first few years, to get through this dangerous period in their life as quickly as possible. The growth of

Be prepared to care for your turtle for the entirety of its long life. In the case of this Galapagos Tortoise, *Testudo* [*Geochelone*] *nigra*, that could mean more than sixty years. Photo by K. H. Switak.

captive specimens often comes to a complete standstill before the turtle reaches its maximum size.

The most inconsistent reports exist on the longevity of turtles. Bellairs considers an age of 200 years to be reachable in individual cases with certain species. Yet this surely could not be the rule. The greatest documented age of an Aldabra Giant Tortoise, *Testudo (Megalochelys) gigantea* [*Geochelone gigantea*], is 152 years. Because it was already an adult when it reached captivity, however, its true age is probably about 180 years. [All records of very old Aldabra Tortoises may be doubtful because of poor records and the possibility that specimens were exchanged without fanfare when one died.] The same author mentions accounts claiming that a Spur-thighed Tortoise lived to be at least 115 years old, an American box turtle 100 years, a European Pond Turtle (*Emys orbicularis*) 70 years, and an Alligator Snapping Turtle

(*Macroclemys temmincki*) at least 58 years. Flower (*Proc. Zool. Soc. London*, 1925 and 1937) gives, among others, the following ages: *Testudo graeca*, 102 years; *Testudo hermanni*, more than 90 years; *Testudo radiata*, 85 years; *Testudo gigantea*, definitely 68, maybe 180 years; *Testudo elephantopus* [*nigra*], more than 100, maybe 150 years; *Terrapene carolina*, 123 years; *Emys orbicularis*, more than 120 years. I have kept emyduras, chelodinas, *Elseya, Kachuga, Testudo* [*Geochelone*] *carbonaria*, and *Pseudemys* species for more than 25 or 30 years. Several of these turtles therefore must have reached an age of 30 years and more.

In 1989, a female *Kachuga tecta tecta* I owned died. I had kept it for 27 years. Because I acquired it when it was about ten years old, it lived to an age of 37 years. Prof. Frank in Hohenheim, Germany, who performed the autopsy, confirmed that the cause of death apparently was old age.

Recognition

DISTINGUISHING CHARACTERS

The arrangement, size, and shape of the dorsal and ventral scutes are of great importance in the identification of the genera and species. Usually several characters are of decisive importance.

The color of the carapace often varies greatly as the turtle ages (age-dependent melanism), making identification extremely difficult. The color of the plastron usually remains more constant, with only the ornamentation or blotches becoming paler with age. The color of the head and legs often changes as well, becoming paler (this also can be dependent on the diet). Thus, we can use these criteria as distinguishing characters only in specific cases with a few species. Softshell turtles are very hard to identify because they do not have a shell with scutes, but rather only a leathery skin. With these turtles the form of the body, head, and legs, as well as the dorsal markings (eyespots, dark borders) or markings on the dorsal side of the head (dark stripes) serve as distinguishing characters.

The form of the shell and legs and the extent of webbing between the toes in part determine the difference between tortoises and aquatic turtles.

With the exception of the Central Asian Tortoise, *Testudo horsfieldi*, and a subspecies of *Kinixys belliana* that have four toes, the front legs always have five toes. In tortoises the legs end in "club feet" from which only the nails protrude. In aquatic turtles, the toes generally have well-developed webbing and the flattened feet are oar-like. In marine and softshell turtles, the feet have evolved into flattened paddles in which independent toes are no longer visible. As many as three sharp claws are present, but even these often are absent.

It is virtually impossible to distinguish the sexes in the juvenile stage, and in some species sexing is difficult even in adults. On one occasion I met Prof. Robert Mertens [a foremost German authority on turtles and other reptiles] in a pet shop. We were buying a "pair" of *Cyclemys dentata*, Asian Leaf Turtles, and we agreed that we had chosen a male and female. A few months later, however, the "male" laid infertile eggs in my facility.

Normally, the tail of the fully grown and sexually mature female is significantly smaller and shorter than in the male. The cloaca in the straightened tail falls within the outer margin of the carapace. In the male the tail is thicker, larger, and longer. The cloaca often falls outside the margin of the carapace. Only in a very few species are differences in the coloration of the turtles useful distinguishing characters. The literature often reports that the plastron of males is concave in the middle. Frequently this is not true even with specimens of the same species. In the sexually mature male, of course, we can determine the sex unequivocally by its behavior: it mounts other turtles (to be sure, it often mounts turtles of the same sex as well) and erects its penis.

IDENTIFICATION KEY TO FAMILIES

The following key is taken from Wermuth & Mertens.

1 Plastron with 11 or 12 large horny plates or the carapace and plastron covered with leathery skin; usually the turtle can at least partially retract the head and does not place it to the side under the carapace: cryptodires (**Cryptodira**)

1' Plastron always with 13 large scutes and, like the carapace, never has a covering of leathery skin; when the turtle retracts the head it always places it to the side under the carapace: side-necks (**Pleurodira**)

CRYPTODIRA

1 The legs roundish or laterally flattened in cross section, but are not conspicuously flattened, flipper-like swimming paddles; at least the front legs with 4 or 5 claws each; carapace always covered with horny scutes: typical turtles (**Testudinoidea**)

1' Strongly flattened legs resemble flipper-like swimming paddles, with maximum of 3 free claws; carapace covered with horny scutes or leathery skin: **2**

2 Snout without trunk-like process; carapace covered either with horny scutes or leathery, keeled skin: marine turtles (**Chelonioidea**)

2' Snout ends in a fleshy proboscis; shell always covered with leathery skin and always unkeeled: softshell turtles (**Trionychoidea**)

TYPICAL TURTLES (TESTUDINOIDEA)

1 Plastron conspicuously small and narrow, approximately cross shaped and rhomboid in outline: **2**

1' Plastron approximately elliptical in outline, approximately as large or only slightly smaller than the ventral opening of the carapace: **3**

2 Head and neck covered with spiny tubercles; tail approximately as long as the carapace; carapace with large saw-toothed scutes: snapping turtles (**Chelydridae**)

2' Head and neck without spiny tubercles; tail shorter than half the length of the carapace, without large saw-toothed scutes on the carapace: mud turtles (**Kinosternidae**)

3 Marginal scutes of the plastron on each side either completely separated by a continuous row of small inframarginal scutes or incompletely by a single inframarginal scute, which extends at least to the middle of the bridge: **4**

3' Marginal scutes at the bridge either touch the abdominal scute or joined to it by a narrow strip of cutaneous connective tissue; axillary or inguinal scutes, when present, neither form a continuous row nor extend to the middle of the bridge: **6**

4 The front and rear parts of the plastron each with a transverse hinge flexibly connected with the rigid middle: mud turtles (**Kinosternidae**)

4' No transverse hinge on the plastron, instead forming a single, rigid plate: **5**

5 Head covered with a few large horny plates and conspicuously massive, so that the turtle cannot retract it under the flat carapace; upper mandible ends in a hook-like, downward-curving tip; tail approximately as long as the carapace: big-headed turtles (**Platysternidae**)

5' The head is not unduly large, and the turtle can retract it completely under the slightly domed carapace; tip of the snout not hook-like and downward-curving; tail much shorter than the carapace: river turtles (**Dermatemydidae**)

6 Front legs laterally flattened and therefore oval in cross section; fingers and toes exposed in their entire length, but usually connected with one another by webbing: pond turtles (**Emydidae**)

6' Front legs approximately roundish in cross section; fingers and toes not visible externally, but rather fused into a club foot, from which only the nails project freely: tortoises (**Testudinidae**)

SIDE-NECKS (PLEURODIRA)

1 The turtle first retracts the head along the longitudinal axis and only in the final part of this movement places it to the side under the carapace; nuchal scute never present on carapace: pelomedusids (**Pelomedusidae**)

1' The turtle never retracts the head along the longitudinal axis, but rather places it to the side under the carapace with the often extraordinarily long neck; only a very few species lack a nuchal scute, but in the genus *Hydromedusa* it can be well back from the border of the marginal scutes, thus simulating an extra sixth vertebral scute: snake-necked side-necks (**Chelidae**)

The Basics of Keeping Turtles

Anyone who wants to keep turtles, whether tortoises or aquatic turtles, must always consider carefully whether he can offer the turtles keeping conditions that to some degree correspond to their natural living space. The beginner must offer the turtles a sufficiently large enclosure, a varied diet, and plenty of time. He must consider that outdoor keeping is at times absolutely necessary with many species (such as the *Terrapene* species) and that aquatic turtles become considerably hardier as a result of a stay during the summer in the outdoor pond. At the very least, we should have a balcony to provide the turtles with a place to sunbathe. From the start, we must be aware that turtles grow very rapidly with proper care and diet. Furthermore, we must be able to transfer the turtles to larger terraria when they have grown too large for the previous enclosure.

We usually make the mistake (in the acquisition of any kind of animal) of buying the animal first and the relevant literature later. We should do this the other way around, because it is better to spend money on a book than to kill an animal out of ignorance.

What must we consider during the purchase?

When we pick up the turtle, it should react by immediately retracting the head and the extremities, unless it has lost all fear during a long time in captivity. When we hold the turtle in our hand so that the front legs rest on the spread index finger and thumb, it must at least be able to hold its legs horizontally, without the body sagging. Very vigorous specimens press themselves above the horizontal. The turtle should be relatively heavy, since "light weights" usually are "goners." The eyes should be clear and not filled with tears or stuck together. The shell should be undamaged and not brittle or cracked. The nose must not have a mucous discharge or be runny. The formation of small bubbles at the nostrils during exhalation is a very bad sign. Rattling sounds when the turtle respires also are an alarm signal and usually indicate pneumonia.

With aquatic and semi-aquatic turtles, also make sure that the shell of juveniles is not too soft. When we place the turtle on its back, it must be able to right itself quickly. We should keep in mind, however, that it usually will stay on its back for a while out of fear. When we put the turtle in water, it should be able to dive immediately without too much effort and to surface again. When swimming at the surface, the turtle must be level in the water. Stuck-together or swollen eyes and mucous or bubbles forming at the nostrils also are disturbing signs. It takes much experience and luck for a hobbyist to nurse turtles with such health problems back to health.

Buying from mail-order dealers has the big disadvantage that you cannot see and examine the turtle. Moreover, when the turtle arrives, often the species, subspecies, or sex does not agree with our order. It always is preferable to be able to see and examine the turtle before you buy it. The beginning hobbyist should ask an experienced turtle keeper for help.

Few hobbyists will have the opportunity to collect turtles in their natural living space. Obviously, no species protected under CITES is a suitable candidate. Wild-caught turtles often suffer from parasitic infestation. Therefore, I recommend an eight-week to ten-week quarantine as well as an examination of the feces.

THE TERRARIUM FOR TORTOISES

An indoor terrarium for tortoises should have approximately the following dimensions: at least 100 centimeters long, 60 centimeters wide, and 60 centimeters high (40 X 24 X 24 inches). Typically there is a glass front and half ventilation screens and half glass on both sides and in the cover. As a substrate we should use dust-free sand with some peat mixed in. Under the substrate install a heating cable (wattage and length depending on terrarium size). In my own practice it has proved very beneficial to install the heating cable permanently, that is, not simply buried in the sand or soil, where the turtles could dig themselves in. There is the added danger, particularly with lead cables (which, to be sure, the pet trade scarcely carries anymore), that the turtles could burn themselves. Therefore, I have always embedded my heating cables in concrete, which also serves to distribute the heat more evenly and to increase greatly the life expectancy of the heating cable. To prevent overheating, we must lay the cables individually and not overlap them, because otherwise they could melt. In place of a heating cable we also can use a heating pad, which I think is an even better choice. The terrarium should have a shallow aquatic section that the tortoises can reach effortlessly to bathe. If possible, we should equip it with a drain.

A healthy turtle must be able to brace itself strongly when held in this position.

The food bowl should be easy to reach. For the greenfood, install a feed rack with not too closely spaced bars slightly above the floor of the enclosure. If we use the usual shallow food bowls, the tortoises march over the food or lie directly in it, which soils everything and spoils much food. In the preferred type of feeding station, metal hoops and cross-bars still allow the tortoises to get at the food, but prevent them from walking through it. The tortoises very quickly become acclimated to this arrangement. Install a spotlight with a reflector under the cover.

THE AQUATERRARIUM FOR SEMI-AQUATIC AND AQUATIC TURTLES
In principle, the aquatic section should make up at least two-thirds of the total area and be at least 40 centimeters, preferably 50 or 60 centi-

meters, deep (16 to 24 inches). I disagree with the prevalent opinion (in the specialist literature as well) that the water level should never be deeper than the width of the turtle's carapace. In the natural habitat, the smallest pond in which aquatic turtles live is significantly deeper than our aquaterraria! Even with the smallest specimens (such as *Sternotherus odoratus* and *Sternotherus minor*) I have never suffered losses because the water was too deep. To the contrary, the young turtles must kick vigorously to reach the surface for air. This strengthens the muscles, increases the appetite because of the musculature exertion, and thus increases the vitality of the turtle and promotes growth.

Various sources have documented that juvenile *Emys, Mauremys, Chrysemys,* and *Pseudemys* in the wild sought out precisely the deepest water.

Adult turtles that always have lived in shallow water acclimate themselves poorly to deeper water. They are in danger of drowning because they can no longer reach the surface. They apparently have forgotten how to use the inhaled air to float in the water and to adjust their swimming depth with slight paddling movements. It is best to build a gradually sloping bank, which unfortunately is not always feasible due to lack of space or for structural reasons. In principle, we should cover the concrete structures with decorative cork, because the hard concrete is dangerous for the often soft plastron, particularly with young turtles. Today, the building industry carries such a wide selection of the most diverse materials (such as plastics, adhesives, and fillers) for furnishing terraria, that I will not discuss them individually here. It is important, however, not to use sand or gravel in the aquaterrarium (except with softshell turtles), because they make cleaning more difficult. To camouflage the bottom of the tank, I glue sand and gravel of various sizes to the bottom with two-component adhesive. When you use plastics, make sure that they are not toxic!

THE AQUARIUM FOR SOFTSHELL AND MARINE TURTLES
We keep softshell turtles, marine turtles, or other nearly strictly aquatic species, such as the Matamata, in an aquarium. Naturally, we do not

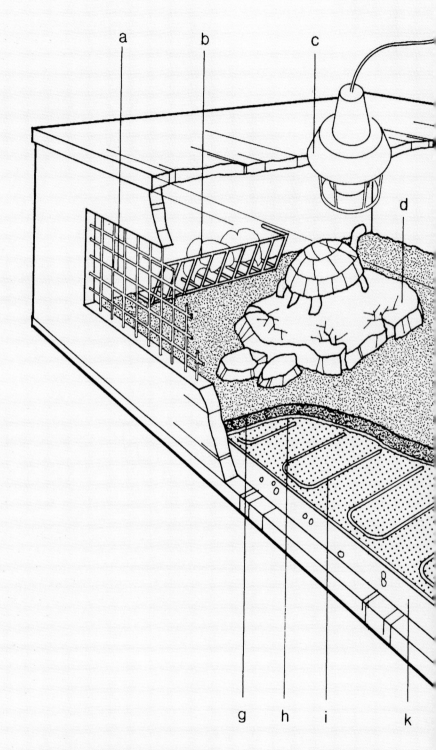

Terrarium for tortoises: a. grille; b. feeding rack; c. lamp; d. flagstone; e. water dish; f. food dish; g. sand; h. sheet asbestos; i. heating cable or mat; k. Styrofoam sheet.

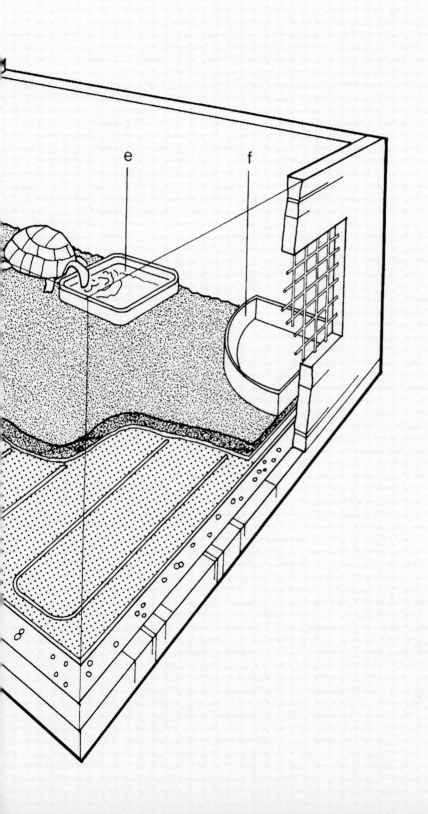

e   f

need a nicely planted and furnished tank here, but rather an aquarium furnished according to the requirements of its occupants.

For nearly all softshell turtles and the Matamata, sand is indispensable as the substrate. I recommend washed river sand with a grain size of 0.5 to 1.5 millimeters. We should avoid all sharp-edged rocks and quartz sand. Resinous bog roots and thoroughly washed driftwood and grape vines make a very good decoration. To keep the turtles in good health, we must wash the sand occasionally (particularly with softshell turtles).

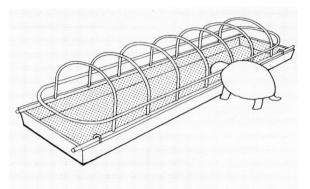

A feeding trough, in which the turtles cannot climb over it and soil the food.

To simplify the washing, I recommend the installation of a flow-through power filter system. With the undergravel filtration plate installed under the substrate, the water returning from the filter can pass down through the substrate, thereby rinsing it effectively. With a sand layer about 8 to 20 centimeters, 3 to 8 inches, deep (depending on the size of the turtles), we need a correspondingly powerful pump. The output should be at least 20 to 30 liters (5.3 to 8 gallons) per minute; an even more powerful filter would be even better.

The following deserves special attention. Even with constant filtration of the water, I recommend changing the water every 10 to 14 days (depending on the tank's population density and size). Even a powerful filter does not remove nitrates, which may be present in high concentrations even in crystal-clear water and which can be toxic to delicate specimens. If we keep adults and expect to breed them, we should use an aquaterrarium instead of an aquarium.

THE OUTDOOR TERRARIUM FOR TORTOISES

We can leave tortoises that do not require particularly warm temperatures at liberty in the garden (if the installation permits it). A prerequisite is that we have a suitable fence to prevent escape. If this is not possible, then we can build an outdoor terrarium.

Select a sunny location protected from wind. The facility should have a minimum area of 4 square meters. Enclose it with boards, wire mesh, or a wall. Remember that some tortoises are excellent climbers. Always design the enclosure so that good climbers cannot escape. Consider also that many tortoises can easily burrow under a normal wire-mesh fence. If you do not have a wall which together with its foundation extends at least 30 centimeters (12 inches) below ground, then bury the wire mesh at least 30 centimeters deep to prevent escapes.

Besides the food station and the water basin, the tortoises also need a shelter, which, if possible, we should furnish with in-floor heating. The advantage of in-floor heating is obvious: during northern summers, which unfortunately are not always particularly warm, we often have periods of cool weather during which we normally would have to transfer the tortoises to a heated terrarium. They can withdraw into a heated outdoor shelter, however, at any time. When the weather is too cool, some turtles hardly make an appearance or stay inside. Construct the shelter, in the form of a large box, as follows. First put down a layer of glass shards (to prevent rats from entering from below). Over that place a layer of sand or gravel, then for insulation a sheet of Styrofoam. The shelter will sit on top of that. Next install a heating cable on the underside of the floor of the shelter by gluing or otherwise fixing it to the floor. A mat also can be installed if you wish. Make sure that the loops of the heating cable do not overlap or they might overheat and melt. I think it is very beneficial to build a small "mountain" with cliffs in the middle of the outdoor terrarium. This gives those species that want to climb the opportunity to do so. It also invites the "wanderer" to take a roundabout, endless journey.

The water basin should be shallow, so that the tortoises can climb in and out easily. Concrete is the preferred material because it is easy to work with and looks the most natural. For larger basins, I advise installing a drain at the deepest point to make it easier to change the water.

THE OUTDOOR POND FOR AQUATIC TURTLES

Anyone who has a garden has unlimited possibilities in the design of the outdoor turtle area. For semi-aquatic and aquatic turtles, the pond naturally plays the leading role.

It makes no difference what material we use to build the pond; the main thing is that it serves its purpose. Several suitable liners are available on the market today. According to manufacturers, all the pond liners offered today are resistant to ultraviolet radiation. To increase their useful life, however, I propose the following. At the pond's edge, where the liner is exposed to sunlight, after a number of years it will lose its elasticity and become brittle. Counter this by, after installing the liner, placing wire mesh on the bank and far enough over the pond's edge that it extends under the water. On top of it place a layer of cement to protect the riparian zone. The wire mesh prevents the cement from cracking.

It always is possible that a concrete basin will crack and leak. Many a swimming pool owner can tell you about that. I consider it best to use a fiberglass-reinforced plastic liner or form, because these liners last practically forever, conduct heat poorly, and are not damaged by freezing. From one company I bought half a plastic

Aqua-terrarium for aquatic turtles. a. outflow; b. outside heater; c. lamp; d. fluorescent lighting; e. decorative cork; f. perforated sheet, bent over on top; g. inflow; h. sand-peat mixture; i. heating cable; k. bottom layer; l. plant roots; m. filter; n. ramp.

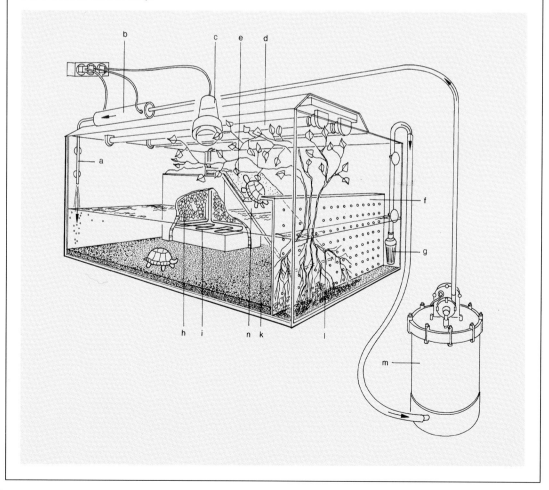

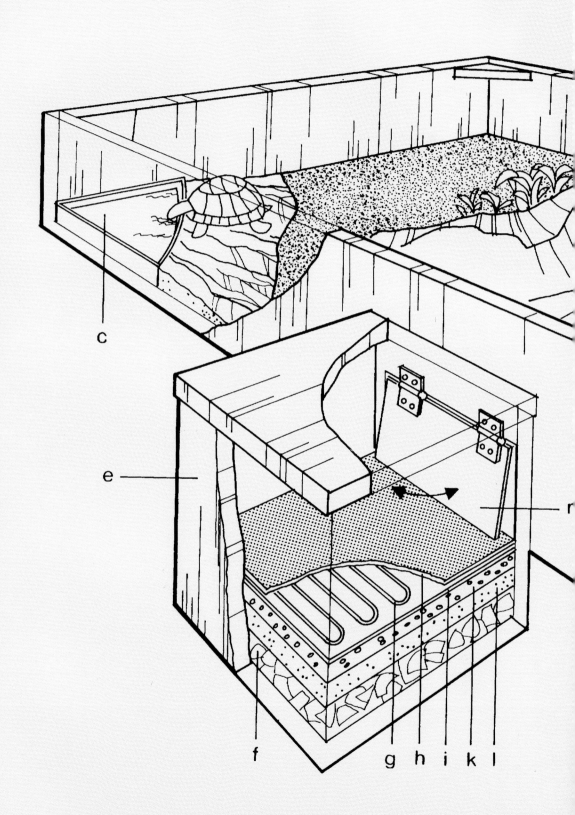

c

e

r

f

g h i k l

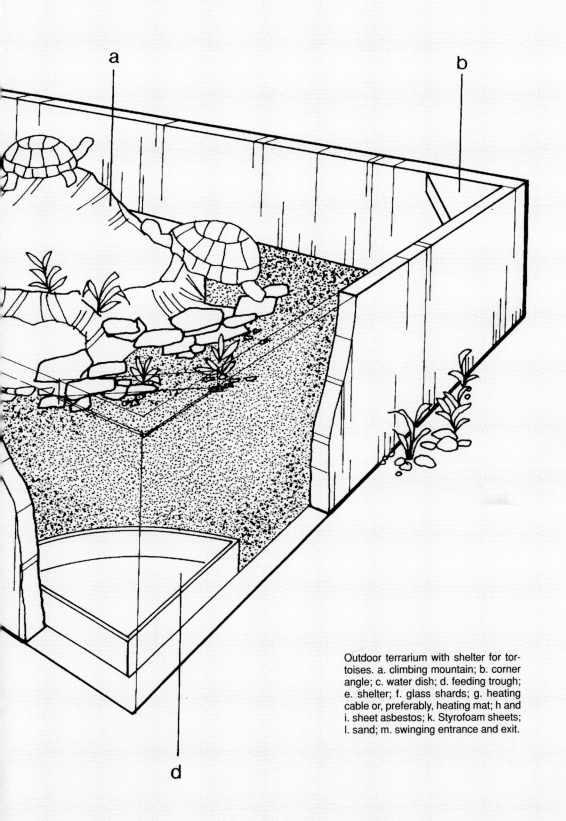

Outdoor terrarium with shelter for tortoises. a. climbing mountain; b. corner angle; c. water dish; d. feeding trough; e. shelter; f. glass shards; g. heating cable or, preferably, heating mat; h and i. sheet asbestos; k. Styrofoam sheets; l. sand; m. swinging entrance and exit.

tank with a normal capacity of 5000 liters (1300 gallons)—it thus held 2500 liters—and installed it in the ground. To break up the outline and to make it easier for the turtles to climb in and out, I used a similar method to the one described for the pond liner. I attached ornamental cork to wire mesh, spread concrete on the pond's edge, and pressed the wire mesh with the ornamental cork into it. I did this in such a way that the ornamental cork extended into the pond and provided the turtles with a soft, easy-to-climb access. I pressed pebbles of various sizes in the part of the cement not covered by the cork. This looks very attractive. An added advantage of the cement border is that it prevents water from running out of the pond.

No one likes to have a cloudy pond in the garden, but when you have a fairly large number of turtles they soon soil the pond. I have found a way, however, to clean the water through biological filtration. Install a filter basin at the same height as the main basin. Fine wire mesh separates it from the actual terrarium. Bend the top of the mesh over (in toward the terrarium) to prevent the turtles from climbing over. Another tip: Galvanized mesh is less conspicuous if you paint it olive-green. As soon as the plants grow luxuriantly, it will be nearly invisible. The filter basin should be about 40 centimeters (16 inches) deep. Install an outlet exactly in the middle of the basin at the deepest point. Poke holes in a shallow plastic tub to form a kind of sieve and place it upside-down on the bottom to create a water chamber. (Those who have had problems with filters know that the clear-water chamber plays an important role in the filtration process. If there is no clear-water chamber, the water simply takes the path of least resistance through the filtration material, and the filtering effect is poor or stops completely.) Now fill the basin with coarse gravel up to the level of the overflow. Cattails, water lilies, and other aquatic plants grow luxuriantly in the constantly fertilized water and simultaneously break down nitrates.

At a depth of 60 centimeters (24 inches), run a hose from the outflow to the water pump. Plastic pipe, which we can permanently connect at the seams with a special adhesive, has an even

longer life. It is best to use an oil-cooled pump, because the pump chamber is underground and a leaky hose or a heavy rain shower could cause water to accumulate there, causing complications with an air-cooled pump. Because I do not like to remove the turtles every time the weather turns cool once I have put them in the outdoor pond, I have connected a homemade flow-through heater between the pump and the inflow, and I use it on cool days. I constructed the return flow to the pond in such a way that the clean and, if necessary, warmed water flows back into the pond in the form of a small stream and in so doing takes up additional oxygen. Because aquatic turtles can take up supplemental oxygen from the water through the cloacal sacs, oxygen-rich water is very important for many species. It also improves the filtration process.

There are many ways to fence in the entire installation, from a concrete or brick wall to fiberglass sheets or a wooden fence. I recommend wood the least, because it is the least durable. It is important to install a sheet-metal or fiberglass angle at the top to prevent accomplished climbers from escaping. It also is essential that the fence extend into the ground so that the digging specialists cannot escape. Escaped turtles usually do not survive in our latitudes. I dispense with a substrate and planting in the pond because the turtles graze and destroy the plants. This also makes it much easier to clean the basin.

SPOTLIGHTS AND HEAT LAMPS

In my opinion the best lighting for larger terraria is a combination of mercury-vapor lamps and fluorescent tubes. Red light plays an important role in luxuriant plant growth. I illuminated my first fairly large aquaterrarium with only two 40-watt, warm-tone fluorescent tubes, and the plants grew poorly. After I exchanged one tube for a plant growth bulb high in the red part of the spectrum, the plants grew very luxuriantly. Of course everything depends on the size of the terrarium, but with the lighting—if you expect the plants to flourish—you can never have too much light.

Even today the literature often claims that turtles require ultraviolet light if sunlight is not

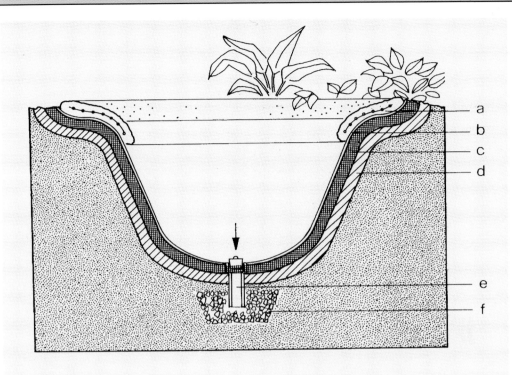

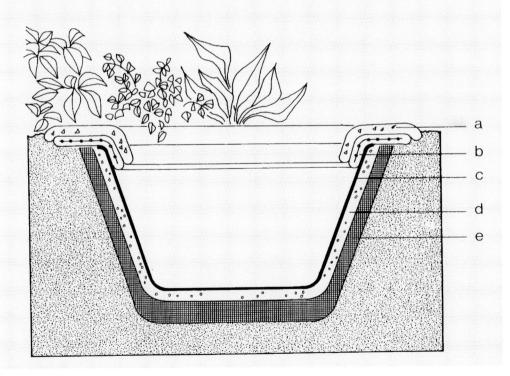

top: Pond with plastic liner for turtles. a. concrete reinforced with wire mesh; b. liner; c. layer of sand; d. layer of loam; e. drain with plug; f. gravel.
bottom: Plastic basin as an outdoor pond. a. decorative cork; b. concrete reinforced with wire mesh; c. plastic basin; d. Styrofoam sheets; e. sand.

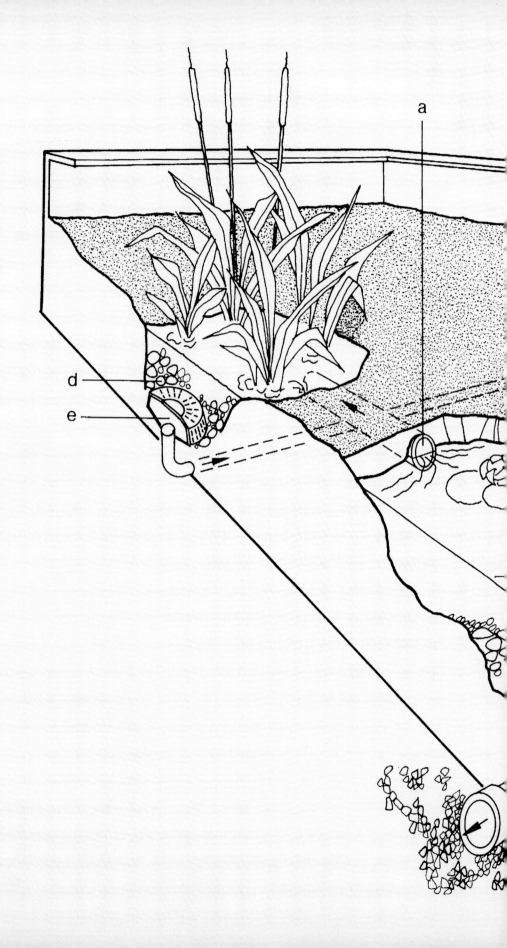

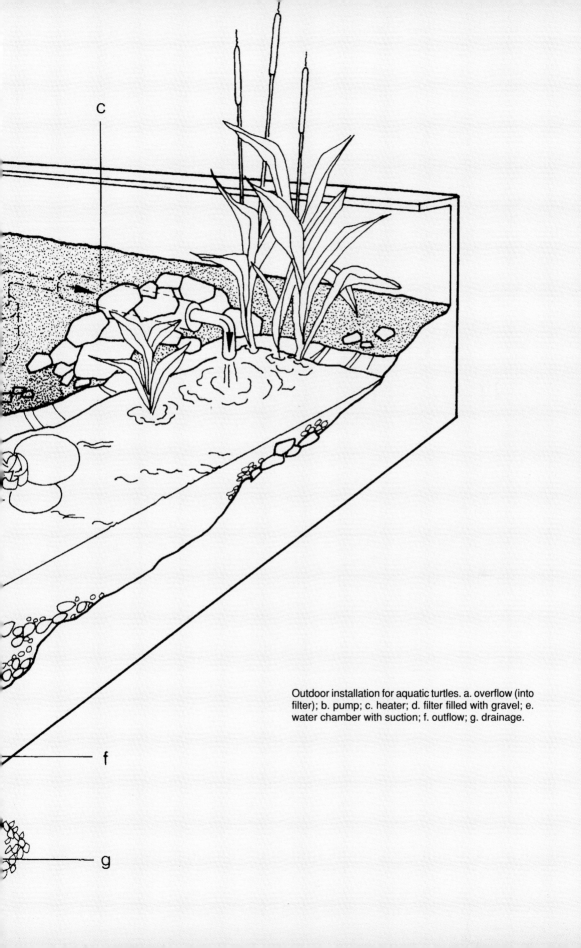

c

f

g

Outdoor installation for aquatic turtles. a. overflow (into filter); b. pump; c. heater; d. filter filled with gravel; e. water chamber with suction; f. outflow; g. drainage.

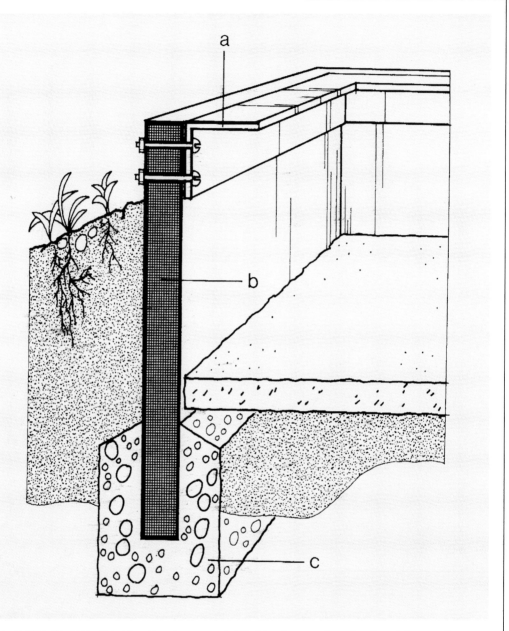

Cross section of a concrete outdoor terrarium. a. angled flashing; b. concrete wall; c. foundation.

available. The literature also contains very inconsistent information about the irradiation period. An amount of ultraviolet light that turtles tolerate easily would cause serious burns in humans. In my early days of keeping turtles, I irradiated a great deal and had to reduce the exposure time only with the *Podocnemis* species. If I irradiated the *Podocnemis* species for more than 15 minutes, the turtles' irises turned gray and visual acuity decreased. After a few days, however, the vision improved and the eyes and behavior returned to normal. None of the other turtles showed a negative reaction to ultraviolet irradiation.

Considering the current availability of fluorescent lamps with an ultraviolet component, separate ultraviolet irradiation no longer is absolutely necessary. This is particularly true if we can expose the turtles to unfiltered sunlight in the warm season in the outdoor terrarium. Today

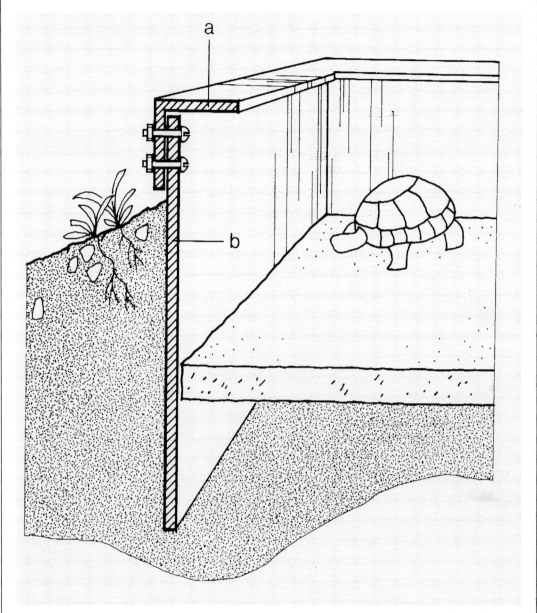

Cross section of a sheet-asbestos outdoor terrarium. a. angled sheet asbestos; b. flat sheet asbestos. Asbestos has become almost unavailable, but other materials, such as melamine, can be used similarly.

pet shops carry a variety of full-spectrum fluorescent lights. These lamps also boast a good color reproduction.

A normal incandescent bulb installed as a heat source over the terrestrial section is indispensable for rearing young turtles. I usually favor lighting or irradiating a terrarium such that each turtle can choose the conditions it wants. Those who keep tropical turtles often do not consider that many species come from bodies of water in the rainforest, where sunlight seldom penetrates the thick vegetation.

FILTRATION

In my turtle tanks, I always filter the water. Yet the pros and cons (filtration or regular water changes) are a disputed issue that can lead to all-night discussions among fanciers.

The opponents consider filtration to be wrong for the following reasons:

1) While it is true that filtration produces clear water, the nitrate component still rises constantly. Moreover, filtration does not always remove other toxic or disease-causing substances in the water. This can lead to poisoning over time if the concentration of the substance exceeds a particular level.

2) The filter material could provide places for pathogens to grow. The pathogens could multiply inside the filter and infect many healthy turtles.

As a proponent of filtration, I advance the following arguments:

1) Of what use is a cloudy "broth" in which I can barely see the turtles? A well-stocked tank, even a large one, turns cloudy in a short time, particularly after feeding.

2) Even in a heavily stocked tank, filtration allows a good view of the turtles. (I also change the water in my tanks every 10 to 14 days.) If you put plants in the filter basin or in a part of the pond that the turtles do not have access to, they will break down or consume much of the nitrate. Recently the pet trade has offered filter materials that break down nitrate, but we do not yet have comprehensive experiences with them.

3) Filtration also offers the opportunity to perform regular preventive treatment and to kill pathogens.

When buying a filter, remember that turtles produce a great deal of filth. Therefore, it is important to select a suitably powerful device with a centrifugal pump. If the manufacturer claims that filtration capacity is sufficient for an aquarium with a capacity of 200 liters (about 53 gallons), I recommend using a filter of at least three times that capacity.

Filters will greatly improve your water quality, which is especially important for turtles that develop fungus and shell rot easily, like the soft-shells. This is an albino Florida Soft-shell, *Trionyx ferox*. Photo by M. Bacon.

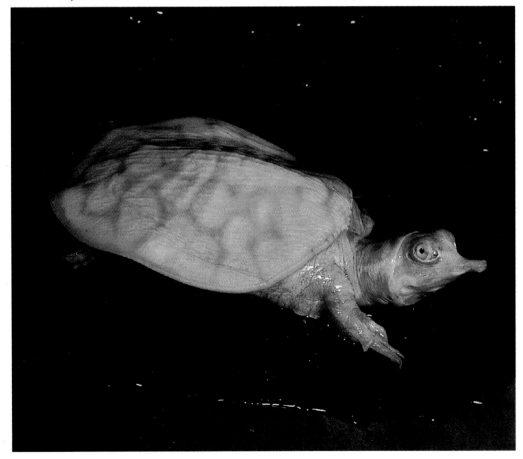

Turtles of the genera *Emys*, *Mauremys*, and *Chrysemys* in a man-made pond. Photo by W. Hemmer.

This is an artificial pond with a plastic liner. With an area of about 100 square meters, it offers optimal conditions for the turtles kept in it. Photo by W. Hemmer.

Breeding Turtles

The crowning achievement of keeping animals is breeding them successfully. A true captive breeding requires that copulation occurred successfully in captivity. It is an even greater achievement, however, when we rear captive-bred offspring and they in turn also produce offspring that continue to breed in subsequent generations.

Outdoor keeping during the warm season certainly is one of the most important prerequisites for breeding turtles, but a very varied diet and of course a suitable mate are equally impor-

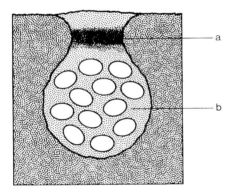

A clutch of turtle eggs. a. strongly compacted layer; b. soil between the eggs, which normally do not move.

tant. Turtles also express sympathies and antipathies between the sexes, and a female will not always accept every male its keeper offers it. I have seen a female reject every male suitor, even when they made every effort to win the female's favor. Then I introduced a new suitor, identical to my eyes, that "came, saw, and conquered."

When we observe the courtship of male turtles, few species exhibit the graceful courtship behavior we see in so many other animal species. The turtle species that do exhibit an elaborate courtship behavior include *Kachuga tecta tecta* and *K. t. circumdata*, as well as various *Chrysemys* or *Pseudemys* species. We must admire the persistence they show in courting the female. Of course, we also find turtle species in which the males exhibit rough courtship behav-

ior. These include *Cuora, Phrynops, Emys,* and others. Tortoises (including *Testudo*) often display a brutal courtship behavior. Here the ramming by rutty males even has cracked the female's shell. Of course, turtles of the same species often show great individual differences.

In my experience, most tropical aquatic turtles usually lay their eggs in the months of November to February. Anyone who knows his turtles well notices immediately when a female is ready to lay her eggs. She becomes restless, leaves the water, and wanders around on land. She also tries to climb the walls (many individuals show an astounding ability to climb), then returns to the water, and so on. This restlessness can continue for eight to ten days. With *Chelodina longicollis*, for example, I observed that the female began to dig following this period of restlessness. When the female finished the nest hole or it was deep enough, she stuck her head down to the bottom of the hole and left it there for a while. If the nest was not up to expectations, the female abandoned the site without laying eggs or even filling in the hole. The female excavated several more holes and behaved in the same way before she found a satisfactory site and laid her eggs there. Unlike the clutches of tortoises, with aquatic and semi-aquatic turtles I no longer remove the eggs from the nest. I merely expose the clutch, remove damaged eggs, replace the sand, and cover it with fine wire mesh. The mesh should be fine enough to prevent the hatching youngsters from getting through and strong enough to protect the eggs from the digging of other females.

The number of eggs turtles lay is highly variable. One of my *Testudo graeca* lays 20 to 22 eggs every year. For years, one *Pseudemys [Trachemys] scripta elegans* laid two clutches of eight to ten eggs, usually in February, at an interval of about two weeks. A *Chrysemys picta dorsalis* that I reared from a youngster usually laid four or five eggs twice a year, but at an interval of at least four to six weeks. (Unfortunately, these were always infertile, because I never obtained a suitable healthy and active male.)

Both *Chelodina novaeguineae* and *Emydura macquarri* usually lay eight to ten eggs twice a year. On the other hand, *Emydura albertisi* lays eight to ten eggs up to five times a year.

As a normal average temperature for the clutch, 25 to 30°C (77 to 86°F) has proved effective. At higher temperatures there is the danger that the embryos will develop too quickly in the eggs and will hatch too soon. According to the most recent findings, the temperature during the maturation of the eggs determines the sex of the hatchling turtle in most genera. At 30°C (86°F), supposedly [in most species] only females hatch. Unfortunately, we often find that many eggs are infertile, and many of the copulations observed are unsuccessful. On the other hand, a single copulation (in various species) can fertilize a female for one to four years, although the number of fertile eggs decreases in each successive clutch. It long ago was observed that, for example, *Terrapene* species only laid infertile eggs starting in the fifth year.

If we cannot leave the eggs in the nest, we absolutely must mark them, because even the slightest change in position can kill the embryo. This may not be true, however, of all species. The literature reports that during World War II, in the Berlin Aquarium, the keepers simply put the eggs of the Matamata in a drawer. When workers opened the drawer weeks later, a healthy, fully developed youngster had hatched.

We immediately must remove any egg laid in the water, because otherwise the embryo will die. [Water of course prevents air from entering the pores of the eggshell.] Even the temporary absence of air may cause deformities.

Incubator. a. plate glass; b. thermometer; c. perforated Styrofoam for ventilating the eggs; d. support; e. heater; f. thermometer in water.

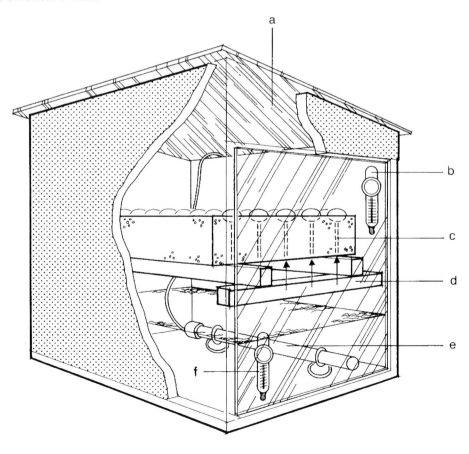

Outdoor installation for adult Snapping Turtles, *Chelydra serpentina*. In such a setup, the turtles can be kept outdoors the whole year in most climates. Photo by M. Mohr.

Clutch of *Emydura macquarri,* the Murray River Turtle, immediately after laying. Notice the marking to prevent the eggs from being turned, which would result in the death of the embryos. Photo by G. Müller.

Hatchlings of Hermann's Tortoise, *Testudo hermanni.* Photo by B. Kahl.

The incubation period of the eggs varies greatly and of course also depends on various factors, particularly temperature and humidity. Temperatures that are too high (above 32°C, 90°F) often cause the turtles to die in the egg or they are not viable after they hatch. On the other hand, scientists have determined that low temperatures of 18 to 20°C (65 to 68°F) are not harmful and merely lengthen the maturation period. As a rule, the eggs require two to three, more rarely three and a half, months to mature. Tortoise eggs usually need even longer, often more than six months! Eggs of *Emys orbicularis* supposedly have overwintered outdoors, the young turtles not hatching until the following year. [Painted Turtles, *Chrysemys picta*, at the northern part of their range often remain in the nest after hatching because the ground has frozen.]

Female Bowsprit Tortoise, *Testudo* (*Chersina*) *angulata,* laying eggs. This species is rarely kept in captivity. Photo by K. H. Switak.

Years ago I stopped using incubators for rearing. In my opinion, any manipulation of the clutch, such as marking, weighing, measuring, and the repeated "having a look," is harmful. When I used incubators in my early years of keeping turtles, I had minimal hatching success. Whole clutches often died or the hatchlings did not develop fully (by the way, this also applies to the lizards I bred, such as *Basiliscus plumifrons, Phelsuma m. madagascariensis, Anolis carolinensis*, and *Chamaeleo dilepis*, among others).

Since I started putting ready-to-lay aquatic turtles or sexually mature females in my large terrarium and let them choose the most suitable laying sites themselves, I have had a hatching rate of nearly 100 percent with fertile eggs. The approximately 1,500 hatchlings that I have reared in about 22 years prove this.

After a female has laid her eggs and covered the hole in one of the two land sections, I uncover the clutch to the point that I can determine the position of the eggs. I then cover the clutch with fine wire mesh so that other ready-to-lay females cannot excavate the eggs and the hatching babies cannot reach the water basin with the adult turtles, which usually eat them. The two land sections consist of a mixture of sand and peat in a 3:2 ratio. They are about 25 centimeters (10 inches) deep. Below them is a layer of gravel for drainage as well as a drain, so that moisture cannot accumulate there. I only use river sand, never quartz sand.

I heat the land sections with heating mats that are impermeable to water and can be used anywhere. They give off a very uniform heat. The temperature in the land section varies from 26 to 30°C (79 to 86°F). I have observed that the females do not always use sites with the same temperature to lay their eggs. This probably affects the sex of the hatchlings.

In turtle breeding, despite diverse experiences, there always are new worlds to conquer. Therefore, I ask all serious hobbyists to publish even seemingly unimportant experiences. Only in this way can other breeders profit from them and achieve breeding successes that could contribute to the survival of a species.

Diet

Unlike many terrarium animals, which need a constant supply of live food (and often need special food animals, such as insects, snails, mice, or even lizards), turtles are easy to feed. It is essential, however, to supply a varied diet that includes all the basic nutriments the turtles need for their well-being. I feed my tortoises dandelion, thistle, unsprayed lettuce, grated carrot, beans, all kinds of fruit (stone fruits with pits removed), and, occasionally as a special treat, banana. From time to time I also feed them animal food, such as earthworms, finely chopped beef heart, or beef liver, which they also are fond of. They also like dry dog and cat food (soften hard food beforehand by soaking), but do not feed too much of this food, because it can cause gout. My *Testudo [Geochelone] carbonaria* are very fond of fish (sardines with head and bones). I feed my aquatic turtles dried shrimp every other day. The shrimp also provide roughage. You can buy them in agricultural feed stores in the form of chicken feed. The shrimp also contain a great deal of calcium, which benefits shell growth. In addition, once a week I feed finely chopped beef heart and frozen sardines (thawed first, of course). I also offer dandelion, lettuce, and sliced banana occasionally, depending on season. Additionally, I give them everything that turns up in the house and garden: caterpillars, maggots, insects, earthworms, slugs, snails, aquatic snails, as well as all kinds of freshwater fishes.

The diet of young turtles requires special attention, because any mistake made here can affect their development. Lasting damage, such as rachitic malformations and deformations, can persist for years and even remain visible forever. I cannot explain, however, how sometimes specimens of the same size, which I reared at the same time, under the same conditions, on the same diet, react completely differently. One individual has rachitic symptoms, whereas another of the same species is completely normal. Because juveniles grow very fast and therefore need a great deal of food, vitamins, and minerals, particularly calcium, we must feed them more often.

I have always fed juveniles a particularly varied diet: very finely chopped beef heart and liver, aquatic crustaceans, chopped earthworms, daphnia, midge larvae, small aquatic snails, and commercially prepared foods including tablets, sticks, and pastes. The most varied food of all is meadow plankton (sweepings), because it consists of so many different kinds of insects.

The gelatin-based turtle food cited by various authors in the literature certainly has great advantages, but it is worth preparing only if you keep a fairly large number of turtles. Various recipes exist for it. I recommend Pauler's "turtle pudding." The recipe yields eight liters (2.1 gallons) of gelatin food.

1 liter milk (low-fat, if possible)

5 eggs

1 kilogram unsprayed carrots

1 kilogram squid (because the tentacles are very hard to process, it is better to use smaller squid or pieces of squid)

1 kilogram lean fish (if possible with scales and bones)

0.5 kilogram shrimp

0.5 kilogram beef heart, beef, possibly a little liver (but not too much, or the food will not set)

4 vitamin supplement capsules

1 tablespoon marine algae flour

approximately 2 liters of water

600 to 800 grams of powdered gelatin (70 to 80 grams per liter) of the best quality, minimum 260 Blum (measure of the binding ability of the gelatin)

Pour the powdered gelatin into a pot and cover it with about 1.75 liters of cold water while stirring. Allow to soak for 15 to 20 minutes, and then dissolve the gelatin over

A European Pond Turtle, *Emys orbicularis*, in the act of hatching. This species is bred frequently in Europe and occasionally in the U. S. Photo by W. Hemmer.

very low heat, stirring occasionally. Steam the carrots for about five minutes and then put them, along with the squid, fish, heart, and shrimp, through the meat grinder (with a large appliance there is no need to cut the ingredients into smaller pieces) or chop it in the blender. Transfer the mixture to a second pot and heat over a low flame. Then add the hot milk, eggs, marine algae meal, and the vitamin capsules (dissolved in a small amount of water) and stir well. Heat the chopped puree to a temperature of about 35 to 40°C (95 to 104°F) (measure with a laboratory thermometer). Now stir this puree in portions into the dissolved gelatin (heated to about 40°C—be sure to measure; if the temperature difference between the two liquids is too great, the gelatin will not set). Transfer immediately to shallow containers and refrigerate. Chill the food thoroughly. After the food sets, divide it into portions and freeze.

Recently several prepared foods that contain a balanced diet for turtles, complete with vitamin and calcium supplements, have become available at pet shops. These foods, often in the form of sticks or tablets, are easy to feed and are accepted by most turtles after just a short adjustment period. Be sure, however, that the brand you feed does not cloud the water; experiment with a few pieces of different formulas. Since I started using this food, I have stopped the time-consuming preparation of the "turtle pudding." Of course, I continue to supplement the diet with greenfood, fruit, dried shrimp, and occasionally with finely chopped beef heart or beef liver as well as freshwater fish or soaked saltwater fish.

With hatchlings I must warn against the feeding of tubifex, the so-called "mud worms." Because this food is harvested from the mud of canals or sewage ditches, there is the danger of an infection with disease organisms and the like.

In the first three months of rearing, I feed, apart from meadow plankton, exclusively a dry food mixture of 50 percent shrimp, 40 percent amphipods or scuds, and 10 percent fish flake food, which also promotes the development of the turtles' coloration. Since then I have achieved a rearing rate of nearly 100 percent, apart from the "runts" that occasionally hatch.

The rule with diet always is the more varied, the better. It is completely wrong to feed only the food that the turtles like to eat. In any case, do not feed adult turtles too often. Twice or three times a week is sufficient, and any leftovers were too much anyway.

Red-foot Tortoises, *Testudo* (*Chelonoidis*) *carbonaria,* with a Leopard Tortoise (left), *Testudo* [*Geochelone*] *pardalis,* at feeding time. Although many tortoises will take beef heart and other meats, feeding such things often can result in gout and shell deformities. Photo by G. J. Seite.

Hibernation

With most turtles from the Northern Hemisphere, experts recommend hibernation for keeping the turtles in good health. Hibernation is not advisable with very young turtles. During hibernation they often die or become so weak that they subsequently remain stunted and never reach adulthood. According to the most recent findings, hibernation is not essential, but affects positively the reproductive ability in some species.

Aquatic Turtles

With aquatic turtles, I particularly recommend hibernation for species from Europe and those with similar climatic conditions with a regular winter. I put the turtles in an enclosure (in which I gradually lower the water temperature to 8 to 10°C, 46 to 50°F) in an unheated room or in the basement, where they remain at this temperature. We must stop feeding the turtles some time beforehand, to make sure that the intestinal tract is empty and feces do not foul the water. The turtles remain in this enclosure until the temperatures have warmed up for good in the spring (beware of premature, temporary warm spells). A "wet" overwintering of aquatic and semi-aquatic turtles is better than a "dry" overwintering.

Tortoises

When the temperature drops in the fall and the tortoises stop feeding, I bathe them in lukewarm water several times to void the intestinal tract. Then I thoroughly dry and grease the tortoises. For this purpose, I use an ointment that simultaneously protects against mites. [Many keepers recommend against ever oiling a tortoise.] I put a layer of slightly moist peat in a suitably large box and then place the tortoises on the peat and cover them with a thick layer of dry leaves or hay. I put the box in the basement or some other frost-free room (not colder than about 6°C, 43°F) and store it there until the tortoises become restless in the spring. Do not be concerned if the tortoises awaken from hibernation prematurely during a warm period. I advise checking the tortoises at about four-week intervals without disturbing them. Before I release the overwintered tortoises in the terrarium or outdoors, I bathe them in lukewarm water. They usually drink deeply while they bathe. Then I dry them thoroughly and grease the shell. I put them outside on a warm, sunny day only after I have kept them completely dry for a day.

OVERWINTERING OUTDOORS

Tortoises

Many hobbyists hibernate their tortoises outdoors, but this practice has its problems. It may work if we do it in a well-watered, leaf-filled hole of suitable size that is protected from rodents with wire mesh. It always is dangerous, however, when tortoises at liberty dig themselves into compost heaps or elsewhere and they are left to their own devices. Then they have absolutely no protection against rats and mice, which often gnaw on the tortoises. The rodents sometimes even manage to pull the tortoises out of the compost pile because the tortoises cannot react in the hibernating state. During warm spells in our latitudes, the tortoises often become active and emerge, but in the cold snap that usually follows, they can no longer dig themselves in quickly and deeply enough and consequently freeze to death.

Aquatic Turtles

Aquatic turtles from suitable habitats definitely can remain outdoors. The pond should be at least 1 meter (40 inches) deep so that it does not freeze to the bottom. If ice forms on the surface, never break it up; this would alarm the turtles, which would then swim around and have to go to the surface for air. This activity stimulates the heart rate, which was at a minimum, and the turtles usually will be unable to return to hibernation. If the hole in the ice then freezes over, this will cut the turtles off from the air and they will suffocate. I recommend highly the oxygenator devices available today for such ponds. They contain 30 percent hydrogen peroxide and, through a catalytic reaction resulting in the breakdown of the hydrogen peroxide, release oxygen into the water. In this way an oxygen supply is present even under a covering of ice that prevents the water from turning over. In a pond with a capacity of about 2500 to 3000 liters (660 to 792 gallons), a one-liter supply lasts about 14 to 16 weeks during the winter.

With larger ponds, I advise installing two oxygenators.

Each hobbyist must choose which method of overwintering to use. In my opinion, indoor hibernation in a box or tank at low temperatures is significantly less risky than outdoor hibernation under largely uncontrollable conditions. I would like to add that hatchlings and young turtles should not hibernate during their first two years of life; instead, we should care for them as usual at slightly lower temperatures during the winter. It is normal for the turtles to eat less and hide frequently during this time. The same also applies to not completely intact or frail turtles.

Many turtles, particularly aquatic turtles, do not necessarily have to hibernate. Hibernation, however, often is a requirement for successful breeding.

Wild Painted Turtles, *Chrysemys picta*, living in the northern part of their range may freeze solid during the winter. In the spring, they thaw out seemingly none the worse for the wear. Photo by W. P. Mara.

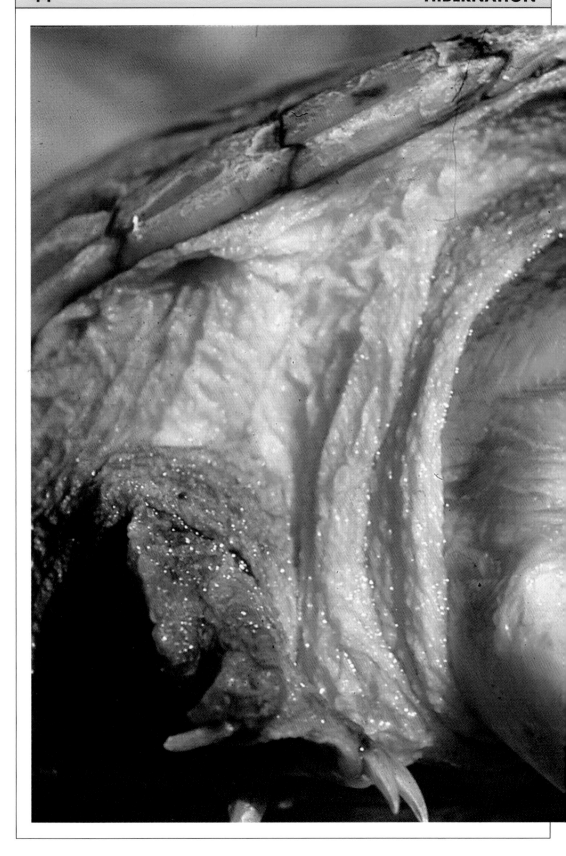

Close-up of the Narrow-bridged Musk Turtle, *Claudius angustatus.* This species is only rarely seen in the terrarium hobby. In the wild, it inhabits slow, muddy streams in Mexico and northern Central America. Photo by MP. and C. Piednoir.

Diseases

Unfortunately, this is one of the most important chapters of my book. Because most veterinarians have a limited knowledge of turtles, I will try to give some instructions for the treatment and prevention of diseases. These measures have proved effective with my own turtles and when used by other experienced turtle keepers.

Most turtles we keep for many years in captivity do not get sick. We also do not have problems with our own captive-bred turtles or those we buy from other breeders. We do, however, find illnesses with imported specimens recently bought from a dealer. Keep in mind that with many of these new imports the stress of capture and transport and the complete change in environment trigger illnesses. These turtles may never have gotten ill in the native biotope, despite the presence of the pathogen. This is particularly true of baby turtles that arrive in a weakened condition and are particularly susceptible to illness.

At the same time, however, I would like to point out how important it is to acquire turtles only if we can offer them an environment comparable to their own biotope, and if we can sacrifice a great deal of effort and leisure time for their well-being. Furthermore, I think it is enormously important to immediately send dead turtles whose cause of death is unknown or not precisely known to a specialist research facility. We should include the following information to help form a useful file on the specimen:

1) The common and scientific name of the turtle.

2) How did you acquire it (did you buy it, breed it in captivity, trade for it, and so forth)?

3) How long did you keep it?

4) Under what conditions did you keep it?

5) What was its diet and what were its eating habits?

6) When did symptoms of illness appear?

7) What other animals did you keep with it?

8) Did you record previously the deaths of other animals?

When shipping, do not pack the turtles in plastic bags or freeze them beforehand. [Turtles, living or dead, cannot be shipped through the mails in the United States. Unfortunately, few hobbyists have a good working relationship with a college or zoo that will perform autopsies on dead turtles. Rising costs and busy personnel also make autopsies unavailable to the general public. Your veterinarian might be able to do a simple posting of a dead specimen, the fresher the better, or be able to refer you to someone who will be able to help you. In any case, be prepared to pay for the service and also for the costs of bacteriological and other laboratory tests.]

The following diseases and conditions are seen with some regularity in captive turtles. Where treatments can be performed by hobbyists, they are mentioned. [Always check with your veterinarian before administering any drugs to a turtle. You should try to find a local vet who enjoys and is capable of working with turtles, and you should try to stay in a good working relationship with your vet. Home diagnosis and treatment of turtle ills seldom is a simple process, and an incorrect guess at any stage may lead to an even worse situation in your pet.]

AMOEBIASIS

The pathogen of this disease is a protozoan, an amoeba. The disease is not transmissible from reptile to human, but it is the most widespread disease in the terrarium. Many zoos and private collections have suffered a death rate of up to 100 percent. With turtles there is the problem that in a terrarium the whole population can be latent carriers of the infection without becoming ill themselves. These chronic carriers can infect newly arrived, possibly weakened specimens, or because of inadequate hygiene also can infect the populations of other terraria and lead to the further infection or loss of specimens. The following precautions apply for the prevention of amoebiasis:

1) Never separate turtles that you have kept together for a fairly long time and transfer them to another tank with other turtles.

2) Never put newly bought or self-caught turtles with fully acclimated specimens. They must undergo a quarantine of about 8 to 12 weeks, preferably in "solitary confinement," as a preventive measure.

During the quarantine period, check the feces for worms and treat the turtles if necessary. [The assistance of your vet for these tests will be necessary.] When you send fecal samples to test for an amoebiasis infection, make sure that not too much time goes by between the time you collect the feces and the examination. Specialist institutes can use another, more direct method. It is not, however, as accurate as culturing.

4) I advise transferring the turtles to the general population only after they have completed the quarantine. The turtles should behave normally and eat and defecate regularly. I must emphasize that no matter how long the turtles spend in quarantine, however, there is no ultimate guarantee that they are not carriers.

5) Use separate furnishings for each cage. Always keep them clean. Depending on the material, wash them in hot water or boil them regularly.

6) If you keep turtles in several terraria, especially in quarantine tanks, wash your hands frequently or, better yet, disinfect them with antibacterial soap and an alcohol bath.

7) Following deaths, disinfect the terrarium thoroughly. This can be difficult, if not impossible, with outdoor facilities.

Symptoms:

Turtles infected with amoebiasis eat little or refuse food entirely. They often have gaping mouths and have convulsions with twitching or turning of the head and the legs. Tortoises drink excessively. If you observe such anomalous behavior, isolate the turtle immediately.

Treatment:

Treatment is possible in the early stage, but confirm an amoebiasis infection by examining the feces or dissecting the dead turtle. A very useful preparation, Clont (Bayer) (1-[beta-hydroxyethyl] 2-methyl-5-nitroimidazol), has proved effective. The preparation also goes by the name Flagyl. The pharmaceutical industry originally developed it for the treatment of trichomonads in humans. Treatment takes 6 to 12 days, depending on the number of tablets you administer. We determine the proper dosage from the dosage for humans, calculating the dosage for the body weight of the turtle. Then we multiply this amount by a factor of five. I recommend pulverizing the tablets and mixing them with a liquid. I administer this solution through a syringe (with a bicycle-tire valve in place of the needle) directly into the mouth and gullet or directly into the cloaca (with extreme caution!). With larger specimens, it is preferable to buy the vaginal form of the tablets and to insert these in the cloaca. The advantage of inserting the tablets in the cloaca is that the medication reaches the amoebiasis protozoans directly, because they usually live in the rectum. Because the body absorbs this preparation relatively poorly and the protozoans also infest the internal organs (mainly the liver), additional treatment often is necessary. A suitable medication for this purpose is Resochin (Bayer), which we administer as follows: Per kilogram of body weight, inject 1 cc of the preparation into the thigh muscle (with specimens weighing less than 200 grams, use 0.4 cc, not 0.2 cc). Repeat the treatment every two to three days for two or at most three weeks. In the following weeks, administer the medication twice a week. This treatment, subsequent to the previous therapy, is the only way we know of to save at least some of the infected charges.

EYE DISEASES

These can have many causes and sometimes are only one of the symptoms of another disease. Inflammation of the eye with swollen eyelids and sometimes a red coloration of the conjunctiva can have various causes.

1) If the patient also has a nasal discharge, it probably has a cold. Causes include drafts, too low keeping temperatures, or a too sudden change in temperature.

Treatment:

Isolate the patient, raise the water temperature, cover the enclosure, use an infrared lamp, and apply an appropriate veterinary eye ointment to the eyes, making sure you apply the ointment carefully under the eyelid. Bathe the patient once a day in diluted chamomile solution or Kamillosan. In persistent cases, I have used the following method with great success: Take an ointment containing volatile oils and menthol such as we use in human medicine as a liniment for colds. Warmth releases fumes that open the air passages and make it easier to breathe. Put some of this ointment in a pot with moderately hot water and dissolve it. Put the turtle in a fairly large colander and cover it with a cloth. Set the colander on the pot and leave it for about an hour. [As with all home remedies, caution is advised, especially with hot water.] In one case, one treatment cured the patient completely. In other cases, I also achieved success after repeating the procedure. To keep the water hot, put the pot on a hot plate. It is important to maintain a constant water temperature; make sure that it does not rise. Following this "steam bath," it is particularly important to put the patient immediately in an isolation tank. Also be sure to protect the patient from drafts (wrap the patient in a hand towel before you transfer it). [If the cold is due to bacteria or viruses, rather than just a symptom of a stress condition, obviously this remedy will not work. Please consult a veterinarian for this and all other possibly complicated conditions.]

2) Other causes of inflammations of the eye include contamination and dirty water.

Treatment:
Isolate the patient, keep it dry, and treat the eyes with a veterinary eye ointment (including sulfonamide or an antibiotic) about three times a day. Every other day put the patient in warm (26 to 28°C, 79 to 82°F), clean water for several hours. Continue treatment until the eyes heal. With tortoises also provide a warm, constant temperature, avoid direct sunlight, and drip eye drops with a pipette directly under the lid (the tortoises usually wipe off the eye ointment).

3) Exposure to ultraviolet radiation at too close or too strong a level often causes cloudy or milky gray eyes. The various species show ex-

tremely variable reactions. When I used to irradiate regularly with ultraviolet lamps, I observed the following: At a distance of 1 meter (40 inches) from the lamp, the *Pseudemys, Chrysemys, Chinemys, Graptemys*, chelodinas, emyduras, *Kachuga, Clemmys*, and *Mauremys* species exhibited no changes at 30 minutes of exposure. I could expose the *Podocnemis* species, however, only for a maximum of 15 minutes. Upon longer exposure, they exhibited the symptoms described above. The turtles's reactions seemed abnormal and they could no longer see clearly. I treated them with eye ointment, and after about a week the eyes were clear again and vision was normal.

4) Eye diseases can also be the result of nutritional deficiencies (rachitis, etc.). I will discuss them in a separate section.

SOFTENING OR DEFORMATION OF THE SHELL
This usually is a result of rachitis and is very serious in the advanced stage.

Symptoms:
The normal turtle shell (except for baby turtles, Pancake Tortoises, and softshell turtles) is hard and does not bend. If the shell is soft and you can push the plastron in with your finger, the patient requires immediate attention. The turtle also often has an inflammation of the eyes. In most cases, the deformation of the carapace and plastron (upward curving margins, formation of humps in species that normally have a smooth carapace, or other deformities) share the same cause: vitamin D deficiency, absence of sunlight or equivalent artificial light, and a one-sided diet.

Treatment:
Prevention is better than a cure! If possible, and if the species does not require very high temperatures, keep the turtle outdoors or on the balcony—at least in summer. Administer multivitamins with a high vitamin D content. Feed a diet that includes plenty of shrimp, earthworms, and snails with their shells, and administer calcium preparations (also cuttlebone). If the turtle does not receive direct sunlight, use ultraviolet irradiation, being sure to follow the previously

described precautions. In the greatly advanced stage, I recommend having the veterinarian inject a water-soluble vitamin preparation containing vitamins A, D3, E, and C.

SHELL INJURIES

Mechanical injuries to the shell caused by falling or carelessness, apart from extreme cases with possible internal injuries, are not tragic. They heal relatively quickly if we apply a cod liver oil ointment to the site and isolate the patient. In some cases, we must treat the turtle with an antibiotic. Shell injuries that suddenly appear in isolated places, at first usually only in the form of dark blotches, are more problematic.

Symptoms:

You easily can lift the affected dorsal scute. Underneath the scute there is damage to the bone and a cheesy, usually foul-smelling, mass is present. In the most serious cases, the bone has been eaten through.

Treatment:

Lift and remove the affected dorsal or ventral scute. With a small spoon, carefully scoop out the soft part until only solid bone remains. Slight bleeding is not serious. Next dab the wound with alcohol, brush with gentian violet (alcohol solution), and dust with terramycin powder. Take care! Use protective gloves, because the "violet" discolors very strongly and stains the fingers for a long time. Repeat the procedure until the patient recovers. Return aquatic turtles to the water, however, every third day. This treatment sometimes takes many weeks.

When we buy turtles, they often have isolated damaged spots on the shell that do not heal on their own, but also do not exhibit the aforementioned symptoms. I recommend brushing these sites (after moistening them first) with silver nitrate, repeating this procedure every other day. The caustic action stimulates the growth of the horny material. I have had excellent success with this method. Sometimes the damaged sites healed completely. Exercise caution when handling the silver nitrate! Do not get it on your hands and do not touch the treated places. This material will cauterize your skin, and skin exposed to silver nitrate will turn black (due to

reaction to light), the blotches persisting for one to two weeks. A prescription probably will be required to obtain silver nitrate.

NECROSIS OF THE SKIN AND SHELL IN AQUATIC TURTLES

Necrotic (dead) spots are due to infectious diseases that affect the skin and shell. In advanced stages, they also affect the toes and claws.

Symptoms:

White botches appear, particularly on the head and legs, more rarely on the shell. If you rub off these necrotic spots, the hypodermis starts to bleed. At first they are small, but often they quickly grow into large blotches, which then turn brownish. These places begin to swell, and with infected toes the claws fall out. The horny margins of the jaws loosen and partially or completely fall out. The affected places grow noticeably larger and the turtle stops feeding because of the deformation of the jaw margins and die of starvation or sepsis. This disease is infectious. It is astounding how different turtles kept in the community terrarium react to it. The *Kachuga* species, *Siebenrockiella crassicollis*, *Chrysemys*, *Chinemys reevesi*, and particularly *Lissemys punctata* as well as *Clemmys guttata* were very susceptible. I did not observe the infection with *Pseudemys, Podocnemis, Pelomedusa, Emydura*, as well as chelodinas (in contrast to other reports in the literature). We do not yet know the true identity of the pathogen, but it probably is some kind of bacterium. Naturally, many other pathogens, such as fungi, also colonize the affected sites as secondary pathogens.

Treatment:

If the infection is not in the advanced stage, treatment is straightforward and promising. In such cases I have used baths with a high table salt concentration and applied pure alcohol (do not get in the eyes) with rather good success. In 1963, for example, from a Swiss pet dealer I received four baby *Chrysemys picta dorsalis* that were in very good condition. However, after four weeks all four specimens exhibited necrotic spots that grew extremely rapidly. The condition soon became so bad that the claws of two specimens started to fall out. I submerged the turtles for ten minutes in a solution of one tablespoon of salt in a quarter liter of water while holding only the head above the water. After that I put them in a small aquarium containing dilute salt water (about 5 grams per liter). The next day I took the babies out, dried them off, and then brushed them with alcohol. After drying them for an hour, I returned them to a weak salt solution. I repeated this treatment several times.

One specimen with very advanced necrosis died. The other three were healthy after a week. When one baby had a slight relapse, I removed it immediately and rubbed it with fine, moistened salt. After the salt acted for a half hour, I rinsed the turtle and the infection never returned. As a preventive measure with aquatic turtles (except in the outdoor pond), I now always add salt to the water (2 grams per liter) with the best of success.

A mixture of two sulfonamides, Marbadal and Debenal-M, also has been used by German keepers. They smeared the patient's whole body with it and kept it out of water for one day. After 24 hours in water, they repeated the procedure. They observed healing a few days later as the skin grew back. Necrosis has been treated successfully with Bayrena, using a dosage of 80 milligrams active agent per kilogram of body weight on the first day and 40 milligrams per kilogram on days two to seven. The solution was injected into the muscle on the outside of the hind leg. (Because of the anatomy of the turtle, I consider the underside to be a better site, but because of the rapid excretion by the kidneys, injection in the upper forearm is more favorable than in the thigh.) In difficult and advanced cases, I recommend using a combination of Supronal and Bayrena. Obviously, we also must thoroughly disinfect the enclosure; Sagrotan has been used in a concentration of 4 percent and an exposure time of four hours, followed by thorough rinsing.

HEXAMITIASIS

This is a chronic disease of turtles that runs its course without specific symptoms. A flagellate is the vector. Hexamites are very fast-moving parasites that survive for a long time in feces and

urine but survive freezing or fairly high temperatures for only a few hours. They have a cosmopolitan distribution. Sources of infection, particularly at high population densities, include both sick and clinically healthy specimens. Hexamites apparently infect aquatic turtles through the water and tortoises through infected food. Cloacal autoinfection, however, also seems possible. Although other reptiles and amphibians also harbor these pathogens, only turtles become infected by hexamites. Various factors are important for the occurrence of the infection: errors in keeping and diet; bacterial, viral, and parasitic infections; stress factors, such as moving turtles to new enclosures during acclimation, and so forth; as well as overcrowding. We do not know the precise incubation period (the time from which the pathogen enters the organism until the first clinical symptoms appear), but apparently it is at least three months. Hexamites are part of the normal intestinal flora (Frank, personal communication). In most aquatic turtles, hexamites are present in the fecal smear, but they do not affect the turtles if the host-parasite ratio is in equilibrium. Only under the influence of the above-mentioned factors is there a change in the intestinal flora that leads to the outbreak of the disease. Only then can we detect a large number of hexamites in the feces or anal smear.

The turtles become increasingly apathetic, lose weight, refuse food, and slowly die. The urine is viscous and slimy or thin and gelatinous.

Treatment:

Resochi, in a dosage of 50 milligrams per kilogram body weight per day for five days, injected in the musculature or under the skin, is an effective chemotherapy. We usually stop the treatment before the course is finished, however, because the preparation attacks the liver and the patient tolerates it poorly. During treatment, the patient looks even sicker than before. Therefore, I recommend administering Clont (metronidazole) over an interval of two to three days (orally two to three weeks), together with a liver-protecting therapy (Methiovertan, injected into muscle). The dosage for Clont is 50 to 100 milligrams per kilogram body weight (about 1 tablet [0.25 gram] per 2 kilograms). Duodegran (Ronidazole) is another preparation I recommend. Administer it orally in a dosage of 10 milligrams per kilogram body weight for eight to ten days.

Prevention:

The most important prerequisites for stabilizing an aquatic turtle population are maintaining strict hygienic measures and decreasing the population density of the terrarium. The same rules also apply to tortoises. Diagnosing a live turtle is difficult without clinical symptoms, because hexamites also infect completely healthy turtles.

MITES AND TICKS

I have never seen a turtle infested with mites, although supposedly it occurs frequently. In any case, ticks are a much bigger problem, particularly with semiterrestrial turtles and tortoises. The ticks, which usually attach themselves on the undersides of the hind legs, are dark, flat, or elongate-oval creatures up to the size of a hazelnut (in large species that are full of blood). On the other hand, mites look like tiny (barely visible) moving red dots.

Treatment:

Spray the turtle and the enclosure with a 2 percent solution of Neguvon (Bayer). Repeat after 8 to 14 days. I must mention that this preparation has fatally poisoned various reptiles (snakes), although turtles seem to be less sensitive. We also can remove a tick easily from the turtle by coating or dabbing it with oil. This causes the tick to suffocate, after which it falls off or can be picked off easily. Never simply try to pull off ticks by hand or with forceps, because the mouth parts usually remain behind and can cause inflammations and festering wounds that can take a long time to heal. Normally, mites and ticks are almost harmless and not fatal.

PNEUMONIA

Turtles kept in the terrarium, particularly in the outdoor terrarium, sometimes get pneumonia, especially following a sudden drop in temperature in the outdoor period or with inappropriate care in the home. A neglected cold, however, also can turn into pneumonia.

Symptoms:

The turtles become listless and spend an inordinate amount of time on land if aquatic. Tortoises suddenly have moist nostrils. During respiration small bubbles form at the nostrils and the turtles emit piping noises. They swim aslant in the water because they can no longer blow out air from the diseased part of the lung (the diseased part always floats higher). In the advanced stage they try to dive in vain. In this stage the turtles are also no longer able to eat. Usually the turtles still seize pieces of food held in front of them, but they can no longer swallow the food, because the swallowing movements are too weak.

Treatment:

Use the "steam-bath" therapy as described under eye conditions. We must, of course, isolate the patient in clean, warm quarters. I also advise irradiation with infrared light (30 minutes) or the Vitalux lamp (10 minutes). Also administer vitamin A and D, if necessary by means of a syringe (with a bicycle-tire valve inserted in place of the needle to prevent injury). The use of Omnacillin has had good success. Injections of tetracylines (terramycin, aureomycin) also have proved effective. The dosage is 50 milligrams per kilogram body weight on the first day, subsequently 30 milligrams per kilogram over the following three to six days. Adding a dash of hydrogen peroxide to the water may do a good job of dissolving the mucus.

TUBERCULOSIS

Tuberculosis bacteria often cause what appears to be pneumonia. The symptoms are similar to those mentioned in the previous section. In this case, however, the small bubbles do not form at the nostrils. Years ago a fully grown, very beautiful female *Chelodina longicollis* of mine died from tuberculosis. I probably was responsible for the death myself, because I had always put dead aquarium fishes directly in the turtle tank. The turtle in question was very agile and therefore always was the first to arrive to snap up this food. The fishes continued to die, and eventually I had several of them tested. They had tuberculosis. This showed that the sick fishes infected the *Chelodina*. Tuberculosis can appear in many forms anywhere in the body, as well as

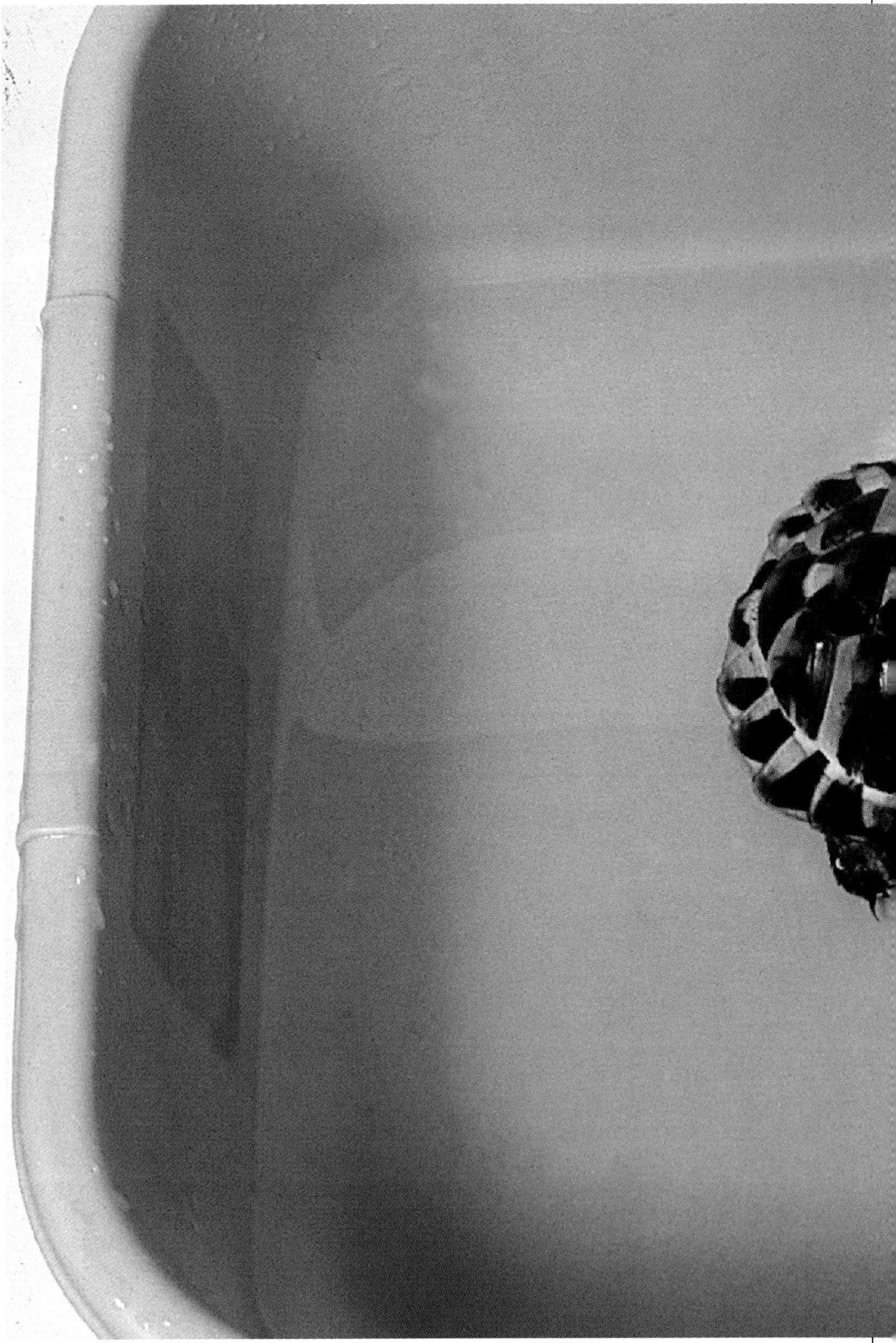

Although many tortoises must be kept in relatively dry conditions, an occasional soak is good for them. Here is a Hermann's Tortoise, *Testudo hermanni*, enjoying a bath. Photo by I. Francais.

externally. Only a bacteriological institute can provide a definitive diagnosis through culture methods.

Treatment:

Medicinal treatment is unknown. In milder cases, however, much warmth and infrared or Vitalux irradiation with vitamin supplements and a good, varied diet can bring the course of illness to a standstill. Preventive measures also are important. Furthermore, specimens that already are weak because of another illness and poorly nourished specimens are far more susceptible to an infection with tuberculosis. As a rule, however, the disease is not easy to transmit.

CANCER

Unfortunately, this insidious disease does not spare turtles either. Usually it manifests itself in tumors that do not heal or grow steadily. When we treat (apparently successfully) a tumor in one place, daughter tumors (metastases) typically turn up somewhere else. In the early stages, surgery may have some success (cauterization or cutting out all the diseased tissue with an electric knife). We, of course, should leave operations of this kind to the expert. Other than such radical methods, I know of no other treatment.

DIARRHEA

Do not feed the turtles for several days. Administer lukewarm chamomile tea in which you have dissolved a Tanalbin tablet. Administering charcoal tablets (crushed, soaked in water, and fed through a tube) has also proved effective. If you diagnose a salmonella infection, administer 50 milligrams of chloramphenicol per kilogram of body weight with the food for about a week. [Of course, only bacteriological culturing can truly diagnose the bacterial causes of diarrhea; see your veterinarian if diarrhea is persistent.]

WORMS

Besides many species of nematode worms (roundworms), tapeworms also occur in turtles. Even the layperson can identify them by examining the feces. Turtles are susceptible to para-

sitic infections because of their habits, particularly since some specimens are fond of eating feces.

Treatment:

For prevention, maintain cleanliness in the water and on the land. Always remove feces. For tapeworms administer a one-time dose of 25 milligrams of Droncit (Bayer) per 1 kilogram body weight. For nematodes administer a one-time dose of 20 to 50 milligrams fenbendazol (Panacur) per 1 kilogram body weight. Certain nematodes, such as *Capillaria*, require that we continue the treatment for five days. Repeat after eight weeks. We seldom use Thibenzol (200 milligrams per kilogram body weight) and Piperazin (100 milligrams per kilogram) anymore. The preparation Molevac from human medicine has proved very effective with pinworms. [Shot-gun treatments for worms may not be the most effective way to handle infections. Most worms can be accurately identified from fecal samples and specific medication suggested by your veterinarian; additionally, some worming drugs may cause serious side-effects if misused; Ivermectin, for instance, may be fatal even in small dosages.]

CONSTIPATION

This malady only affects tortoises and is caused by a one-sided diet.

Treatment:

Administer warm baths daily. Feed dandelion and lettuce generously, but do not offer banana. Give the tortoises plenty of room to move. In serious cases, a warm-water enema is helpful.

INJURIES

Bites and other injuries occur regularly among turtles. To prevent this, with my specimens I transfer or give away inveterate "biters" whenever possible. Very often, aggressive males are the instigators because they bite the female on the neck when mounting. These wounds heal poorly (unlike other injuries), because the males repeatedly tear open the wounds before they heal. "Solitary confinement" is the only solution here. I also recommend spacious quarters, particularly those with hiding places. A favorable sex ratio—several females per male—also is beneficial.

Treatment:

Dust the wound with "Refobacin" powder or smear it with an appropriate soothing antibiotic ointment. Isolate the patient and keep aquatic turtles dry for a few days. Place several layers of moistened newspaper in the enclosure. This is particularly important with patients being treated for wounds on the plastron. Normal newspapers (not magazines) are particularly suitable for this purpose. With longer treatment, occasionally return aquatic turtles to the water for a day.

BURNS

With small burns, use 1 percent tannin ointment or a similar soothing ointment. With larger and more serious injuries, a veterinarian should carry out the treatment, because he may have to stitch or clamp the wound.

In closing, I cannot stress too strongly that we can prevent many illnesses by employing preventive measures. Always isolate sick turtles and always quarantine new arrivals. Practice extreme hygiene with all terraria and equipment. Whenever possible, keep the turtles outdoors.

Close-up of shell-rot in a Painted Turtle, *Chrysemys picta*. This is a serious and common problem in captive aquatic turtles that often requires veterinary attention. Photo by W. P. Mara.

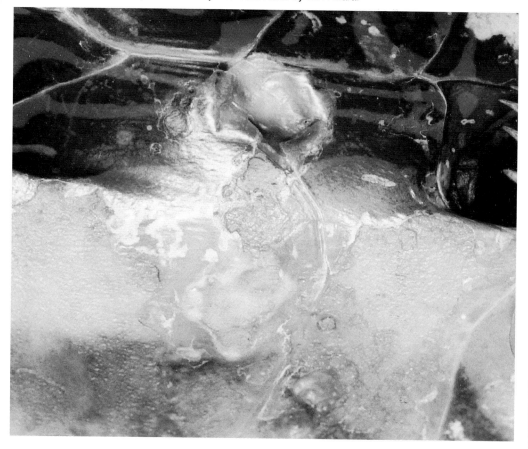

SPECIES DESCRIPTIONS

In the descriptions of the species that have subspecies, I will discuss only the nominate form. The other subspecies will be mentioned only for the sake of completeness, and I will discuss in detail only any special features that may be present.

FAMILY: Dermatemydidae
River Turtles

DERMATEMYS
Dermatemys mawi
Central American River Turtle

The carapace is brownish, the plastron lighter in color. The whole shell is very bony. A wide bridge connects the smooth carapace with its three longitudinal keels to the stiff plastron. The most diagnostic character is the complete row of inframarginal scutes separating the scutes of the carapace and plastron.

Up to 40 centimeters (16 inches).

Eastern Mexico, Guatemala, Belize, and Honduras.

This sluggish turtle lives on the bottom of large rivers and rarely leaves the water except to lay its eggs; it seldom basks. Its diet consists strictly of aquatic plants. The female is reported to lay up to 20 eggs in the immediate vicinity of the water.

The Central American River Turtle is extremely rare in captivity. A specimen lived for eight years in London. As far as I know, Hausmann also kept it for several years in Stuttgart, Germany. It is probably of no importance in the terrarium hobby, since it is almost impossible to keep and, to my knowledge, captive breeding has not occurred.

A Common Snapping Turtle, *Chelydra serpentina serpentina.* This female weighs over 17 pounds. The name is not unjustified, for it immediately snaps at a reaching hand. Photo by M. Mohr.

FAMILY: Chelydridae
Snapping Turtles

CHELYDRA

Chelydra serpentina
Common Snapping Turtle

Chelydra serpentina serpentina
Common Snapping Turtle

The carapace is dark to blackish brown, the plastron yellow brown. The legs are olive gray. The triangular, blunt head has an almost parrot-like beak. Juveniles have tubercles on the neck and head that gradually become less prominent with age. There are two barbels on the chin. The front and hind legs have very sturdy claws but only inconspicuous webbing. The distinctly arched carapace has three longitudinal keels and radiating, converging lines that become indistinct with age. The tail is very long, about the length of the carapace. The plastron is in the shape of a cross. A narrow bridge of inframarginal scutes connects the plastron to the carapace. The legs protrude somewhat from the shell and lend even juveniles an ungainly appearance. The powerful jaws do full justice to the Common Snapping Turtle's name, because even the youngest specimens open the mouth into a wide gape at the slightest provocation and bite immediately.

Up to 50 centimeters (20 inches).

Southeastern Canada and the eastern and central United States (excluding peninsular Florida). The species ranges south through Mexico into northern South America (Ecuador).

The Common Snapping Turtle lurks for prey in rivers, lakes, marshes, and even large ditches. It usually waits hidden in the muddy bottom, superbly camouflaged by a thick growth of algae. It feeds on any animal food it can find, even aquatic birds. Because it is a poor swimmer, it often walks on the bottom of the body of water and searches for carrion, of which it is very fond. For variety it often also feeds on dying aquatic plants.

The Common Snapping Turtle is not especially fussy about temperature. The species is suitable for year-round outdoor keeping, and many hobbyists have done it successfully for a number of years. A prerequisite, however, is that

Underside of a Common Snapping Turtle, *Chelydra s. serpentina*. Note the "bikini" plastron. Photo by M. Mohr.

the pond is sufficiently large and above all deep (at least 80 centimeters, 32 inches). In addition, the pond should have a layer of mud or debris on the bottom into which the turtles can burrow.

As a juvenile, it is a good candidate for the terrarium. Because it grows fast, it soon will need larger quarters and will soon exceed the limits of the indoor terrarium. For that reason, particularly beginners should consider if they can offer the turtle appropriate keeping conditions in a full-grown state as well as when it is just a baby.

Do not keep adult males together. It is best to keep one male with several females. This species has been bred in captivity, but the normal hobbyist would probably have a difficult time breeding the turtles because of the size of the adults and the large quarters they require.

Chelydra serpentina acutirostris
South American Snapping Turtle

Central America (Honduras to Panama) and northern South America (Colombia to Ecuador).

Chelydra serpentina osceola
Florida Snapping Turtle
   Southeastern United States (the Florida peninsula).

Chelydra serpentina rossignoni
Central American Snapping Turtle
   Central America (Veracruz, Mexico south to Honduras).

MACROCLEMYS
Macroclemys temmincki
Alligator Snapping Turtle
   The carapace is blackish brown. Tubercular, backward-tapering scutes form three longitudinal keels. The carapace is very strongly serrated. In juveniles the three scutes between the costal and marginal scutes are a good character for distinguishing the species from the genus *Chelydra*. The cross-shaped, small plastron is yellow brown. The legs are gray. The head is massive, with very powerful jaws and a strongly hooked beak. The toes are webbed and end in very sturdy claws. A peculiarity is the pink process on the tongue that resembles a worm and functions as a lure for attracting prey. The turtle usually rests half-buried in mud or sand. With mouth agape, it moves the "lure," and when a fish swims to the supposed prey, the turtle snaps it up and swallows it.
   Up to 75 centimeters (30 inches).
   Southern United States (central Texas to Illinois and northern Florida).
   This species usually lives in the mud of rivers, larger streams, and lakes and requires somewhat higher temperatures than does the Common Snapping Turtle. Its diet consists mainly of fish, but it also feeds on larger aquatic insects and snails, but not plants. In captivity it readily takes beef heart, beef liver, and dead fish.
   In captivity the Alligator Snapping Turtle is easy to keep at a room temperature of about 23°C (73°F). Outdoor keeping is possible in summer if the temperature does not fall below 20°C (68°F). Unfortunately, we seldom get a glimpse of it in the pond as it stays hidden in the bottom during the day and hunts mostly at night. It is easy to keep in roomy quarters with specimens of the same size.

FAMILY:Kinosternidae
Musk and Mud Turtles

STERNOTHERUS
Musk Turtles
   [Several workers consider *Sternotherus* to be a synonym of *Kinosternon* on the basis of molecular evidence, but other workers (especially paleontologists) disagree. Most hobbyists continue to treat the musk and mud turtles as separate genera.]

Sternotherus carinatus
Razor-backed Musk Turtle
   As the name indicates, the olive-brown carapace is even more highly arched than in *Sternotherus odoratus* and is roof-like with strongly sloping sides. There is a keel running along the middle of the carapace. The individual dorsal scutes have radiating lines that continue to be visible in older specimens. The plastron is yellow. No gular scute is present. There are numerous black dots and streaks on a pale olive background, particularly on the head and neck. This species has sturdy legs with sharp claws and webbed toes. As in *S. odoratus*, there is a hinge between the scutes of the plastron.
   Up to 15 centimeters (6 inches).
   Southern United States (central Texas and Oklahoma to southern Mississippi).
   This species scarcely differs from *S. odoratus* in behavior, but it basks more often on land, which is a behavior that I have never observed in *S. odoratus*. It also is similar to *S. odoratus* in diet, temperament, and other habits. The same is true of keeping in the terrarium, with one qualification: *S. carinatus* prefers somewhat higher temperatures in the terrarium than many more northern *S. odoratus*.

Sternotherus minor
Loggerhead Musk Turtle

Sternotherus minor minor
Loggerhead Musk Turtle
   Unlike the Razor-backed Musk Turtle, this species has three distinct longitudinal keels. The carapace is flatter, particularly with age. Old males have a relatively large head. In coloration

and other points it is reasonably similar to *S. carinatus*.

10 to 12 centimeters (4 to 5 inches).

Southeastern United States. [Southeastern Alabama to central Georgia and northern Florida.]

The Loggerhead Musk Turtle does not swim much. It lives in swampy bodies of water with a moderate current and usually stays hidden on the bottom, where it crawls along in search of food. With one adult male that I kept, I noticed the following peculiarity: The turtle sometimes hides for weeks (up to six weeks) in the dense planting of the rainforest terrarium (peaty, constantly very wet substrate, humidity 100 percent), and then appears suddenly in the aquatic section to feed. While there it eats everything it can find, stays for two or three days in the water, and then disappears again for a few weeks among the plants. These habits have served this turtle well for eight years; it is healthy and of normal weight. The water is 55 centimeters (22 inches) deep in the terrarium and causes it no trouble at all. This species needs higher temperatures than *S. odoratus* but otherwise has similar keeping and dietary requirements. This species has been bred regularly in captivity.

Sternotherus minor depressus
Flattened Musk Turtle

The conspicuously low carapace becomes concave in the middle with age. The head markings consist of a dark netting on a light ground color. [American herpetologists consider this form, restricted to the Black Warrior River system of northern Alabama, to be a full species. It has legal protection but the rivers in the area have been greatly modified by man. Hybrids with *S. minor* have been reported.]

Sternotherus minor peltifer
Stripe-necked Musk Turtle

There is only one dorsal keel, which is still present in older specimens. On the sides of the head there are alternating dark and light-colored longitudinal stripes. [Tennessee and Virginia south to the Gulf of Mexico.]

Sternotherus odoratus
Stinkpot or Common Musk Turtle

The carapace, which has three longitudinal keels in juveniles, is very strongly arched and dark olive in color. The small plastron is yellow-brown and only slightly movable (gular scutes are present). In *Sternotherus odoratus* the gular scutes are more prominent than in *S. carinatus*, where they often are completely absent. The dark olive to nearly black head has two pale longitudinal stripes on the sides, but sometimes it is almost completely dark and unmarked. The turtle has relatively strongly scaled legs with sharp claws and webbing on the hind feet. The plastron is somewhat wider in males than in females [and has much more exposed skin between the widely separated scutes. This is our only musk turtle with barbels on the throat as well as the chin.]

Up to almost 14 centimeters (5.3 inches), [but more commonly only 10 centimeters (4 inches)].

Found from eastern Canada near the Great Lakes over most of the eastern and central United States, from central Texas to Wisconsin and Maine.

This turtle lives primarily in shallow lakes, bays with little current, and oxbow lakes with abundant vegetation. It goes on land only to lay its eggs [but often basks on low branches well above the water]. It usually crawls on the bottom in search of food and is something of an aquatic sanitation engineer, because it primarily feeds on carrion along with insects and snails. A captured or otherwise alarmed musk turtle emits a secretion with a musk-like, penetrating smell to which it owes its name. Both males and females have this ability. After the turtle lives in captivity for some time, however, it ceases to emit the musk. The female lays the relatively small, hard-shelled eggs (corresponding to the size of the turtles) in excavated or existing holes. Sometimes, however, she simply lays them on the ground and covers them with leaves or similar material.

This species, as well as all other species of the genus, is a very good candidate for terrarium keeping and provides much enjoyment. The turtle is omnivorous, so feeding presents no problems. They are not as fond, however, of vegetable foods. Keeping at room temperature is completely adequate. During the warm season, I keep my turtles in the garden pond, which suits them splendidly. The water temperature there

top: An Alligator Snapping Turtle, *Macroclemys temmincki*, can grow to a length of 30 inches and is suitable only for large tanks.
bottom: Underside of an Alligator Snapper, *Macroclemys temmincki*. Note the same "bikini" shape as the plastron of the Common Snapper. Both photos by W. Hemmer.

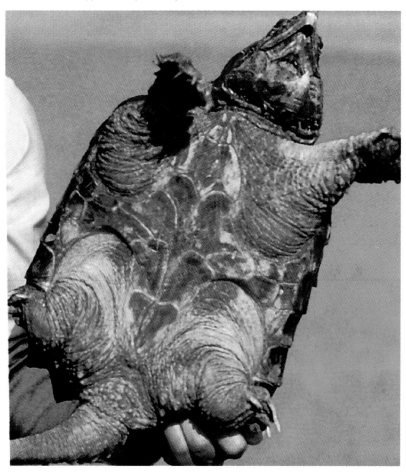

The Stinkpot, *Sternotherus odoratus*, as well as most of its family, is most active at dusk. The author has always kept all *Sternotherus* species at water depths of 16 to 20 inches with good results, instead of the shallow water the hobby literature usually recommends. Photo by B. Kahl.

The Yellow Mud Turtle, *Kinosternon flavescens*, from the central U. S. and northern Mexico, often aestivates during the hottest season. Photo by J. C. Drews.

does not drop below 20°C (68°F). I want to emphasize that the shallow water level recommended throughout the literature for keeping musk turtles is absolutely unnecessary. I have always kept my turtles (including *Sternotherus minor*) with no problems at water depths of 50 to 60 centimeters (20 to 24 inches and in ponds even at a depth of 85 centimeters (34 inches). I have had problems only with turtles obtained from other hobbyists who had kept their specimens for a fairly long time at shallower water levels. In this case an acclimation period is necessary. Except at feeding time, Stinkpots normally get along with one another if the tank is large enough. I recommend highly this species to the less-experienced hobbyist. Captive breeding is a regular occurrence.

KINOSTERNON
Mud Turtles

The genus *Kinosternon* consists of 19 species that, along with the many subspecies, I will present here only for the sake of completeness. On the other hand, I will discuss the more familiar species in more detail. All species and subspecies can raise the front and rear of the plastron up against the carapace, thereby sealing the shell completely and thus protecting the soft parts. Most adult mud turtles bite readily. Keep them either singly or in very large quarters with numerous hiding places. If you meet this requirement, as well as their requirements concerning temperature and a varied diet, the turtles do well in the terrarium. [American workers recognize about 15 species in the genus once *Sternotherus* is removed for the musk turtles. The arrangement of species and subspecies varies quite a bit from the listing presented below.]

Kinosternon abaxillare
Central Chiapas Mud Turtle
Up to 15 centimeters (6 inches).
Central Chiapas, southern Mexico. [This form now is considered a subspecies of *K. scorpioides* by most workers.]

Kinosternon acutum
Tabasco Mud Turtle
Up to 10 centimeters (4 inches).
Southeastern Mexico, Belize, and Guatemala.

Kinosternon alamosae
Alamos Mud Turtle
Northwestern Mexico.

Kinosternon angustipons
Narrow-bridged Mud Turtle
Caribbean Central America from the border between Nicaragua and Costa Rica south to Almirante, Bocas del Toro, Panama.

Kinosternon bauri
Striped Mud Turtle

Kinosternon bauri bauri
Three longitudinal stripes run along the horn-colored to black carapace. The yellowish to olive plastron is more or less deeply concave and smaller than the ventral opening of the carapace, so that the turtle cannot close it completely. The relatively small head has two light-colored lateral stripes.
Up to 12 centimeters (5 inches).
Lower Florida Keys. [Endangered.]
This species lives mainly in small, shallow ponds. It often leaves these bodies of water and crawls through the adjoining wet meadows in search of animal food. It is not fussy concerning diet and takes carrion and other scraps, so it also is undemanding in the terrarium and easy to feed on a somewhat varied diet. Although it is omnivorous in the wild, it refuses vegetable foods in the terrarium. In accordance with its natural range, it requires temperatures above 22°C (72°F).

Kinosternon bauri palmarum
Southeastern United States (chiefly Florida).This subspecies is differentiated from the previous subspecies by having the horny scutes of the carapace translucent, revealing the underlying bony sutures. It is somewhat more dependent on water than is the nominate form.
[American herpetologists have not recognized subspecies in the Striped Mud Turtle since 1978. The characters distinguishing *bauri bauri* and *b. palmarum* are not constant and appear in populations from throughout the range. Recently the species has been recorded from southeastern Virginia south to the Carolinas as well as the traditional range

from Georgia and Florida. Northern specimens are almost impossible to distinguish from *K. subrubrum* except by minor ratios of shell measurements.]

Kinosternon creaseri
Creaser's Mud Turtle
Up to 12 centimeters (5 inches).
Eastern Mexico on the Yucatan Peninsula.

Kinosternon cruentatum
Red-cheeked Mud Turtle
The usually dark olive carapace has three closely spaced dorsal keels; the large, brownish plastron usually has a radiating hatching. The movable front flap of the plastron is longer than the rigid central part. The soft parts have conspicuous red markings, especially the cheeks, although sometimes the red spots are absent from the sides of the head.
Up to 15 centimeters (6 inches).
Eastern Mexico (Tamaulipas) south to Honduras.
This form does not differ in habits from the other species of the genus; at most the species may need slightly higher temperatures. [This form now is considered a subspecies of *K. scorpioides* by most workers.]

Kinosternon dunni
Dunn's Mud Turtle
Up to 15 centimeters (6 inches).
Pacific coastal drainages of Colombia, from the basin of the Rio San Juan to the Rio Baudo.

Kinosternon flavescens
Yellow Mud Turtle

Kinosternon flavescens flavescens
Yellow Mud Turtle
The carapace is smooth, centrally flattened, usually olive-green and unmarked. With age it usually (but not always) develops a longitudinal keel. The plastron is yellowish to brown; the seams of the individual scutes are dark. The legs are unmarked and yellow to gray. The head is flat with a hooked jaw that normally is whitish to yellow and may have speckling. All feet have webbing between the toes.
Up to 15 centimeters (6 inches).

Central United States (Nebraska to New Mexico) as well as northern and northeastern Mexico.
This species usually lives in quiet bodies of water such as lakes, slow-flowing streams, and ponds with muddy or sandy bottoms and abundant vegetation. It likes fairly warm temperatures from 18 to 32°C (65 to 90°F), but continues to feed even at 16°C (60°F). During the hottest time of year, *K. f. flavescens* often estivates. It often comes on land to bask or forage for food and occasionally migrates overland between bodies of water. An omnivore, its menu features insects, crustaceans, snails, amphibians, carrion, and aquatic plants. It is not fussy in the terrarium either, and takes prepared foods as well as all kinds of animal foods, such as heart, liver, and worms. It also takes bananas, dandelion, lettuce, and other greens, although vegetable foods are always the second choice. This species probably should be kept singly, especially in small terraria.

Kinosternon flavescens arizonense
Arizona Mud Turtle
Southwestern Arizona and Sonora, Mexico. [This subspecies formerly was called *stejnegeri*.]

Kinosternon flavescens durangoense
Durango Mud Turtle
Northwestern Mexico.

Kinosternon flavescens spooneri
Illinois Mud Turtle
Up to 15 centimeters (6 inches).
Prairie remnants in southwestern Illinois as well as adjoining parts of Iowa and Missouri. [Though considered endangered, this subspecies recently has been treated as a synonym of *K. f. flavescens*. This opinion is not accepted by all workers, however.]

Kinosternon herrerai
Herrera's Mud Turtle
Up to 12 centimeters (5 inches).
Eastern Mexico.

Kinosternon hirtipes
Rough-footed Mud Turtle

top: The Striped Mud Turtle, *Kinosternon bauri*, is a highly aquatic turtle. The terrarium for one, therefore, does not need a large land section. Photo by H. Reinhard.
bottom: The Red-cheeked Mud Turtle, *Kinosternon cruentatum* lives mainly in the southern United States, as well as in Mexico and Central America. Photo by J. C. Drews.

Kinosternon hirtipes hirtipes
Valley of Mexico Mud Turtle
 Up to 15 centimeters (6 inches).
 The Valley of Mexico.

Kinosternon hirtipes chapalaense
Lake Chapala Mud Turtle

Kinosternon hirtipes magdalense
San Juanico Mud Turtle

Kinosternon hirtipes megacephalum
Viesca Mud Turtle

Kinosternon hirtipes murrayi
Mexican Plateau Mud Turtle
 Up to 15 centimeters (6 inches).
 Southwestern Texas south over the Mexican plateau to Mexico state.

Kinosternon hirtipes tarascense
Patzcuaro Mud Turtle

Kinosternon leucostomum
White-lipped Mud Turtle
 Up to 15 centimeters (6 inches).
 Southeastern Mexico (Veracruz) over central and Caribbean Central America to Colombia and Ecuador. [Commonly two subspecies are recognized, *K. l. leucostomum* from Veracruz to Nicaragua and *K. l. postinguinale* from Nicaragua to Ecuador. Almost all American workers treat *K. spurrelli* as a synonym of this species.]

Kinosternon oaxacae
Oaxaca Mud Turtle
 Southwestern Mexico.

Kinosternon scorpioides
Scorpion Mud Turtle

Kinosternon scorpioides scorpioides
Amazon Mud Turtle
 The greenish to dark brown carapace is oval and high-domed. It has a distinct central keel and two weaker lateral keels across the costal scutes that usually disappear with age. The plastron is brownish yellow with dark seams between the scutes. The head usually has yellow speckling on the sides. The generally gray legs end in toes with robust claws and webbing.
 Up to 20 centimeters (8 inches).
 Southern Central America and northern and central South America, from Panama to Colombia, Venezuela, and the Guyanas south to northern Brazil and northern Peru. This is the most widely distributed *Kinosternon* species.
 K. s. scorpioides prefers slow-flowing or standing waters and frequently goes on land, more to forage for food than to bask. It feeds on snails, crustaceans, large insects, and fishes. Naturally, it also takes carrion, but only some individuals show an interest in aquatic plants or other greenfood. It needs fairly high temperatures, and even water and air temperatures of 20°C (68°F) are too low. The optimal temperature range is 24 to 28°C (75 to 82°F). In the terrarium it is more delicate than most of its relatives and therefore is unsuitable for the beginner. Except for fights at feeding time, usually it is peaceful toward turtles of about the same size.

Kinosternon scorpioides albogulare
White-throated Mud Turtle
 Up to 14 centimeters (5.5 inches).
 Central America, Honduras to Panama.

Kinosternon scorpioides integrum
Mexican Mud Turtle
 Up to 12 centimeters (5 inches).
 Western and southern Mexico from Sonora to Oaxaca and Tamaulipas. [This form now is considered a full species by many workers.]

Kinosternon scorpioides pachyurum
 Bolivia. [Now usually considered a synonym of *K. s. seriei*.]

Kinosternon scorpioides seriei
Argentine Mud Turtle
 Northern Argentina [and Bolivia].

Kinosternon sonoriense
Sonora Mud Turtle
 The carapace is olive to dark brown with darker growth rings. The underside of the marginal scutes and the bridge are yellowish to

top: The White-lipped Mud Turtle, *Kinosternon leucostomum*, has no subspecies. This species is occasionally imported from South America.
bottom: *Kinosternon scorpioides albogulare,* The White-throated Mud Turtle, ranges widely through Central America. Including this subspecies, this species has eight subspecies. Both photos by J. C. Drews.

brown with dark speckling. The plastron is yellow to brownish with dark seams between the scutes. The skin is gray and there is dark speckling on the head, neck, and legs. The head is flat and all four feet have webbing.

Up to 14 centimeters (5.5 inches).

Southwestern United States from southeastern California east to southwestern New Mexico and northern Mexico in Sonora and Chihuahua. [A second subspecies, *K. s. longifemorale*, sometimes is recognized from the Rio Sonoyta basin in southern Arizona and adjacent Sonora, Mexico.]

This species lives in rivers, streams, ponds, ditches, and water holes, predominantly in forests. We know little about its habits, since it leads a very secretive existence and only occasionally leaves the water to bask. Captive specimens take fishes of all kinds as well as all sorts of meat. One individual lived 21 years and 9 months in the Philadelphia Zoo.

Kinosternon spurrelli
Spurrell's Mud Turtle

Up to 13 centimeters (5 inches).

Western Colombia. [This form usually is considered to be a synonym of *K. leucostomum postinguinale*.]

Kinosternon subrubrum
Common Mud Turtle

Kinosternon subrubrum subrubrum
Eastern Mud Turtle

The yellowish olive to brown or even black carapace has a keel only in juveniles. The plastron is yellowish with clearly visible growth rings. The head is medium in size and normally has dark brown to yellow speckling. Usually there are two light yellow stripes on each side of the head and neck. All four feet are webbed. The males have diagnostic horny scales inside the hind legs. The short tail ends in a blunt spine.

A very popular turtle, the Common Mud Turtle, *Kinosternon subrubrum*, has three subspecies and lives primarily in the eastern and southeastern United States. Photo by J. C. Drews.

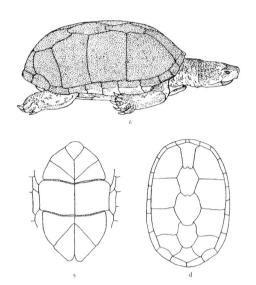

Eastern Mud Turtle, *Kinosternon subrubrum subrubrum*. Illustration: E. Bobbe in Wermuth/Mertens: Schildkröten — Krokodile — Brückenechsen.

Up to 12 centimeters (almost 5 inches).

Eastern and southeastern United States, Illinois and New York to Mississippi and northern Florida.

This mud turtle prefers slow-flowing waters, lakes, ditches, ponds, and pools with abundant vegetation; it even can live in salt marshes. It does not require high temperatures (it remains active even at 16°C, 60°F), although a temperature of about 24°C (75°F) is best for feeding and circulation. The Eastern Mud Turtle is not a particularly good swimmer and more often crawls along the bottom. In early morning and early evening, in particular, it likes to go on land. It is rather timid and remains so in captivity. Though it is an omnivore, it apparently prefers animal food, especially in captivity. This species is fairly pugnacious and therefore should be kept only with animals of the same size in roomy quarters with many hiding places.

Kinosternon subrubrum hippocrepis
Mississippi Mud Turtle

Up to 12 centimeters (almost 5 inches).

The Mississippi basin of the United States, from Missouri to southern Mississippi and west to central Texas.

Kinosternon subrubrum steindachneri
Florida Mud Turtle

Up to 12 centimeters (almost 5 inches). The Florida Peninsula.

CLAUDIUS
Narrow-bridged Musk Turtles

Claudius angustatus
Narrow-bridged Musk Turtle

The olive to dark brown carapace has three fairly indistinct longitudinal keels. The rhomboidal yellow to yellow-brown plastron is very small and covers only about a third of the ventral side. A very narrow strip of membranous connective tissue joins the plastron to the carapace. The turtle has a conspicuously large head. Females usually are smaller than males (unusual in turtles).

Up to 18 centimeters (9 inches).

Eastern Mexico (Veracruz) to Guatemala and Belize.

This species leads a hidden life in slow-flowing bodies of water and ponds, becoming most active when foraging for food at night. Besides snails, crustaceans, and other kinds of meat, it also takes carrion. This turtle is easy to keep in an aquaterrarium with a large aquatic section and hiding places. The average water temperature should be 25°C (77°F). Because of its habits, a basking light is unnecessary. The turtles are very aggressive and prone to bite, so it is advisable to keep them singly. Supervise all mating attempts. They breed regularly in captivity.

STAUROTYPUS
Giant Musk Turtles
Staurotypus salvini
Pacific Coast Giant Musk Turtle

The dark olive to blackish brown or black carapace has three high, ridge-like longitudinal keels. Sutures join the carapace and plastron rigidly; the plastron cross-shaped. The humeral scutes are the longest scutes of the plastron and the abdominal scutes are much wider than long. The plastron covers only about one-third of the underside, so some hobbyists call it a "bikini."

Up to 25 centimeters (10 inches).

Pacific slope of southwestern Mexico, southern Guatemala, and El Salvador.

The Pacific Coast Giant Musk Turtle is nocturnal and rarely goes on land except to lay its eggs. At the start of the dry season the turtles bury themselves on land for long periods of estivation. This species needs fairly warm surroundings, the optimal average temperature being 25°C (77°F). Avoid at all costs a fall in temperature below 20°C (68°F) even briefly because it may seriously injure the turtle. This is particularly important to keep in mind when shipping the turtles. There have been several successful breedings. An incubation temperature that is too low (only 24°C, 75°F) can lead to a relatively long incubation period of 127 to 161 days, so I would recommend a temperature of 28 to 30°C (82 to 86°F). It is particularly important to avoid extreme fluctuations in temperature. Neither juveniles nor adults are problematic regarding diet. Besides vegetable foods, they take almost everything: freshwater or marine fishes, beef heart, liver, dried shrimp, prepared food, snails of all kinds—with and without shells—and baby mice.

I recommend keeping this species singly even during the breeding season. The turtles are incompatible with one another (and with other turtle species as well) and are extremely prone to bite. Therefore, put them together for mating only under supervision.

Staurotypus triporcatus
Mexican Giant Musk Turtle

The Mexican Giant Musk Turtle differs from the previous species in its larger size; its pectoral scutes that have the longest medial seam in the plastron; and the abdominal scutes that are as wide as long.

Up to 38 centimeters (15.5 inches).

Southern Mexico (Veracruz), Guatemala, Honduras, and Belize, all on the Caribbean slope.

Its habits are the same as those of *S. salvini*. Because of its larger size, however, it can manage larger pieces of food or food animals. Years ago I reared four babies of this species that had been bred in captivity. It was amazing how voracious these turtles were and how unbelievably quickly they converted the food into growth. Unfortunately, at the time I was unable to mea-

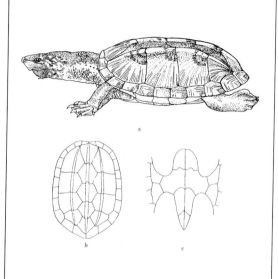

Mexican Giant Musk Turtle, *Staurotypus triporcatus*. Illustration: E. Bobbe in Wermuth/Mertens: Schildkröten — Krokodile — Brückenechsen.

sure and weigh them regularly, but I still recall clearly that the average turtle 6 centimeters long (2.4 inches) (the ruler placed along the carapace) had grown in about eight months to the length of a man's hand without exhibiting any signs of rachitis. I noticed that they became fully active only at dusk and that they usually spent the day in hiding. Furthermore, I discovered that single keeping is advisable. This prevents the turtles from biting one another constantly (not just at feeding time) and sometimes being badly injured. The Mexican Giant Musk Turtle definitely is unsuitable for community keeping and is completely unsuited for keeping with smaller animals of their own or other species.

In conclusion, the following applies to the entire family Kinosternidae (musk and mud turtles). In the terrarium, I advise caution with community keeping, except with the *Sternotherus* species. Therefore, I advise single keeping or keeping in very large tanks with numerous hiding places. The mud and musk turtles are a very interesting group and even today we know relatively little about many of the subspecies.

top: The Mexican Giant Musk Turtle, *Staurotypus triporcatus*, is mainly crepuscular. Keep it by itself, because it is very prone to bite.
bottom: Underside of *Staurotypus triporcatus*. Note the so-called bikini plastron. Both photos by G. Müller.

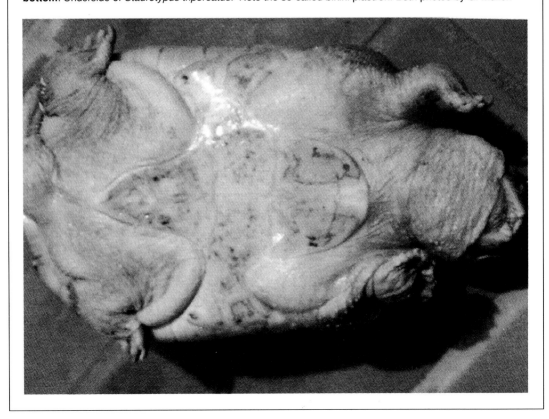

top: *Platysternon megacephalum vogeli*, the Thai form of the Big-headed Turtle, is probably the rarest of the four subspecies. Photo by W. Hemmer.
bottom: According to the author, the European Pond Turtle, *Emys orbicularis*, has not disappeared entirely in Germany. However, the past and current attempts to reintroduce the species have yet to produce the hoped-for success. Photo by G. Fischer.

FAMILY: Platysternidae
Big-headed Turtles

Platysternon
Big-headed Turtles

Platysternon megacephalum
Platysternon megacephalum megacephalum
Chinese Big-headed Turtle

The head is conspicuously large (and cannot be retracted into the shell) with a uniformly bluntly rounded outline of the bridge of the snout. From the side it resembles a hawk's bill. In adults the usually reddish brown carapace has smooth scutes with a smooth, nonserrated trailing edge that is olive-brown, sometimes with light speckling. They cannot completely withdraw the extremities and tail under the carapace, although large scales cover the exposed places. In juveniles the carapace features a low longitudinal keel that disappears with age. The robust feet end in sharp claws. The tail has spiny scales, is unusually long, and nearly equals the length of the carapace.

Up to 20 centimeters (8 inches).

Southern China from Kwangsi and Kwangtung Provinces, including Hainan Island, and north along the coast to Futschau.

This nocturnal, pugnacious turtle lives mainly in mountain streams. It tolerates fairly cool temperatures, although it certainly accepts higher temperatures, as decades of terrarium keeping show. The formerly much-cited 12°C (54°F) likely is not the preferred temperature, since even at 25°C (77°F) the turtles appeared healthy and took food voluntarily. They are strictly carnivorous and are especially fond of earthworms, but they also take larger aquatic insects, fish, beef heart, and beef liver. On the other hand, Big-heads are not particularly fond of snails and take them only in extreme hunger, although the specialist literature reports that they have the ability (because of the hooked snout and powerful jaws) to detach snails and crush the shells. To my knowledge, they have not bred successfully in captivity. The female apparently lays two or three eggs, but we know little about the incubation period, hatching, and rearing. Most breeding attempts probably have failed because of the incompatibility of the turtles.

Big-headed Turtles are accomplished climbers. Normal wire mesh or screening and ornamental bark or cork walls are no obstacle for them, which we must consider when furnishing the terrarium. Also keep in mind that this species ranges widely on land at night.

Platysternon megacephalum peguense
Burma Big-headed Turtle

The head has a narrow, almost beak-like snout. The carapace has concentrically furrowed scutes and a distinctly serrated trailing edge. The plastron has a sharply defined, symmetrical, dark blotch along the middle, its lateral branches following the transverse seams between the scutes.

Southern Burma and southern Thailand.

Platysternon megacephalum tristernalis
Yunnan Big-headed Turtle
Yunnan, China.

Platysternon megacephalum vogeli
Thailand Big-headed Turtle

Distinguished from the nominate subspecies by the conspicuously narrow, uniformly tapered, wedge-shaped dorsal outline of the snout, as well as the dark blotches on the plastron. Distinguished from *P. m. peguense* by the less beak-like snout in front of the eyes; the smooth, nonserrated trailing edge of the carapace; and the dark, extensive blotch on the plastron that often covers most of it.

Up to 20 centimeters (8 inches).

Northwestern Thailand.

FAMILY: Emydidae
Pond Turtles and Their Allies

EMYS
European Pond Turtles

Emys orbicularis
European Pond Turtle

The oval, only slightly convex carapace varies in color from dark olive through dark brown to black. The scutes have more or less pronounced yellow dots and streaks. The head, neck, and legs also exhibit yellow speckling on a dark brown to dark olive background. The plastron has a yellowish tinge and sometimes has dark spots, which can cover large areas. There is no rigid connection between the plastron and the carapace. An unusual feature is a transverse hinge in the middle, making both halves movable. Nevertheless, it cannot close its shell completely, unlike the mud turtles and box turtles. The tail is very long. On the front and hind legs there are sturdy claws and webs between the toes.

Up to 25 centimeters (10 inches).

Central and southern Europe, western Asia, and northwestern Africa. [Two subspecies have been recognized, *E. o. orbicularis* from all the range except the high plains of Turkey, where *E. o. luteofusca* occurs. Recently several other perhaps doubtful forms have been described in addition.]

This species likes standing or slow-flowing waters, ponds, lakes, and oxbow lakes, as well as fairly small pools. It prefers secluded waters with abundant aquatic and riparian vegetation. The turtles are unbelievably shy in the wild and react to the slightest noise by diving into the water. Therefore, I, along with some experts, believe that *Emys orbicularis* probably is more common in Germany than is generally assumed, but has maintained its numbers only in secluded and hard-to-reach reedy and boggy parts of bodies of water located far from industry and intensive agriculture.

The diet consists of any animal in the water that the turtle can capture, such as aquatic insects, aquatic and terrestrial snails, and fishes of all kinds. Healthy fishes that can swim normally certainly do not fall prey to *Emys orbicularis*, and thus they are not pests of commercial fisheries, unless they can get at fish eggs. They seldom take vegetable foods.

The temperature requirements of this species correspond to a moderate summer climate, whereby the optimum would be 22-24°C (72 to 75°F). Keep the European Pond Turtle in the terrarium only if you can keep it outdoors in a garden pond in the warm season. In this case, however, you must consider its ability to escape. It is such an excellent climber that wire-mesh fences, walls with rough plaster, and even wooden fences are not insurmountable obstacles. I speak here from my own experience, for these Europe-

ans have escaped from me on more than one occasion. I have never seen my own turtles feed out of the water, as is described in the specialist literature. They sometimes take or catch food on land, but ultimately they eat it in the water. Also, concerning the slow growth of the young, as is often reported in the specialist literature, I can only report contradictory findings based on having followed the growth of various baby turtles (*Pseudemys, Chrysemys, Graptemys*, and *Emys*) monthly over a period of two years. According to these findings, slow juvenile growth seems totally out of the question. My *E. orbicularis* increased its weight 25-fold in two years, and in the first year alone grew 7 centimeters (almost 3 inches)!

Emys orbicularis has bred regularly in captivity, so I would like to discuss its reproductive behavior in detail. Sexually mature males are at least 12 centimeters (4.8 inches) and females about 15 centimeters (6 inches) long. A sufficiently large terrarium with adequate swimming space in the aquatic section should be available. In this instance, of course, a garden pond offers great advantages. No universal recipe exists for the construction of the terrestrial section for egg-laying. As I have observed regularly, the turtles often chose a site for egg-laying that I would have never thought they would choose.

A female lays up to 12 eggs. In our latitudes it is advisable after laying to put the eggs in an incubator and it is best to transfer the eggs immediately after the female lays them, because turning them at this time does them no harm. The young turtles hatch after 51 to 90 days. In the wild, particularly in a cool summer, the eggs supposedly overwinter and the babies do not hatch until the following spring. The time when the juveniles take their first food mainly depends—based on my observations—on whether the yolk sac was still present at hatching and on how big it was. The larger it is, the later (sometimes not until four weeks) food intake becomes necessary. I also have observed that at hatching there normally is no yolk sac present, and that these specimens grew much more rapidly than those that hatched with a yolk sac (this generally is true of most turtles).

I have described *Emys orbicularis* in such detail in the hopes of encouraging as many hobbyists as possible to breed it, so that reintro-duction can take another step forward.

EMYDOIDEA
Blanding's Turtles

Emydoidea blandingi
Blanding's Turtle

Years ago this species was classified in the genus *Emys*, but because of its different skull structure it was placed in its own genus. In most respects it is very similar to the European Pond Turtle. The carapace, however, is somewhat more convex, and the dots and spots (particu-larly in younger specimens) are bright yellow. The often uniformly yellow throat is usually visible when the turtle raises its head out of the water, a behavior that I never have observed in other turtles.

Up to 26 centimeters (almost 11 inches).

Southern Canada and the northern and cen-tral United States.

Its habits are scarcely distinguishable from those of *Emys orbicularis*. However, Blanding's Turtle requires higher temperatures, for I once lost a very attractive adult female kept outdoors when the temperature fell to about 16°C (60°F) and the sun did not shine all day. (This cooling did not harm many other species of *Chrysemys, Pseudemys, Kachuga*, emyduras, chelodinas, *Graptemys, Mauremys*, and of course *Emys*.) [Extreme temperature sensitivity is unlikely in Blanding's Turtle, as it is known to be active and comfortable at 15°C (59°F) and has been re-ported actively searching for food at 10°C (50°F) in nature; it also is unlikely that one day of exposure to slightly lowered temperatures could cause death. The loss of the author's specimen may have been due to other causes not noticed at the time.]

E. blandingi often goes on land, where it ranges widely. The diet is the same as with *Emys*, except that *Emydoidea* takes more greenfood. It is not easy to keep and is not a turtle for the

A European Pond Turtle, *Emys obicularis*, with a conspicuously heavy pattern of yellow dots. Some individuals, however, have only a few of them. Photo by W. Hemmer.

A male Blanding's turtle, *Emydoidea blandingi*. This interesting little turtle has a hinged plastron, allowing partial closure of its shell. Photo by W. Hemmer

beginner. [It is widely protected in the United States but still has many admirers among advanced hobbyists. However, it is disappearing from much of its range in the Great Lakes region.]

DEIROCHELYS
Chicken Turtles

Deirochelys reticularia
Chicken Turtle

Deirochelys reticularia reticularia
Eastern Chicken Turtle

The olive to brown carapace has a net-like pattern of yellow-green lines. It has a slight keel only in juveniles. The lines sometimes disappear with age as the carapace becomes darker, strongly convex, and completely rounded. The marginal scutes and plastron are uniformly yellow. The relatively blunt head, the long neck, and the legs are gray-green. The toes have wide webs and sharp claws. A clearly visible orange-yellow stripe begins under the eye and extends along the neck. The head, neck, and legs have additional thin, longitudinal stripes in this color.

Up to 25 centimeters (10 inches).

Southeastern United States, excluding peninsular Florida.

This shy turtle lives in slow-flowing, secluded bodies of water and lakes. It also wanders on land and is not strictly aquatic. Its diet consists of aquatic insects, aquatic snails, and earthworms as well as vegetable foods. We must consider this in the terrarium and keep plants only in terraria with juveniles (juveniles are more carnivorous than adults). It is a fussy eater that often has very individual tastes about food. It does not require particularly high temperatures and displays an appetite at a water temperature of 17°C (63°F); however, the preferred temperature is from 20 to 25°C (68 to 77°F).

The Chicken Turtle is seldom offered in the pet trade, and it is not exactly a turtle for the beginner. It is peaceful toward other turtles but never loses its innate shyness.

Deirochelys reticularia chrysea
Florida Chicken Turtle

The Florida Peninsula.

Deirochelys reticularia miaria
Western Chicken Turtle

Southern United States from southern Missouri to central Texas and Louisiana.

CHRYSEMYS
Painted Turtles

Chrysemys picta
Painted Turtle

Chrysemys picta picta
Eastern Painted Turtle

The carapace, except for the marginal scutes, is unkeeled and the trailing edge is not serrated. The marginal scutes have red markings both above and below. The costal and vertebral scutes stand in nearly regular, transverse rows and have horn-colored stripes on the leading edges. The head and legs have attractive stripes and markings. The plastron has a yellow ground color with a dark, large, and usually symmetrical blotch along the medial seam.

Up to 18 centimeters (7 inches).

From southeastern Canada (southeastern Quebec and New Brunswick) across the eastern United States south to northern Alabama and northern Georgia.

The Eastern Painted Turtle prefers quiet, slow-flowing or standing waters with abundant vegetation, both in the water as well as on the shore. They like to sun themselves on projecting logs or the like. Though they prefer animal food, occasionally they also take tender plants and in captivity they will take lettuce, bananas, or other sweet fruits. The required temperature depends strongly on the provenance of the turtles. The same is true of a possible hibernation at lowered temperatures, which, however, should not be allowed to drop too much. The turtles' provenance is always decisive here; nevertheless, dealers provide accurate information about this only in the rarest of cases.

Chrysemys picta belli
Western Painted Turtle

The color of the unkeeled, not serrated, and very flat carapace is a bright olive-green in juveniles, turning dark olive to olive-brown with increasing age. In addition, in the juvenile stage there is a net-like yellowish red to red pattern. The plastron is yellowish red to red. It has a dark blotch that sends out lateral branches from the medial seam along the transverse seams. The head, neck, and legs are greenish gray and the

head and neck have a pattern of yellow lines. On the front and hind legs, which have webbing and sturdy claws, there are red longitudinal lines or dots.

Up to 25 centimeters (10 inches).

Southwestern Canada (southern British Columbia east to southern Ontario) and western and central United States.

This subspecies has the widest range of any form of the species. In its biotope, its dietary requirements, and so forth, it does not differ from the nominate form. In my opinion it is the most beautiful turtle of all. Unfortunately, all my specimens proved hard to keep, and I consider it to be the most delicate of all *Chrysemys* species.

Chrysemys picta dorsalis
Southern Painted Turtle

The olive to blackish carapace has an orange to yellow longitudinal stripe down the center. The plastron (the lateral margins of which are reddish in juveniles) is whitish yellow and almost unmarked. The color of the visible body parts is dark gray to black. The head and neck have attractive yellow streaks and markings and the legs have orange-red stripes.

Up to 14 centimeters (almost 6 inches).

Southern United States from southern Illinois to the Gulf of Mexico.

It is identical to the other subspecies in its requirements concerning biotope and diet. The turtles in my terrarium have flourished ever since they grew out of their baby stage, but I feel sorry for all the many small juveniles of this turtle that die in the hands of beginning hobbyists who have difficulty rearing them. Therefore, I will discuss in detail the care of these attractive turtles. First, rear the youngsters in water that is not too soft. To guard against fungal infections, add about 2 grams of sea salt to each liter of water. (In principle, I do this with all species of young turtles and have had good results with it.) In addition, offer them plenty of swimming space (with a water depth of at least 30 centimeters, 12 inches), a flat shore or an easy-to-climb cork island, and, if possible, natural sunlight. The diet should be as varied as possible: daphnia and other small aquatic crustaceans, drowned meadow plankton, young aquatic snails or their spawn, the smallest freshwater fishes (such as guppies), caddisfly larvae, midge larvae, a little shaved beef heart or beef liver, and prepared turtle food of the smallest flake size. I also strongly recommend taking aquatic plants from a pond and stirring them vigorously in a bucket of water. You will be surprised by the number of all sorts of aquatic animals that you can harvest in this way. Not to be overlooked are earthworms (large ones finely chopped), but not foul-smelling dungworms. If you also provide a constant water and air temperature of about 25°C (77°F) and always keep the water fresh and healthy, rearing will be successful if the turtles did not come to harm beforehand (during transport or through inappropriate keeping), because then all efforts are in vain.

I myself once bought four baby *C. p. dorsalis* from a dealer, reared them in this way, and only lost one baby (through fungal infection, hence the salt). Because I had three females, I gave two to another hobbyist. The third female is still in my care and is in the best of health. Its initial weight of 4 grams and carapace length of 29 millimeters (1.2 inches) have increased in two years to 323 grams and 151 millimeters (6 inches). It lays five or six eggs (at an interval of about eight weeks) twice a year, usually in November and January. Unfortunately, these eggs are always infertile, because so far I have been unable to obtain a healthy, potent male of this species. I keep my turtle from May to October in the garden pond at water temperatures that vary from 17 to 26°C (63 to 79°F), depending on the summer. However, the temperature rarely falls below 20°C (68°F), because I can heat the pond on critical days.

Chrysemys picta marginata
Midland Painted Turtle

In *C. p. marginata*, in contrast to the nominate subspecies, the dorsal scutes are not aligned in rows and the bright coloration of the margins often is absent. The usually orange plastron has a broad, dark medial stripe without lateral arms. Otherwise the coloration strongly resembles that of *Chrysemys picta belli*.

Up to 20 centimeters (8 inches).

The north-central United States and adjacent Canada.

PSEUDEMYS
Cooters and Sliders

The turtles of the genus *Pseudemys* live exclusively in North, Central, and South America, including the Caribbean islands. Their keeping requirements therefore vary at most with respect to temperature requirements, corresponding to their provenance; otherwise they are largely the same. I will therefore limit myself to listing the species and subspecies and to discussing in more detail only the most familiar species and those that turn up in the pet trade. I also would like to point out that, because of their different carapace coloration, I consider *Pseudemys* and *Chrysemys* to be two separate genera, as do a number of very famous herpetologists.

[Not only are *Pseudemys* and *Chrysemys* now considered full genera, but *Pseudemys* has been split into two as well. The cooters, *P. concinna* and allies, remain in the genus *Pseudemys*, while the sliders are placed in the genus *Trachemys*. The sliders consist of the North American *T. scripta* and its tropical American allies as well as the species of the Caribbean. Differences between the genera are minor anatomical and biochemical features that are not easily seen externally, so it is best to think of the genera in terms of their species.]

Pseudemys concinna
River Cooter

Pseudemys concinna concinna
Eastern River Cooter

Up to 32 centimeters (13 inches).
Southeastern United States.

Pseudemys concinna hieroglyphica
Hieroglyphic Cooter

The relatively flat carapace, rich green and keeled in juveniles, has pale to bright orange-yellow markings resembling hieroglyphics. Unfortunately, they disappear with age and a dark olive to black color replaces them. The plastron has a dark blotch on a pale yellow ground color. The head and neck are dark gray and have yellow, longitudinal, parallel stripes, as do the legs. The toes have webs and sharp claws. In sexually mature males, the front claws are about three times as long as in females.

top: *Chrysemys picta belli,* the Western Painted Turtle. Young specimens, in particular, have exquisite colors.
bottom: *Chrysemys picta belli.* The bright red color of the plastron fades or disappears entirely with increasing age. Both photos by W. Hemmer.

top: This Southern Painted Turtle, *Chrysemys picta dorsalis,* shows the normal coloration. The stripe along the midline can vary from red to pale orange.
bottom: *Chrysemys picta dorsalis.* This specimen's coloration differs completely from the norm and is a peculiarity. Both photos by W. Hemmer.

Up to 38 centimeters (15 inches).

Southern United States.

This turtle lives mainly in quiet rivers, lakes, and ponds with abundant vegetation both in the water and on the shore. The Hieroglyphic Cooter is not delicate or fussy about diet. The predominantly carnivorous diet of the juvenile shifts with age to a predominantly herbivorous diet.

This turtle, like all *Pseudemys* species, likes to bask a great deal and makes use of every ray of sun in the pond or the outdoor terrarium. It does not need high temperatures and does well with water and air temperatures that vary from 20 to 28°C (68 to 82°F). The turtles do not hibernate in the terrarium. They do, however, engage in a sort of winter rest when the turtles bury themselves on land under moss or leaves and stay there for several weeks without actually hibernating. [This subspecies, itself questionable, usually is interpreted as including *P. c. mobilensis*.]

Pseudemys concinna suwanniensis
Suwannee Cooter

Peninsular Florida along the western coast. [This subspecies now is considered to be a full species by several workers.]

Pseudemys concinna texana
Texas River Cooter

Up to 32 centimeters (13 inches).

Central Texas.

For the most part, all *P. concinna* subspecies have the same habits, except for *P. c. texana*, which allegedly is almost strictly carnivorous. [Most workers today consider *texana* to be a full species restricted to several drainages in central Texas west of the range of *P. concinna*. Also closely related to *P. concinna* is the Rio Grande Cooter, *P. gorzugi*, of the Rio Grande basin from southern Texas to New Mexico. Neither of these forms is distinctly more carnivorous than the River Cooter.]

Pseudemys dorbigni
Orbigny's Slider

This turtle, particularly in the juvenile stage, is the most beautiful species of the genus *Pseudemys*. The slightly convex, green carapace has yellow bars. Each marginal scute has a bright yellow central spot with black borders. The plastron has a large, dark, branched blotch that covers it almost completely. The head has a bright orange patch behind the eye. The neck and legs have a pattern of yellow-orange to yellow patches and streaks on a dark gray ground color.

Up to 21 centimeters (8.5 inches).

Extreme southern Brazil, Uruguay, and northeastern Argentina.

This is the most southerly distributed slider species. It differs at most from the remaining species in requiring, because of its geographic range, somewhat higher temperatures. The water and air temperature should not fall below 20°C (68°F). The optimum temperature is probably about 26°C (79°F). It does not hibernate. Concerning diet and other requirements, however, it corresponds to the other sliders.

[This species now is placed in the genus *Trachemys*. Two subspecies, *T. d. dorbigni* from Argentina and Uruguay and *T. d. brasiliensis* from Porto Alegre, Brazil, sometimes are recognized, and a supposedly distinct related species also exists the area. Additionally, there are doubtful records of the species from much of southern Brazil, possibly based on introduced pets or food animals. It does not live in especially warm areas, as Argentina and extreme southern Brazil may have quite cold winters.]

Pseudemys floridana
Common Cooter

Pseudemys floridana floridana
Florida Cooter

In juveniles, an attractive pattern of yellow streaks on each scute covers the green carapace. This pattern disappears with age and a dark olive to black color replaces it. Only the second costal scute retains a more or less pronounced, vertical, light-colored stripe. The safest character for the *floridana* subspecies is that the carapace slopes steeply to the front and that its highest point therefore is in front of the midline. The plastron is unmarked or slightly marked. The extremities are dark brown to black with a pattern of yellow streaks.

Up to 40 centimeters (16 inches).

Southeastern United States except peninsular Florida.

These highly gregarious turtles often live in groups of 20 to 30 individuals. Together with other *Pseudemys* species, it basks in hard-to-reach riparian zones, on projecting logs, or on small islands. Like all *Pseudemys* and *Chrysemys* species, it is very fond of basking. It is one of the more warmth-loving species. In the garden pond (where I kept them from late April to early October), my *P. floridana* continued to feed and showed no listlessness even at a temperature of 18°C (65°F). The preferred temperature, however, is probably at least 23°C (73°F). Regarding the other requirements, such as diet, terrarium keeping, and sociability, it does not differ from other cooters.

Pseudemys floridana hoyi
Missouri Slider

As in the nominate form.

Southern United States.[This taxon now is considered to be unrecognizable and the range in the Mississippi Valley falls within the range of *P. concinna*. The taxonomy of the cooters, as you can see, is quite confused.]

Pseudemys floridana peninsularis
Peninsula Cooter

As in the nominate form.

Peninsular Florida. [This form often is considered a full species. Some workers, in addition, consider *floridana* to be a subspecies of *concinna*.]

Pseudemys grayi
Gray's Slider

The ground color of the carapace usually is dark olive. There is an eyespot on the costal scutes that remains visible even in adults. The yellowish white plastron usually is slightly mottled. Behind the eye there is a bright orange-red, narrow temporal stripe. The snout tapers to a point; the chewing surfaces of the upper jaw have a strongly serrated ridge. The nostrils are well below the tip of the snout. A light-colored medial stripe on the underside of the throat usually forks to the rear. The feet have sturdy claws and full webbing.

Up to 35 centimeters (14 inches).

The Pacific slope of southern Mexico and Guatemala to El Salvador.

We know little about this very attractive turtle because it is an extremely rare import; consequently, hobbyists rarely keep it. The habits and requirements in captivity, however, resemble those of the other slider species.[This form now is referred to *Trachemys*. It is one of over a dozen Central American forms related to the Red-eared Slider, *T. scripta*, but of uncertain relationships. It is very similar to *T. ornata*.]

Pseudemys ornata
Ornate Slider

[This species now is assigned to *Trachemys*. *T. ornata* is the oldest name for the large number of closely related sliders found from the Rio Grande south into northwestern South America. Often these subspecies are considered part of *T. scripta* from North America, but they have been considered one or several full species as well. The taxa considered part of *ornata* or at least closely related include: *callirostris, cataspila, chichiriviche, emolli, gaigeae, grayi, hartwegi, hiltoni, nebulosa, ornata, taylori, venusta,* and *yaquia*, plus a few other undescribed populations. Few of these taxa are available to hobbyists.]

Pseudemys ornata ornata
Ornate Slider

The carapace usually is dark olive with a pattern of stripes and netting. The dorsal scutes have large, circular yellow or reddish eyespots with dark borders. The surface is fairly smooth. The plastron usually is light yellow, unmarked, and has lines that become paler with age. The snout projects only slightly. The nostrils are well below the tip of the snout. The light-colored longitudinal stripes on the throat are unforked and extend forward to the margin of the horny lower jaw. The feet have full webbing and sturdy claws.

Up to 35 centimeters (14 inches).

Southern Mexico over all of Central America (except range of *grayi* as used here).

In its habits, diet, and keeping requirements, it does not differ from the other slider species. This also is true of the remaining subspecies.

The Midland Painted Turtle, *Chrysemys picta marginata*, is not as nicely colored as some of the other subspecies, and, consequently, it is infrequently offered for sale. In the U.S. specimens found in yard and pond are often kept by beginning hobbyists. Photo by W. Hemmer.

The Caribbean sliders are rare turtles in the pet trade. Although the author considers these turtles to be subspecies, the current trend is to recognize the varieties as individual species. This is the Jamaican Slider, *Pseudemys* [*Trachemys*] *terrapen*. Photo by G. Müller.

The Yellow-blotched Sawback, *Graptemys flavimaculata*, is an attractive turtle that only rarely appears in the pet trade. The author reports that it is more difficult to keep than some of the others in the genus. Photo by B. Kahl.

Graptemys kohni, the Mississippi Map Turtle, is a good candidate for the terrarium and does not require nearly as high temperatures as is often reported in the literature. This turtle is commonly offered for sale. Photo by H. Reinhard.

Pseudemys ornata callirostris
Colombian or Venezuelan Slider
It differs from the nominate form in that the longitudinal stripes do not extend all the way to the margin of the lower jaw. Instead, isolated, circular, dark-bordered yellow blotches or chin spots separate them from the jaw.
Up to 35 centimeters (14 inches).
Northern South America, in Colombia and Venezuela.

Pseudemys ornata nebulosa
Baja California Slider
Like the nominate form, *P. o. nebulosa* has large, circular, light-colored blotches on the costal scutes. They have black borders but do not have a dark center. [The distinctions between *nebulosa* and *ornata* are minor and not as obvious as stated above.]
Up to 35 centimeters (14 inches).
Baja California Peninsula, northwestern Mexico.

Pseudemys ornata yaquia
Yaqui Slider
A few interior river basins of Sonora, Mexico.

Pseudemys rubriventris
Red-bellied Turtle

Pseudemys rubriventris rubriventris
Red-bellied Turtle
The brown to black carapace has red or yellow markings on the costal scutes. The carapace is oblong, highest in the middle but widest behind the middle, and is generally rather flat. The trailing edge is serrated. The plastron is red or reddish, at least on the margin. The dark olive legs have yellow stripes, as do the head and neck. This species also has sharp claws and full webbing on the toes.
Up to 40 centimeters (16 inches).
Eastern coast of the United States, from New Jersey to North Carolina.
In its habits *P. r. rubriventris* does not differ from the other species of this genus. It goes on land mainly to bask. The juveniles are predominantly carnivorous. Following the growth period they switch to a more herbivorous diet. This species is not hard to keep in the aquaterrarium.

Pseudemys rubriventris alabamensis
Alabama Red-bellied Turtle
Up to 35 centimeters (14 inches).
Mobile Bay region of southern Alabama. [Endangered. This taxon usually is considered a full species though closely related to *P. rubriventris*.]

Pseudemys rubriventris bangsi
Massachusetts Red-bellied Turtle
Up to 35 centimeters (14 inches).
Restricted to eastern Massachusetts. [Most workers no longer recognize this subspecies as distinct from *P. rubriventris* of New Jersey to North Carolina; the population is considered endangered, however.]

Pseudemys rubriventris nelsoni
Florida Red-bellied Turtle
Up to 35 centimeters (14 inches).
Florida and barely entering Georgia. [American workers and hobbyists treat the Florida Red-belly as a full species.]

Pseudemys scripta
Northern Slider
[This species now is placed in *Trachemys*.]

Pseudemys scripta scripta
Yellow-bellied Slider
Up to 27 centimeters (11 inches).
Southeastern United States from Virginia to northern Florida.

Pseudemys scripta elegans
Red-eared Slider
The relatively flat carapace, which is bright green in juveniles, later turns olive to yellow-brown. With age it continues to exhibit a highly variable mottled pattern. The eyespots on the marginal scutes also become indistinct with age, but never disappear. The common name refers to the bright red oval elongated blotch behind the eyes. This blotch is bright yellow in the subspecies *P. s. troosti* and a jagged yellow vertical blotch in *P. s. scripta*. The head, neck, and legs also have white and light-green streaks. The feet have sharp claws and are webbed. This species is doubtless among the most beautiful turtles of all. Unlike

other turtle species, the adults usually retain their handsome coloration and markings.

Up to 30 centimeters (12 inches).

The central United States (from Illinois and Indiana to Alabama and New Mexico) and extreme northeastern Mexico.

This turtle, which the pet trade formerly handled in massive numbers, is one of the most widely distributed turtles in the United States and lives in nearly all kinds of waters except for cold mountain streams. Therefore, it is very important for the hobbyist to know from which climate the specimen in question comes. Unfortunately, we can determine this in only the rarest of cases.

The turtles spend most of their time in the water and leave it only to lay their eggs or to bask. They are not fussy about diet, as is true of all slider species. Keep in mind, however, that adults take more vegetable foods than do young. With this species as well, I cannot stress too much the importance of a varied diet.

Although many hobbyists keep this species today, they still breed it relatively infrequently. It seems reasonable to assume, however, that captive-bred specimens would be easier to rear than the stressed babies from turtle farms. I always recommend keeping them outdoors in the summer. Hibernation is not absolutely necessary. Specimens from suitably cold biotopes hibernate on their own. An attractive captive-bred albino is widely available, as in a colorful "pastel" form.

Pseudemys scripta gaigeae
Big Bend Slider

Up to 25 centimeters (10 inches).

Upper Rio Grande drainage of western Texas and New Mexico plus adjacent Mexico. [This form commonly is considered a full species or a subspecies of *T. ornata*.]

Pseudemys scripta troosti
Cumberland Slider

Up to 25 centimeters (10 inches).

Cumberland River drainage of eastern Tennessee and adjacent states.

Pseudemys terrapen
Antillean Slider

The seven different *P. terrapen* subspecies have rarely reached the hands of hobbyists. Their requirements in the terrarium, however, do not differ from those of the other *Pseudemys* species. They do not require temperatures as high as would be expected from their provenance.

[The Caribbean sliders now are referred to the genus *Trachemys*. The most recent revision considers them to be full species: *T. decorata* (Hispaniola), *T. decussata* (Cuba and Caymans), *T. stejnegeri* (Great Inagua, Puerto Rico, Hispaniola), and *T. terrapen* (Jamaica).]

Pseudemys terrapen terrapen
Jamaican Slider

Only juveniles have a strongly arched carapace. The carapace is olive-brown to black and often has a rough surface with longitudinal furrows. The plastron is predominantly pale yellow with several irregular black blotches in the rear third. The undersides of the marginal scutes have black, somewhat faded, circular blotches with light-colored centers. The gular scutes have a straight leading edge and do not project. The sides of the snout are uniformly round in cross-section. The head, neck, and legs have an olive-black or dark gray color with light yellow longitudinal stripes that become paler with age. The feet have pointed, sharp claws and full webbing.

Up to 25 centimeters (10 inches).

Greater Antilles (Jamaica), apparently also introduced to Cat Island and a few other islands in the Bahamas.

These turtles prefer still or slow-flowing bodies of water, lakes, ponds, or pools with abundant vegetation in the water and on the shore. They leave the water only to bask and to lay their eggs. In my experience, they do well in the terrarium and, despite their provenance, do not require high temperatures. During the warm season, when the water temperature normally does not fall below 20°C (68°F), we can keep them without further ceremony in the garden pond. Even in cool weather in the summer, when the temperature suddenly fell to 17°C (63°F) in the pond, I had no problems.

Feeding is completely without problems, although adults continue to prefer animal food and

The Alabama Map Turtle, *Graptemys pulchra*, is one of the most difficult to keep of the map turtles. Only expert turtle keepers should work with this species. Photo by K. H. Switak.

only occasionally take a little banana, lettuce, or dandelion. I primarily feed dried shrimp, with both beef heart and fish once a week. The turtles also readily take slugs from the garden and canned and dry dog food in the form of kibble. Unfortunately, I have never been able to obtain a male. In 1985, however, after repeated copulations with a male *Pseudemys scripta scripta*, the females laid several clutches of eggs (two or three eggs in each case) that in part were fertile. After 72 to 78 days, a total of five young hatched from these clutches. They grew into robust turtles in 17 to 19 months. Recently I have seen the largest specimen, a male about 14 centimeters (almost 6 inches) long, copulating with the mother in the garden pond.

With the remaining subspecies treated below, keep in mind that they are very hard to tell apart. There is great variability even within each subspecies because of age-related melanism. For more details, consult the relevant specialist literature.

Pseudemys terrapen decorata
Hispaniolan Slider
Up to 20 centimeters (8 inches).
Western Hispaniola: Haiti and the Dominican Republic. [Now considered a full species.]

Pseudemys terrapen granti
Up to 25 centimeters (10 inches).
Grand Cayman. [Now considered a synonym of *T. decussata angusta*.]

Pseudemys terrapen malonei
Up to 20 centimeters (10 inches).
Bahamas (Great Inagua Island). [Now considered a subspecies of *T. stejnegeri*.]

Pseudemys terrapen rugosa
Up to 25 centimeters (10 inches).
Cuba and Isle of Pines. In this subspecies, individual specimens—independently of sex—exhibit completely different coloration. For example, in one specimen the entire carapace, head, and legs have a conspicuous pattern of dark streaks and squiggles that is indistinct in other specimens. [The name *rugosa* presently is considered unidentifiable. The species found on Cuba and the Isle of Pines is now called *T.*

decussata, with the subspecies *angusta* occurring on the Caymans.]

Pseudemys terrapen stejnegeri
Antillean Slider
Up to 25 centimeters (10 inches).
Puerto Rico. [The related *malonei* and *vicina* are considered subspecies.]

Pseudemys terrapen vicina
Dominican Slider
Up to 25 centimeters (10 inches).
Dominican Republic. [Now considered a subspecies of *T. stejnegeri*.]

GRAPTEMYS
Map Turtles
The map turtles are restricted to the central and eastern United States, many of the species being restricted to specific river systems in the southern states. From the genus *Graptemys*, the pet trade usually offers only the species *G. kohni* and *G. pseudogeographica* in large numbers (though other species, especially *G. pulchra* and *G. nigrinoda*, may be seasonally available). Therefore, I will discuss in detail only these two species. In any case, the other species scarcely differ from them regarding keeping and other requirements. The males are always significantly smaller than the females.

Graptemys barbouri
Barbour's Map Turtle
Females up to 32 centimeters (13 inches), males up to 14 centimeters (5.5 inches).
Apalachicola and Chipola drainages of southeastern Alabama, southwestern Georgia, and western Florida.

Graptemys caglei
Cagle's Map Turtle
Females up to 18 centimeters (7 inches), males up to 10 centimeters (4 inches).
Guadalupe and San Antonio river systems in southern Texas.

Graptemys flavimaculata
Yellow-blotched Sawback
Females up to 20 centimeters (8 inches), males up to 10 centimeters (4 inches).

Pascagoula River drainage in Mississippi.

Graptemys geographica
Common Map Turtle

Females up to 31 centimeters (12.5 inches), males up to 16 centimeters (6.5 inches).

Southeastern Canada and interior eastern United States south to northern Louisiana.

Graptemys kohni
Mississippi Map Turtle

In juveniles, the light brown carapace usually displays a fine, net-like pattern that disappears with age. The trailing edge of the carapace is strongly serrated. Along the midline there is a keel with backward-facing spines with dark-brown tips. The plastron is light yellow. There is a dark blotch in the middle with lateral arms extending along the seams of the scutes; this is present only in juveniles. On the middle of the gray-brown head a bright yellow stripe extends back from the tip of the snout and a crescent-shaped yellow stripe extends from the middle of the head and ends under each eye, preventing yellow stripes on the neck from reaching the eye. The eye is bright pale yellow or white without a horizontal black bar. The neck and legs have numerous light yellow longitudinal stripes. The toes are fully webbed and end in sharp claws.

Females up to 27 centimeters (11 inches), males up to 12 centimeters (almost 5 inches).

Central and southern United States in the Mississippi Valley. [This species often is considered a subspecies of *G. pseudogeographica*, but not all workers are convinced.]

This species prefers slow-flowing bodies of water, lakes, ponds, and pools with abundant vegetation. It is an avid sun bather. Depending on the season, we can keep these turtles at temperatures from 5 to 30°C (41 to 86°F). In my experience, these turtles are absolutely insensitive to cold [many keepers would disagree with this, and it always is better not to stress an animal by subjecting it to unnecessarily cool temperatures]. I have even overwintered *G. kohni* in an ice-covered garden pond. In early March it already sunned itself at a water temperature of about 10°C (50°F) and an air temperature of about 14°C (57°F). Accordingly, my Mississippi Map Turtle normally is always outdoors from April to October and has never lost its liveliness.

Except for the occasional banana, it exclusively eats all sorts of animal food: dried shrimp, beef heart, fish in any form, even canned dog food and turtle aspic. It has, however, never lost a certain shyness. Particularly in the garden pond, although I have kept it for 12 years, it still maintains a flight distance of 6 to 8 meters (20 to 26 feet). In any case, all *Graptemys* species are very lovable and peaceful charges in their youth. Adults can be very aggressive at times, especially *Graptemys versa*.

Graptemys nigrinoda
Black-knobbed Sawback

Graptemys nigrinoda nigrinoda
Northern Black-knobbed Sawback

[Black-knobbed Sawbacks have very high knobs in a row down the middle of the carapace and a deeply serrated back edged of the carapace. Like other sawbacks, it is found in highly oxygenated flowing rivers with sandy bottoms. This species recently has become fairly common in the pet trade.]

Females up to 21 centimeters (8.5 inches), males up to 12 centimeters (5 inches).

Northeastern Mississippi and central Alabama.

Graptemys nigrinoda delticola
Southern Black-knobbed Sawback

Females up to 26 centimeters (10.5 inches), males up to 13 centimeters (5 inches).

Southern Alabama.

Graptemys oculifera
Ringed Sawback

Females up to 20 centimeters (8 inches), males up to 10 centimeters (4 inches).

Pearl River drainage of southern Mississippi and eastern Louisiana. Protected. *G. oculifera* is a handsome turtle but seldom reaches the hands of hobbyists. It is scarcely available in the pet trade because it lives in a relatively small area. In its habits it differs little from *G. kohni*; at most it needs slightly higher temperatures.

Although map turtles are popular in the hobby, wild-caught ones can be difficult to acclimate to captivity. It would be wise to be sure that a potential purchase is eating well in the store. This is the Common Map Turtle, *Graptemys geographica*. Photo by I. Francais.

Graptemys pseudogeographica
False Map Turtle

*Graptemys pseudogeographica
pseudogeographica*
False Map Turtle
This species is somewhat similar in appearance to *G. kohni* except that the crescent-shaped mark ends behind the eyes so pale stripes on the neck reach the eye. In contrast to *G. kohni*, a dark horizontal bar runs through the iris.

Females up to 27 centimeters (11 inches), males up to 14 centimeters (4.5 inches).

Northern central United States in the Mississippi and Missouri drainages.

The habits are largely the same as those of the species *G. kohni*. I keep it from April to October in the garden pond at water temperatures from 18 to 27°C (65 to 81°F), depending on the summer. It presents no problems regarding diet. It refuses vegetable foods, except for a little banana occasionally. [This appears exceptional, as the species generally consumes soft aquatic plants to about half of its diet; large females may specialize in snails and clams.] I recommend it highly for the terrarium. For some time, several hobbyists have bred it successfully.

Graptemys pseudogeographica ouachitensis
Ouachita Map Turtle
Females up to 22 centimeters (9 inches), males up to 11 centimeters (4.5 inches).

Central United States, Louisiana to West Virginia and Minnesota.[Many workers recently have accepted *ouachitensis* as a full species with the subspecies *sabinensis*. This is not accepted by all workers. Some feel that *sabinensis* also should be listed as a full species.]

Graptemys pseudogeographica sabinensis
Sabine Map Turtle
Females up to 16 centimeters (6.5 inches), males up to 10 centimeters (4 inches).

Sabine River drainage between Louisiana and Texas.

Graptemys pseudogeographica versa
Texas Map Turtle
Females up to 20 centimeters (8 inches), males up to 10 centimeters (4 inches).

Central Texas in the Colorado River drainage. [Most herpetologists accept this as a full species.]

This turtle is unsuitable for the beginner. It is in my opinion the most aggressive member of its genus. So far, only Sachsse and Stamm (Engert, oral communication) have bred it regularly.

Graptemys pulchra
Alabama Map Turtle
Females up to 30 centimeters (12 inches), males up to 13 centimeters (a bit over 5 inches).

Gulf of Mexico drainages from eastern Louisiana to northern Georgia. According to Shealey, there are five different forms of *G. pulchra* that occur in different river systems. It requires extremely high temperatures and is very delicate; thus, it is not a turtle for the beginner. [Recently this species has been broken into three full species: *G. ernsti* from Pensacola Bay drainages in Florida and Alabama; *G. gibbonsi* from the Pascagoula and Pearl River drainages of Mississippi and eastern Louisiana; and *G. pulchra* from Mobile Bay drainages in Alabama and northwestern Georgia. The three species are similar in general appearance but have slight differences in head and shell patterns.]

In closing I would like to mention that hobbyists in Germany and Austria have bred all the species except for *Graptemys geographica, Graptemys pulchra*, and *Graptemys caglei*.

MALACLEMYS
Diamondback Terrapins

Malaclemys terrapin
Diamondback Terrapin

Malaclemys terrapin terrapin
Northern Diamondback Terrapin
The black to brown carapace has slightly humped, very strongly grooved scutes lacking sharply defined central blotches. The humped form results because the turtle does not shed the older horny plates. Instead, they remain attached to the growing, larger scutes. This growth pattern also produces annual rings, which provide information on the turtle's age. [Growth rings on turtle scutes do not provide a record of age that can be read

directly, but when the width of rings is treated mathematically in relation to another shell measurement such as plastron length, information on relative age can be obtained.] The entire underside of the plastron is light orange to greenish, with scattered black blotches. The plastron is always lighter in color than the carapace. The highest point of the carapace is approximately in the middle. The leading edge of the gular scute does not have a notch or has only a slight notch in the middle. The anal scutes are a step lower than the femoral scutes. The upper lip generally is light-colored. The sturdy front and hind legs end in sharp claws.
Up to 25 centimeters (10 inches).

Brackish to marine bays and estuaries of the northeastern United States from Massachusetts to North Carolina.

Diamondback Terrapins live in brackish water near the coast. Their diet consists of saltwater fishes and hard-shelled mollusks; they do not eat plants. The turtles are able to excrete excess salt taken in with the food by means of specialized glands.

Formerly, people considered this turtle to be a delicacy, and even today a few turtle farms still rear it for this purpose in ponds in the United States. It is difficult to keep in captivity. I am unaware of any instance in which the turtle survived for an extended period in the terrarium. In any case, it is not suitable for the beginner. [Many American hobbyists have had good luck with this species and do not consider it especially difficult. Perhaps stress from exportation to Europe causes it to be more difficult to maintain there.] In the aquaterrarium (aquatic section 80 percent), it is essential to add about 10-12 grams of sea salt per liter of water. The air and water temperature should not fall much below 20°C (68°F); the optimal temperature is 25°C (77°F). It is advisable to feed the turtles unrinsed salt-water fish, shrimp, and mollusks.

[Currently there are seven recognized subspecies of Diamondback Terrapins. They replace each other geographically from Massachusetts to Texas and usually are very difficult or impossible to distinguish without long series of specimens. Preliminary genetic studies seem to indicate that the currently recognized subspecies do not represent the true level of variation in this species. Hobbyists would be well advised to ignore subspecies level in this turtle.]

Malaclemys terrapin centrata
Carolina Diamondback Terrapin
Up to 20 centimeters (8 inches).
Southern North Carolina to northeastern Florida.

Malaclemys terrapin littoralis
Texas Diamondback Terrapin
Up to 20 centimeters (8 inches).
Coast of eastern and central Texas.

Malaclemys terrapin macrospilota
Ornate Diamondback Terrapin
Up to 20 centimeters (8 inches).
Western coast of Florida to the panhandle.

Malaclemys terrapin pileata
Mississippi Diamondback Terrapin
Up to 24 centimeters (9.5 inches).
The Texas-Louisiana border to the western Florida panhandle.

Malaclemys terrapin rhizophorarum
Mangrove Diamondback Terrapin
Up to 20 centimeters (8 inches).
Florida Keys.

Malaclemys terrapin tequesta
Florida East Coast Diamondback Terrapin
Up to 22 centimeters (9 inches).
East coast of Florida from Volusia County south to Dade County.

The aforementioned subspecies do not differ in keeping requirements from the nominate form. The only difference is that specimens from the more southerly parts of the United States require somewhat higher temperatures.

MALAYEMYS
Malayan Snail-eating Turtles

Malayemys subtrijuga
Malayan Snail-eating Turtle
The arched, chestnut-brown carapace has three distinct longitudinal keels. The marginal

The Diamondback Terrapin, *Malaclemys terrapin*, is an active and persistent species if kept in brackish water. The photograph shows the nominate form of the seven subspecies. Photo by B. Kahl.

left: The Malayan Snail-eating Turtle, *Malayemys subtrifuga*, is one of the most beautiful, but also most delicate, aquatic turtles. It is virtually unavailable to the average hobbyist. Photo by B. Kahl.
right: *Mauremys caspica leprosa*, the Mediterranean Turtle, lives even in the smallest puddles and ditches, often even in sewage ditches in North Africa. Photo by W. Hemmer.

Mauremys [Sacalia] bealei, Beal's Eyed Turtle. A lovable, although rather quiet, charge in the aqua-terrarium. These can be kept at rather cool temperatures. Photo by G. Müller.

Mauremys caspica caspica. The Eastern Caspian Turtle is the most attractive of the three subspecies. Some European hobbyists breed it regularly. Photo by W. Hemmer.

scutes of the carapace have light-colored blotches on their outside borders. These blotches, together with the dark margins, produce a very attractive pattern. The plastron is yellowish with dark markings on some scutes. The dark brown head with whitish yellow longitudinal lines and dots is very attractive. The dark brown, yellow-bordered limbs have sturdy claws. The toes are webbed.

Up to 20 centimeters (8 inches).

Scattered over Southeast Asia from Thailand to Vietnam and to Java and Sumatra.

This very quiet and sluggish turtle, which usually hides during the day and becomes active only at twilight, lives in the wild primarily in marshy regions with smaller pools or ponds. It is a snail specialist that can crack even the hardest shells, which shows what immense jaw pressure this relatively small turtle generates. Although it specializes on snails, in captivity we can acclimate it gradually to other aquatic-turtle foods, such as dried shrimp, earthworms, chopped beef heart, or fish, but mollusks should predominate. Do not keep this turtle with more active turtles because it has quiet and contemplative habits and otherwise will barely get anything to eat.

I have observed something interesting with the specimen I have kept: It "plays possum." If I suddenly grab the turtle and remove it from its quarters, it becomes completely rigid and looks dead. After I return it to its quarters, it remains stiff for some time before suddenly moving normally again. The literature reports the same behavior with the Big-headed Turtle (*Platysternon*). The optimum temperature is 24 to 28°C (75 to 82°F).

In summary, the Malayan Snail-eating Turtle is a problematic charge that only truly experienced hobbyists should attempt to keep, but even then it is questionable. An appropriate diet based on snails seems to be essential.

MAUREMYS
Striped-necked Turtles

Mauremys (Sacalia) bealei
Beal's Eyed Turtle

[*Sacalia* is considered a good genus by most American herpetologists. A second species, *S.*

quadriocellata, the Four-eyed Turtle, usually is recognized.]

The light brown, slightly arched carapace has numerous dark specks. The trailing edge is not serrated and the carapace has a weak longitudinal keel. The plastron is yellowish with scattered, irregular brown streaks and blotches. The soft parts are light yellow; only the outermost parts of the head, legs, and tail are brownish olive. The light olive top of the head also has numerous dark specks. The occiput has one, two, or three pairs of yellow eyespots with dark borders and a black center. The top of the neck has a longitudinal light yellow central stripe and two lateral stripes. The feet end in claws and have webbing.

Up to 15 centimeters (6 inches).

Southeastern China and Hainan.

Beal's Eyed Turtle prefers smaller pools and ponds with abundant vegetation and also lives in rice fields. It wanders on land, but does not leave the wet region. It is not particularly temperature-sensitive (20 to 26°C, 68 to 79°F) and likes to take long sun baths. It is not fussy about diet and takes all kinds of animal food, whether dead or alive. It is less fond of vegetable foods, but it sometimes takes banana or other fruits, rarely lettuce or dandelion.

In captivity it is a lovable but quiet charge. In summer I keep it in the garden pond, where the temperature seldom falls below 20°C (68°F). There are no reports of captive breeding, but it certainly should be possible in the terrarium. Cool overwintering is unnecessary.

Mauremys caspica
Caspian Turtle

Mauremys caspica caspica
Eastern Caspian Turtle

The elliptical carapace is fawn, olive-brown, or olive-green. It is unkeeled and is not serrated. The plastron is orange to orange-yellow with black blotches. The bridge is orange-yellow and unmarked, in contrast to *M. c. rivulata*, in which it is dark except for a few light blotches. In *M. c. leprosa* [now treated as a full species by many workers] the bridge has two large black blotches. The trans-

top: The Yellow-necked Pond Turtle, *Mauremys nigricans*, is scarcely available in the pet trade despite still being abundant in the wild. Breeding them is usually unproblematic.
bottom: The Western Caspian Turtle, *Mauremys caspica rivulata*, is an easily kept turtle. Popular in Europe, it is seldom available in the U. S. Both photos by W. Hemmer.

verse seams between the marginal scutes are black. The gray legs and the head have orange to yellow markings. The black iris is particularly conspicuous. The legs end in sturdy claws with webbing between the toes. The nominate form, with its elegant form and attractive markings, is a beautiful turtle. It does not suffer in comparison with the North American Painted Turtle.

Up to 25 centimeters (10 inches).

Arabia and the Middle East to the Caspian Sea.

It lives in streams, rivers, ponds, and lakes (in Iran it is particularly common in rice fields); it is not particularly fond of fast-flowing water. In rivers it lives more often in bays and stream mouths or in shallow places with little current. An ideal turtle for keeping in a protected garden pond or in some other outdoor installation, it is highly aquatic and comes on land only to bask (which it does very readily and for long periods) or to lay its eggs. Unfortunately, these attractive and elegant turtles are scarcely obtainable, but they would be ideal charges, even for the beginner.

They feed mainly on aquatic insects, snails (aquatic and terrestrial), fish, prepared dog food, earthworms, beef heart, and beef liver. Although it takes little vegetable food in captivity, offer it regularly. Besides animal food, however, my turtles ate only bananas. An examination of the feces showed that freshly caught (adult) specimens apparently were strictly herbivorous.

One peculiarity (displayed by all *Mauremys* species) deserves mention. Soon after capture or while being weighed and measured, alarmed turtles emit a penetrating musky odor (as I have also observed with *Siebenrockiella crassicollis*). Acclimated turtles, however, rarely emit this scent.

The required temperature range is 18 to 28°C (65 to 82°F). The turtles' provenance plays a large role here. In my opinion, a winter rest at lowered temperatures is better for the turtles than hibernation. This turtle has bred successfully in captivity.

Mauremys caspica leprosa
Mediterranean Turtle

Up to 25 centimeters (10 inches).

Southwestern Europe and northwestern Africa.

In captivity this subspecies probably differs from the nominate form in that it requires somewhat higher temperatures. It has a heavier build and a far less elegant appearance than does *M. c. caspica*. It is able to perform unbelievable climbing feats, which must taken into account in the terrarium and especially in outdoor facilities. [Many workers now treat *leprosa* as a distinct species. In northern Africa it occurs in oases many miles from the Mediterranean.]

Mauremys caspica rivulata
Western Caspian Turtle

Up to 20 centimeters (8 inches).

Southeastern Europe (southern Yugoslavia, Albania, southern Bulgaria, Greece, Ionic Islands, and Cyclads) and the Near East (Turkey, western and southern Anatolia, Syria, Israel, Crete, and Cyprus, possibly Transjordan).

In appearance and keeping requirements, it is more similar to the nominate form than to *M. c. leprosa* and also is a highly recommended charge. It breeds regularly in captivity. I advise a winter rest, as with the nominate form. Feeding is not difficult because it is an omnivore.

Mauremys japonica
Japanese Pond Turtle

The Japanese Pond Turtle has a light brown carapace, the scutes with concentric grooves and radiating lines. The rear marginal scutes are doubly serrated. The scutes of the plastron are yellowish on the margins but otherwise black. The plastron has a round notch on the leading edge and a deeper, triangular indentation on the trailing edge. The sides of the head and the neck are yellow and otherwise unmarked. The webbing is fuller than in the previous species.

Up to 18 centimeters (7 inches).

The three islands of southern Japan.

This lively turtle is highly aquatic, but some authors have claimed that it spends much time on land. As we find time and again, there often are astounding differences in behavior within the same species. In its homeland, *M. japonica* lives in small ponds and lakes with abundant vegetation. It requires temperatures from 20 to 26°C (68 to 79°F). The pet trade imports it rarely, but it would make a very good charge. There are no reports of successful breeding in captivity. It has the same dietary requirements as *Mauremys c. caspica.*

[Two other species of *Mauremys* are recognized by some workers. The Yellow Pond Turtle, *M. mutica*, occurs in southeastern China, Vietnam, Hainan, Taiwan, and the Ryukyus. Its status as a distinct species or as a synonym of *nigricans* has long been in debate, as has its generic status. *M. iversoni*, the Fujian Pond Turtle, recently was described from southeastern China. The relationships between the Far Eastern *Mauremys* and the species placed in *Chinemys* remain controversial, and species float back and forth between these generic names.]

Mauremys nigricans
Yellow-necked Pond Turtle

[Recently this species has been moved to the genus *Chinemys*, where it is placed alongside Reeves's Turtle. This move has not been accepted by all workers as yet.]

This pond turtle has three black longitudinal keels on its chestnut-brown carapace, of which the middle one is more conspicuous. [The two lateral keels often are so weak as to be considered absent.] The plastron is orange to sulfur-colored and has a large black blotch on the outside hind border of each scute. Directly behind the eye there is a broad horizontal yellow band that often has black borders. The throat is yellow. The sturdy legs end in sharp claws. The toes are slightly webbed.

Up to 18 centimeters (7 inches).

Southeastern China and possibly Hainan and northern Vietnam.

The turtles live in a wide range of habitats, from forest streams at high elevations to pools and ponds of swampy regions or low-lying areas. They certainly need higher temperatures than the previously mentioned species. The temperatures should be 22 and 28°C (72 to 82°F). In captivity they are grateful charges, but they seldom are imported and offered, although they are still common in their homeland. They have bred in captivity.

TERRAPENE
Box Turtles

[Though widely collected and occasionally captive-bred, recent agitation and concern about over-collecting for the American and overseas markets have led to proposals to list the box turtles under appendix II of CITES, meaning they would require paperwork for each transaction. Box turtles are protected in several states, which do not allow their possession as pets.]

Terrapene carolina
Eastern Box Turtle

Terrapene carolina carolina
Eastern Box Turtle

The high-domed, brown carapace has a slight keel. It has a pattern of yellow spots and stripes, some of which resemble letters of the alphabet. (In the subspecies *T. c. bauri* the slightly raised scutes have radiating lines.) The plastron is yellowish and sometimes has dark blotches. Box turtles get their name from the movable, cartilaginous hinge in the middle of the plastron. This makes it possible to close the front and rear parts of the plastron against the carapace and to protect the drawn in extremities and soft parts. The robust legs have sturdy claws and the feet are thick, with reduced webbing. Particularly striking is the hook-like upper jaw, which frequently is overgrown into a hawk-like beak.

Up to 16 centimeters (6.5 inches).

Eastern United States, from Illinois and Massachusetts south to Georgia.

The turtles live in moist to rather dry areas (including upland forests), usually near waterbodies ranging in size from shallow pools or puddles to lakes. They are omnivorous, although juveniles are predominantly carnivorous. In the terrarium, it takes virtually anything: beetles, cockroaches, mealworms, wood lice, snails of all kinds, young mice, beef heart, dog and cat food, dandelions, any kind of fruit, leaf lettuce, and mushrooms.

Box turtles live many years in the terrarium if we keep them outside part of the year; otherwise, they often die suddenly for no apparent reason. We should keep them in terraria that are not too small (at least one square meter per pair), because they are very

top: The Japanese Pond Turtle, *Mauremys japonica*, is rare in the pet trade, but is a very highly recommended turtle for the terrarium.
bottom: Plastron of the Japanese Pond Turtle. Both photos by W. Hemmer.

Terrapene carolina triunguis, Three-toed Box Turtle, at the start of copulation. The male clasps the trailing edge of the female's plastron with its hind legs, so that copulation does not end prematurely. Photo by G. Janson.

lively and always wander around a lot. Their behavior is highly variable individually. Some specimens are strictly terrestrial, others prefer a wet biotope where they splash around in the water and even rest in it. One particular *T. c. carolina* was reported to be in the habit of swimming about four times a day in an outdoor pond for aquatic turtles and basked with them on an island. The required temperatures are from 20 to 28°C (68 to 82°F) and should not fall below 20°C (68°F) for long. In the outdoor facility, we should offer them a heated shelter that the turtles can seek out during periods of cooler weather, although they can tolerate fairly cool temperatures for short periods of time. [In nature, most Eastern Box Turtles spend the winter months brumating in mud and debris at the edges of streams and lakes. The young are very aquatic, the adults less so during most of the year.]

During copulation, which often lasts for hours, the male climbs on top of the female, digs the claws of his hind legs into the edge of the female's carapace, and tips itself to the rear. Copulation often takes place in shallow water. Breeding has succeeded regularly in captivity. The clutches of four to six eggs have a maturation period of 70 to 80 days. The young are not particularly hard to rear.

Terrapene carolina bauri
Florida Box Turtle
Up to 15 centimeters (6 inches).
Florida.

Terrapene carolina major
Gulf Coast Box Turtle
Up to almost 22 centimeters (8.5 inches).
Southern United States along the Gulf Coast from southeastern Louisiana to western Florida. [The head of this, the largest living box turtle, often is white, while the legs may lack all reddish markings.]

Terrapene carolina mexicana
Mexican Box Turtle

This is one of the the largest box turtle and also one of the most attractive and colorful. The seams of the carapace have broad, dark markings. On the dorsal scutes there are yellow streaks on a dark background, in part in the form of radiating lines. The head has an attractive yellow, red, and brown coloration. In contrast to the subspecies *T. c. yucatana* (with four claws on the hind feet), this subspecies as a rule has only three claws.

Up to 17 centimeters (7 inches).

Northeastern Mexico.

Formerly this turtle was rare in captivity, but since the adoption of the import ban (into England and northern Europe) on European tortoises, the pet trade has carried it more often. (We hope that it also reached the right hands.) The habits and keeping requirements are the same as with *Terrapene c. carolina*, but it may need slightly higher temperatures. [Mexico currently is closed to legal exportation of its fauna, including box turtles. This subspecies is very similar to the Three-toed Box Turtle of the southern United States, and some in the terrarium hobby may be misidentified.]

Terrapene carolina triunguis
Three-toed Box Turtle

Three-toed Box Turtle, *Terrapene carolina triunguis.* Illustration: E. Bobbe in Wermuth/Mertens: Schildkröten — Krokodile — Brückenechsen.

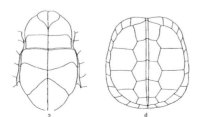

Up to 18 centimeters (7 inches).

Central and southern United States in the Mississippi Valley west to eastern Texas.

Terrapene carolina yucatana
Yucatan Box Turtle

Up to 16 centimeters (5.5 inches).

The Yucatan Peninsula and Quintana Roo, eastern Mexico.

Terrapene coahuila
Coahuilan Box Turtle

Unlike most other *Terrapene* species, the horn-yellow carapace is unmarked and the seams between the scutes do not have dark borders. The elongated-oval carapace is at least half again as long as wide. The plastron is uniformly light in color and unmarked. The hind feet are distinctly webbed.

Up to 15 centimeters (6 inches).

Northeastern Mexico, restricted to the Cuatro Cienegas series of remnant streams and oases.

The literature reports scarcely any information on this species in the private terrarium, and it is protected under Appendix I of CITES. It is much more aquatic than other box turtles and needs higher temperatures. [The species has been well-studied in nature, but its protected status keeps it out of private hands.]

Terrapene nelsoni
Spotted Box Turtle

Terrapene nelsoni nelsoni

The carapace is marked with small yellow spots and does not have yellow radiating lines. The upper mandible has smooth margins and does not have a notch in front.

Up to 15 centimeters (6 inches).

Northwestern Mexico, Nayarit.

We know little about this turtle. Its keeping requirements are probably similar to those of the other *Terrapene* species.

Terrapene nelsoni klauberi

Similar in form to the other *Terrapene* species, but the hooked snout is not as prominent. Numerous small, sharply defined, circular yellow spots cover the dark carapace. The plastron is uniformly yellow.

Up to 14 centimeters (5.5 inches).

Northwestern Mexico, southern Sonora.

Much like *T. c. carolina*, but needs higher temperatures.

Terrapene ornata
Ornate Box Turtle

Terrapene ornata ornata
Ornate Box Turtle

The carapace is considerably flatter than in the majority of *Terrapene* species, is brownish black, and has a very attractive pattern of radiating lines, as does the dark plastron. The head and legs have yellow to orange and even red speckling. The irises of males are red, in contrast to the yellow irises of females. *Terrapene ornata* certainly does justice to its names! In most males the inner claw of the hind leg is thickened and curved to help hold the female's carapace.

Up to 15 centimeters (6 inches).

The Great Plains of the central United States east to Indiana and Louisiana and south through all of eastern Texas.

This turtle is less dependent on a moist biotope than the other *Terrapene* species. It lives in prairies, grazed pasturelands, and in places with sandy soil, but not always near water. It is most active in the morning and evening when temperatures are relatively low. The required temperature range is 18 to 22°C (65 to 72°F). In the terrarium it is advisable to let the temperature fall at night. We should always keep the turtles outdoors, as is true of all *Terrapene* species. I do not consider hibernation to be absolutely necessary; a rest period in winter at reduced temperatures is sufficient. The diet is the same as that of *T. c. carolina*.

Terrapene ornata luteola
Desert Box Turtle

Up to 15 centimeters (6 inches).

Southwestern United States (Arizona to western Texas) and adjoining northern Mexico.

CLEMMYS
American Pond Turtles

Clemmys guttata
Spotted Turtle

The weakly arched carapace is black and becomes smooth with age. The scutes have scattered, sharply defined yellow spots. The back edge is not serrated. The plastron is black with an irregular light yellow border and sometimes scattered pale blotches. The top of the head and the legs usually are black with scattered yellow spots. The underside of the head often is a yellowish tan color. The pattern of yellow spots is extremely sparse in some specimens, both on the carapace and the head and legs. The legs have webbing between the toes and end in sharp claws.

Up to 12 centimeters (5 inches).

Northern and eastern United States, from northeastern Illinois east to Maine and south along the coast to Georgia and northern Florida.

The Spotted Turtle lives in boggy ponds and pools and is more highly aquatic than are the other *Clemmys* species. In my opinion it is very hard to keep in the terrarium. As I have heard from many hobbyists, the turtles did not live very long in captivity, which is an experience that I unfortunately share. According to the most recent findings, however, the water supply apparently caused these failures. According to its provenance, keep *C. guttata* in acid water (filter through peat). The optimum temperature depends on the provenance of the turtles; hobbyists had good success both with cool keeping temperatures (water temperature of 18 to 22°C, 65 to 72°F) and with very warm keeping temperatures (water temperature of 28 to 30°C, 82 to 86°F). The turtles require a straightforward diet: aquatic insects, aquatic snails, earthworms, crustaceans, beef heart and liver, prepared food for turtles, bananas, and occasionally aquatic plants, leaf lettuce, and dandelions. The specimens I kept, however, did not show much interest in vegetables.

Outdoor keeping—except during the winter months—is always important. Because of the persistent attempts by the males to copulate, the females usually get no rest, making it necessary to keep the male turtles separately and to put them with the females only temporarily. A number of hobbyists have bred this turtle successfully.

Spotted Turtles, *Clemmys guttata*, grow to a length of only 5 inches. Separate the males from the females periodically, as the females will get no rest because of the persistent breeding attempts. Photo by H. Reinhard.

Clemmys insculpta
Wood Turtle

The dark brown carapace has a distinct longitudinal keel and the trailing edge is not serrated. The scutes have concentric growth ridges crossed with beaded radiating ridges. The plastron is yellow with a black blotch present on the outer margin of each scute. The tops of the head and legs are dark olive-brown and the undersides are reddish. Some specimens have distinct red markings on the head and legs. The legs end in sturdy claws with only a suggestion of webbing.

Up to 23 centimeters (9.5 inches).

Northeastern United States and adjacent Canada, Minnesota to the Atlantic.

The Wood Turtle has more terrestrial habits and spends more time on land than other pond turtles. It lives in forests or meadows, but never too far from water. It usually overwinters in the water or in riparian regions. It needs a roomy terrarium with a large land section and does very

well in the garden pond or outdoor terrarium. Always be sure to secure the enclosure, because it is very fond of digging and could escape in this way. It also climbs very well. The diet consists of both vegetable and animal foods and should be as varied as possible. It takes more vegetable foods than does the Spotted Turtle. It is very fond of snails of all kinds, including slugs.

Wood Turtles do not require high keeping temperatures, and a range of 10 to 24°C (50 to 75°F) is acceptable. Under suitable keeping conditions, breeding presents no problems in captivity.

The Wood Turtle is not hard to keep in the terrarium and is suitable for the beginner. Always keep the turtle outdoors in the warm season. I leave my turtles outside until early November. When there is the danger of frost, however, I cover the terrarium at night. In the meantime they have become a good value in the pet trade and have bred regularly. One specimen lived 38 years in captivity. [Though captive-bred specimens of Wood Turtles are rather easy to find, this species is protected by law in several states and may need special permits for their keeping.]

Clemmys marmorata
Western (Pacific) Pond Turtle

Clemmys marmorata marmorata
Northwestern Pond Turtle

The flat carapace is olive, dark brown, or nearly black (the coloration is highly variable in individual specimens). The undersides of the marginal scutes and the bridge have dark blotches and lines along the seams. The yellow plastron has irregular blotches or lines that often are indistinct. The skin is gray. In the nominate subspecies the sides of the head are dark and the chin and throat are yellow. This is in contrast to the subspecies *C. m.* *pallida*, in which the sides of the head, chin, and throat are uniformly brownish. In the nominate form the inguinal scutes are large; in *C. m. pallida* they are small or absent.

Up to 18 centimeters (7.5 inches).

Southwestern Canada and western United States to central California.

This *Clemmys* species is the most highly aquatic of the genus and leaves the water only to bask or to lay its eggs. In its range it usually lives in quiet, often muddy, lakes and ponds with abundant vegetation. It also lives in fast-flowing rivers and streams up to altitudes above 2000 meters and in brackish water near the coast. In many areas its populations have been greatly reduced through human impact such as draining waterbodies and pollution.

It would make a suitable terrarium animal but seldom is available in the pet trade. It is protected in part of its range. Its temperature requirements are modest: 18 to 24°C (65 to 75°F)

The Asian Leaf Turtle, *Cyclemys dentata*, is a marsh turtle which is almost strictly aquatic. It is a well-suited charge for the terrarium. Photo by B. Kahl.

would probably be adequate. Collectors have found the turtle at a water temperature of 8.3°C (about 47°F), with a body temperature of 9°C (48°F).

In its dietary requirements it differs from other *Clemmys* species only in that it is almost strictly carnivorous.

Clemmys marmorata pallida
Southwestern Pond Turtle

Up to 18 centimeters (7.5 inches).

The Pacific coastal region from southern California to northern Baja California, Mexico.

Clemmys muhlenbergi
Bog Turtle

This smallest member of the genus *Clemmys* has a brown, arched carapace. The trailing edge is not serrated. The plastron is dark brown to black with lighter blotches along the midline. It is unmistakable because of the large, rather triangular bright orange blotch on each side of the brown head behind the eyes. The skin is brown and may have red specks on the legs. Males have a long, thick tail and a distinctly concave plastron. Females have a higher domed, broader carapace and a flatter plastron.

Up to 11 centimeters (4.5 inches).

The eastern United States in two distinct areas, one from Pennsylvania and New York to Massachusetts and Maryland, the other in the western Carolinas and Virginia.

It lives mainly in shallow pools, lakes, or ponds in boggy or marshy meadows, where it spends about half the time on land and half in the water. An old saying about this species is that it is found only where its feet can be wet but its carapace dry. As a typical omnivore, it takes anything it finds on land or in the water, and takes considerable vegetable food.

Because the Bog Turtle is listed in Appendix II of CITES, all we can say about terrarium keeping is that experienced hobbyists considered the turtles to be delicate, but they have kept and bred them successfully for years. [Captive-bred specimens are available to individuals with proper permits, though keeping this animal is greatly restricted in the United States. Many specimens still are collected illegally for exportation to the Far East.]

ANNAMEMYS
Annam Leaf Turtles

Annamemys annamensis
Annam Leaf Turtle

Though once believed to possibly be extinct, importers recently have offered it again.

The nearly circular olive-brown carapace is relatively flat and has three longitudinal keels, of which the middle one is particularly prominent. The trailing edge of the carapace is slightly wavy but not serrated. Each scute of the yellowish plastron has a black blotch, some separate and some running together, producing a symmetrical pattern. The sides of the head have several straight light yellow longitudinal stripes that contrast sharply with the black-brown ground color. The upper jaw has a central notch. The toes are strongly webbed.

Up to 17 centimeters (7 inches).

Central Vietnam.

The Annam Leaf Turtle lives in small rainforest lakes, pools, and marshy areas. Freshly caught specimens hiss when picked up and spray out the contents of their cloacas (as also is done by several other species). This behavior quickly subsides in captivity, however, and the turtles soon become tame.

The Annam Leaf Turtle is predominantly vegetarian and is fond of fruits of all kinds, particularly when they are sweet and juicy. It eats so much of them that the water in the aquaterrarium soon turns into a dungy brew if we do not use a powerful filter. I know of no reports of captive breeding.

CYCLEMYS
Asian Leaf Turtles

Cyclemys dentata
Asian Leaf Turtle

The brown carapace is flat. The dorsal scutes have light-colored radiating lines that, however, usually disappear with age. The undersides of the marginal scutes have shallow indentations, and there is only a slight displacement between them and the adjoining scutes. The scutes of the pale brown plastron have dark radiating lines. In babies and juveniles the rigid plastron fuses with the carapace on the sides, but connective tissue replaces this rigid, bony connection as the turtles age. In the same manner a hinge forms at the midline of the plastron. This allows the turtles to close the plastron against the carapace in the same way as with the *Terrapene* and *Cuora* species. Closure is not as complete as with these two genera, however, but rather only permits partial closing. The head and the legs are brown with some speckling. A conspicuous feature is that all the soft parts located under the carapace are yellowish white.

Up to 25 centimeters (10 inches).

Southeast Asia, Sumatra and Java, Borneo, and the Philippines.

In its homeland this turtle lives in pools in marshy areas and forests, flooded areas, and rainforest lakes. As juveniles they are nearly strictly aquatic, but later they are said to spend more time on land in marshy areas. The specimens I kept, even when fully grown, left the water only occasionally to bask or to lay eggs. The five eggs laid by the females were infertile because no male was available. Later I gave the turtles to another hobbyist, and I never obtained offspring from this species. This turtle is a highly recommended terrarium animal and does well in captivity. The temperature should be from 22 to 26°C (72 to 79°F).

With my specimens the diet consisted of aquatic and terrestrial snails, dried shrimp, beef heart and liver, earthworms, fish fillets, freshwater fishes, and dog food. They also took bananas, but they largely ignored lettuce and dandelion.

Experts formerly considered *Cyclemys mouhoti* to be a second species of the genus, but according to recent findings it belongs in its own genus, *Pyxidea*, where it is treated here.

Cyclemys tcheponensis
Stripe-necked Leaf Turtle

The carapace is blackish brown on the sides and becomes completely black toward the midline. There is a prominent central longitudinal keel with only indistinct lateral keels. The trailing edge is serrated. The plastron is ivory-colored and has a conspicuous pattern of radiating lines. The color of the head, neck, and legs is a light yellow-brown with conspicuous pink stripes and squiggles, which, however, become paler with age. In the Asian Leaf Turtle the stripes stop at about the level of the corner of the mouth, while in this species the stripes continue to the eye and sometimes the snout. The toes end in very sharp claws.

Up to 20 centimeters (8 inches).

Thailand eastward to Vietnam.

This turtle is very rare, or at least importations have been extremely rare, and we know almost nothing about its habits in the wild, but there is some information about its behavior in captivity. [It is reported to live in streams in mountainous areas and to be partially terrestrial.] In captivity, it often moves between water and land and takes all kinds of fruits as well as beef, horse meat, fish, and dried shrimp (this not as readily). The turtles feed both in the water and on land and use their front legs to shove scraps of food into the mouth. In so doing the turtles occasionally bite their own legs, which is a behavior that I have observed in other turtle species. The temperature range is from 18 to 25°C (65 to 77°F), and they may have a good appetite even at 19°C (66°F). It has been suggested that this species occurs in the same biotope as *Geoemyda spengleri*—mountain forests at high altitude—but is more highly aquatic than is the other species.

PYXIDEA
Keeled Box Turtles

Pyxidea mouhoti
Keeled Box Turtle

The highly arched carapace is very flat along the midline and has three distinct longitudinal keels. Because of the raised, fine chiseling of the individual dorsal scutes, it appears hand-carved. *Pyxidea* has a movable hinge in the plastron but is unable to close its shell completely. The brown, relatively large head has a pair of indistinct streaks on the sides and a conspicuous beak that strongly resembles that of the *Terrapene* species. The brown legs end in sharp claws, and there is only slight webbing.

Up to 20 centimeters (8 inches).

Eastern India through northern Southeast Asia and southern China to the island of Hainan.

The Wood Turtle, *Clemmys insculpta*, is a highly coveted turtle that is heavily protected at the state level. Most offered for sale probably were taken illegally and should not be purchased. Photo by W. E. Burgess.

This is a turtle of the tropical rainforest, where it lives very secretively in shallow pools or in moist ground cover. Because of these secretive habits it is hard to find, and only recently has the pet trade offered it more frequently. It is an omnivore and in my care took fruits, particularly bananas, just as readily as softened dog food, beef heart, tender lettuce leaves, and dandelions. It does not dive at all, but rather paddles around in the water like the *Terrapene* species. Its entire behavior and feeding habits, in fact, parallel closely those of the American box turtles. It has bred regularly in captivity.

GEOCLEMYS
Spotted Pond Turtles

Geoclemys hamiltoni
Spotted Pond Turtle

The rather high-domed, brown to blackish brown carapace has three longitudinal keels. The arching of the costal and vertebral scutes forms the keels, which never disappear completely even with age. On the dorsal scutes are lively yellow spots and broad, sometimes ovoid streaks. In their entirety they form a radiating pattern, but also are very irregularly distributed. The plastron is brownish with pale blotches. The head and legs are gray-brown and have yellow spots that are smaller on the legs.

Up to 40 centimeters (16 inches).

Pakistan across northern India and Nepal to Bangladesh.

This attractive turtle lives in inlets of rivers, slow-flowing bodies of water, streams, pools, and marshy regions, as well as in rice fields. It is diurnal but very secretive in its behavior. It requires a temperature of at least 22°C (72°F) and even can tolerate 30°C (86°F) or above, depending on its provenance.

This would be an easy turtle to keep in a large aquaterrarium, but it rarely is imported because it currently is listed in Appendix I of CITES. It takes the varied diet described for other aquatic turtles, but it prefers animal foods and seldom takes vegetables. Keep this turtle outside only during the summer months and bring it inside immediately during cool periods. The literature contains no information about captive breeding.

CHINEMYS
Chinese Pond Turtles

Chinemys kwangtungensis
[This name usually now is considered a synonym of *Chinemys nigricans*, in this book treated as a species of *Mauremys*.]

The slightly arched, nearly black carapace has only one longitudinal keel. The trailing edge is not serrated. The dorsal scutes have shallow grooves that resemble annual rings. The plastron has large black blotches that sometimes cover it almost completely. Beginning behind the eye, two narrow, parallel, horizontal stripes extend back on each side of the gray-brown head. Only the hind feet have a slight webbing, which indicates that it is not a very good swimmer. The gray legs are unmarked.

Up to 25 centimeters (10 inches).

Northern Vietnam and southern China (Kwangtung).

This turtle scarcely differs from the species *C. reevesi*. However, it probably is somewhat more temperature-sensitive, and outdoor keeping during the warm season would be advisable. It has bred regularly in captivity.

Chinemys megalocephala
Chinese Thick-headed Turtle
[Most authorities now consider this name to represent a synonym of Reeves' Turtle.]

It differs from the previous species mainly through the conspicuously large head and the three dark longitudinal stripes on the brown carapace, which is considerably wider in the back than in the front. The plastron also has dark blotches, but they are not as large.

Up to 20 centimeters (8 inches).

China, Nanking Province.

Its behavior probably differs little from that of the other two species of the genus. There is nothing reported about it in the literature, and there are no reports of keeping in captivity.

Chinemys reevesi
Reeves' Turtle
The slightly arched, oval carapace has three distinct longitudinal keels that do not disappear with age. Concerning the color of the carapace and plastron, adult males have a

black to gray-black carapace with light-colored seams and a completely black, slightly concave plastron. Females, on the other hand, have a pale brown to brown carapace (also with light-colored seams) and a dark plastron, in which, however, the edges of the ventral scutes, particularly on the bridge, have light-colored borders. On each side of the head, beginning behind the eyes, are bright yellowish, hieroglyphic-like markings that to the rear change over into streaked or dotted longitudinal lines. These lines also are present on the throat and neck. Males later lose all head markings as they turn black in color. The head is massive, although it is not as large as that of *C. megalocephala*. The legs are unmarked and slight webbing is present only on the hind feet.

Up to 18 centimeters (7.5 inches).

Central and eastern China from Szechwan east to Kiangsu (the natural range in the south uncertain), Taiwan, Korea, and Japan.

This species has a wide distribution and lives mainly in shallow bodies of water, marshes, pools, and ditches. It also occurs regularly in rice fields. I would like to emphasize that the length of 12 centimeters (5 inches) for this "small turtle" nearly always cited in the literature is incorrect, and the turtles can easily grow to 18 centimeters (7.5 inches). One of my males grew in one year from a carapace length of 4.8 centimeters (2 inches) and a weight of 25 grams (under an ounce) to a length of 12.2 centimeters (5 inches) and a weight of 285 grams (10 ounces). I then gave it away, after which it continued to grow to a length of about 18 centimeters (7.5 inches). Reeves' Turtle is a voracious feeder and is not fussy at all about diet. It is almost strictly carnivorous and at most occasionally takes some banana. Normal aquatic turtle food provides satisfactory nourishment. Occasionally supplement the diet with calcium and vitamins (the easiest way to do this is to use a gelatin-based food.)

C. reevesi is not sensitive to cool temperatures or to temporary heat waves. It easily tolerates temperatures from 12 to 30°C (54 to 86°F), although in my opinion the optimum temperature is from 20 to 25°C (68 to 77°F).

It has overwintered at our latitudes at rather cold temperatures, and it occasionally survives if introduced into ponds in the northern United States and Canada. An excellent candidate for keeping outdoors, it often digs itself in (for no apparent reason) in the middle of the summer for a while and then suddenly appears again. Hibernation is not absolutely necessary but is recommended for breeding, which has succeeded regularly in captivity. Overwintering should take place in a moist substrate at lowered temperatures; overwintering in water has had negative results at times. The young turtles are easy to rear, as long as you feed them a varied diet. *C. reevesi* is a highly recommended charge, particularly for the beginner.

OCADIA
Chinese Stripe-necked Turtles

Ocadia sinensis
Chinese Stripe-necked Turtle

[A second species, *Ocadia philippeni*, has been described from Hainan Island, China. It has only four yellow stripes on the neck. Still another species, in description, is reported from Vietnam.]

The dark olive, arched carapace has three longitudinal keels in juveniles. The lateral keels are indistinct or disappear entirely in older specimens. The head and neck have numerous [about eight] fine, contrasting, yellow longitudinal stripes that give the turtle a very attractive appearance.

Up to 25 centimeters (10 inches).

Vietnam and Laos over southeastern China and Taiwan, including Hainan.

Although it supposedly is still abundant in China, the literature contains virtually no recent information about this species. Keep it in the same way as *C. reevesi* and give it the same diet with a strong emphasis on animal foods. It requires somewhat higher temperatures than Reeves' Turtle, and in the summer it benefits from outdoor keeping. It is peaceful toward other terrarium inhabitants and has bred regularly in captivity. It is not problematic under the right keeping conditions, therefore I can recommend it to the beginner.

NOTOCHELYS
Malayan Flat-shelled Turtles

Notochelys platynota
Malayan Flat-shelled Turtle

The carapace, which is green to green-brown in younger specimens, regularly has six or seven vertebral scutes rather than the five of most other turtles. It is relatively flat, darkens with age, and then turns a brownish olive. The trailing edge of the carapace is strongly serrated, the tips of the marginal scutes looking like spikes but becoming less pronounced with age. The head lacks conspicuous markings, and the robust legs end in sturdy claws.

Up to 30 centimeters (12 inches).

Southern Vietnam (possibly west to Burma) to the Malayan peninsula and south over Sumatra, Java, and Borneo.

This distinctive turtle lives in small lakes and swampy forests with scattered pools. It leads a rather secretive existence but is active during the day. Freshly caught specimens are rather irritable, hiss, and in self defense spray out the contents of their cloaca. Probably because of their secretive habits, they seldom reach captivity, but when they do so they are hardy and soon lose their shyness. Soon they learn to appear as soon as anything edible is available. My specimens mainly took dandelion, lettuce, and fruits of all kinds. They were especially fond of banana, and they also ate earthworms and chopped beef liver occasionally. The always hungry *Notochelys platynota* has a correspondingly active digestion, so use a powerful filter in the terrarium or perform regular water changes. Otherwise, the water in the tank will soon become fouled, particularly, of course, with adults.

Malayan Flat-shells require temperatures from 24 to 28°C (75 to 82°F). They are very peaceful and prefer a rainforest terrarium. Keep them outdoors only at summertime temperatures.

The Spotted Pond Turtle, *Geoclemys hamiltoni,* is a quiet species that requires rather high temperatures. Protected under Appendix I of CITES. Photo by G. Fischer.

There is little information in the literature about breeding in the terrarium.

Siebenrockiella
Thick-headed Turtles

Siebenrockiella crassicollis
Black Thick-headed (Marsh) Turtle

The relatively flat, usually completely black carapace has a slight central keel that disappears with age. The trailing edge is slightly serrated. The yellow plastron has a dark blotch that spreads more and more in older specimens and displaces the yellow color. There is a light yellow to white blotch on each side of the black head. The quite sturdy legs and remaining soft parts also are black.

Up to 20 centimeters (8 inches).

Southern Burma to Vietnam, through the Malayan Peninsula to Sumatra, Borneo, and Java.

This very quiet turtle likes to hide and lives in pools, ponds, and the inlets of slow-flowing waters in rain forests and savannas. Considering its tropical living space, it requires temperatures of 25 to 28°C (77 to 82°F). Although it is an omnivore, my turtles preferred meaty food. The

Chinemys reevesi is a recommended turtle even for the beginner. Reeves' Turtles are diurnal and very active. Photo by B. Kahl.

Notochelys platynota, the Malayan Flat-shelled Turtle. Illustration: E. Bobbe in Wermuth/Mertens: Schildkröten — Krokodile — Brückenechsen.

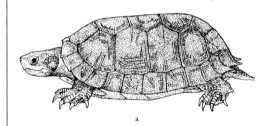

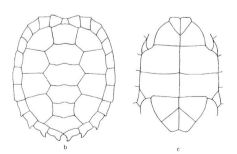

pet trade regularly offers the Black Thick-headed Turtle, but because of its secretive nature it seldom is visible in the terrarium. It is most active at twilight and appears during the day only at feeding time. This turtle is not fond of basking, but rather prefers to walk around the terrarium or to swim around slowly in search of leftover food. My turtles never became aggressive during feeding and are very peaceful even toward significantly smaller and weaker turtles of the same or other species.

The only captive breeding I am aware of is one from the Zurich Zoo (over a number of years). Outdoor keeping in summer is possible but is not necessary, since, as I mentioned, it does not bask. I also have noticed that this species is highly susceptible to necroses. Otherwise, it is not hard to keep, but the aquatic section of the aquaterrarium should make up at least four-fifths of the surface area.

MORENIA
Eyed Turtles

Morenia ocellata
Burmese Eyed Turtle

The brown carapace has a large black, approximately circular blotch with yellow borders on each costal scute. The plastron is uniformly yellow and unmarked. The dark gray head has two thin yellow longitudinal stripes, the upper stripe extending back from the nostrils horizontally over the eye. The lower stripe begins behind the eye (at the ventral margin) and extends back parallel to the upper stripe. The legs and soft parts are gray and unmarked. In these turtles the jaw has broad supplemental chewing surfaces that clearly mark them as herbivores.

Up to 21 centimeters (8.5 inches).

Southern Burma.

This species is nearly strictly aquatic and usually lives in shallow pools and lakes. When the waters dry up in the hot season, the turtles migrate in search of other waters. They require temperatures of 26 to 28°C (79 to 82°F) and are strictly herbivorous.

The pet trade has practically never offered these turtles because they are listed in Appendix I of CITES. There thus is almost no information

on keeping them in the terrarium. They have bred in captivity.

Morenia petersi
Indian Eyed Turtle

The olive-brown carapace is significantly darker, sometimes nearly black, than in the other species. Black specimens have yellow rings in place of the black blotches on the costal scutes. In all other characters, however, it does not differ greatly from *M. ocellata*.

Up to 18 centimeters (7 inches).

The Ganges River basin of Bangladesh and northeastern India.

It appears to be similar to the Burmese Eyed Turtle.

CUORA
Asian Box Turtles
Cuora amboinensis
Southeast Asian Box Turtle

Its dark brown, very highly arched carapace has three distinct longitudinal keels in juveniles, but these disappear with increasing age so only an indistinct central keel still is present in adults. The yellow to pale yellow plastron has a dark blotch on each scute. The top of the head is dark brown, and on each side of the head above the eye a yellow stripe extends back from the tip of the snout. Below and parallel to it there is a wide brown band. The ventral half of the head and the throat are yellow with irregular narrow brown longitudinal stripes. The legs are dark brown, unmarked, and end in sharp claws. There is only slight webbing between the toes. The turtle's name refers to the transverse hinge across the middle of the plastron that allows the turtle to close both the front and rear parts of the plastron against the carapace. The turtle can retract completely and protect the head, legs, and soft parts.

Up to 20 centimeters (8 inches).

Burma and eastern India south through the southern part of Southeast Asia over Sumatra, Java, Borneo, the Celebes, the Philippines, and many islands in the general area.

This aquatic turtle lives in standing bodies of water. Despite the form of its carapace, which resembles that of a tortoise, it is almost strictly aquatic and usually leaves the water only to bask or to lay its eggs. It eats anything: insects, snails (particularly aquatic snails), fishes, prepared food, soft-leafed plants, and fruits.

The males are extremely brutal during courtship. I once kept a pair in which the female mostly stayed outside the water out of fear of the male. The turtle later died from egg binding because the extended, forced stay on land had a negative effect. Otherwise *Cuora amboinensis* is a recommended terrarium charge, although it requires fairly high temperatures of 22 to 28°C (72 to 82°F). You can safely keep it outdoors in summer at a water temperature of about 25°C (77°F) and if possible not below 22°C (72°F). It has bred in captivity.

Cuora flavomarginata
Yellow-margined Box Turtle
The highly arched carapace is dark brown. It usually has a yellow-brown blotch in the middle of the costal and vertebral scutes and a yellow stripe along the midline. The plastron is dark, with a complete yellow border. The head is completely yellow in most specimens, with only the hint of dark shading on the top and sides. The heavy brown legs end in sharp claws and the toes are only slightly webbed.

Up to 18 centimeters (7 inches).

Southeastern China, Taiwan, and the Ryukyus.

In contrast to *C. amboinensis*, this species is almost exclusively terrestrial and in nature prefers moist and marshy areas with shallow pools. A specimen from Taiwan was reported to have stayed almost exclusively in deep water, but this behavior probably is the exception to the rule.

It prefers a vegetable diet and is fond of sweet fruits of all kinds and bananas. It also takes animal food. On land *C. flavomarginata* is very quick and agile and is always a nose ahead of other turtles, and it is a very highly recommended terrarium charge. It has the same temperature requirements as *C. amboinensis*. Keep it outdoors only on warm summer days.

Cuora galbinifrons
Indochinese Box Turtle
At first glance this species looks almost like a *Terrapene* species. The very highly arched

carapace (higher than in the other *Cuora* species) has a brownish yellow ground color. The carapace has numerous irregular brown blotches and streaks, particularly on the vertebral and marginal scutes. The plastron is completely black with only a few scattered yellowish blotches. The head has a brownish yellow ground color with a dark brown snout and irregular brown markings on each side. The conspicuously long legs are brownish and have large scales on the outside. It has been reported that the male has a yellow and the female an orange iris, but my most recent experiences indicate that this is not always true.

Up to 19 centimeters (7.5 inches).

Northern Vietnam to adjacent China and Hainan.

Recently the pet trade has offered this turtle species more regularly than it has the previous species, but little information on it exists in the literature. One keeper reported that he kept the turtles in a terrarium (100 x 60 centimeters, 40 x 24 inches) with one-third water approximately 4 centimeters (1.8 inches) deep and the remaining two-thirds consisting of a thick carpet of moss. A large piece of bark served as a hiding place. The turtles (male about 16 centimeters, 6.5 inches, and female about 15 centimeters, 6 inches) were still juveniles. The male took such fruits as pears, bananas, and tomatoes in addition to earthworms and gelatin-based food. The female never took fruit, but preferred mice, gelatin food, earthworms, and beef. Though quiet, because of their long legs the turtles can move very fast and are good diggers. After the thorough daily bath, they usually buried themselves in the moss. Only the head protruded and the conspicuous eyes alertly observed the surroundings. The turtles were kept at temperatures of 22 to 24°C (72 to 75°F).

Cuora trifasciata
Chinese Three-striped Box Turtle
The arching of the carapace is significantly lower than in *C. amboinensis* and the ground color is lighter brown. The dorsal scutes have somewhat blurred dark streaks. There are three characteristic black longitudinal stripes, the middle one of which runs directly along the slight central keel. The plastron is almost com-

Ocadia sinensis, the Chinese Stripe-necked Turtle, does well in the terrarium. Unfortunately, the pet trade carries it very rarely, and the turtle probably has rarely bred in captivity. Photo by G. Janson.

Siebenrockiella crassicollis. The Thick-headed Turtle is a very quiet species, which becomes active only at dusk. It is very peaceful toward other turtles. Photo by B. Kahl.

pletely black with only a narrow yellow border. The scutes of the bridge are yellow with a black blotch at the trailing edge. This turtle can close its shell completely with the aid of the hinge on the plastron. The entire top of the head is bright yellow. A horizontal brown band extends back from the tip of the snout, and parallel to it there is a thinner stripe at jaw height. The underside of the head and the throat are yellow. The legs are gray-brown with a reddish suffusion and are

Cuora yunnanensis
Yunnan Box Turtle

Probably about 20 centimeters (8 inches).

Southern China.

[In addition to these species of *Cuora*, several other species recently have been described, and some are available in the terrarium hobby. They include *C. aurocapitata*, the Yellow-headed Box Turtle; *C. mccordi*, McCord's Box Turtle; *C. pani*, Pan's Box Turtle (including *C.*

Several species of *Cuora* are found in the U. S. pet shops. The Indochinese Box Turtle, also called the Flower Turtle, *C. galbinifrons*, is one of the prettiest. This species is one of the more terrestrial of the Asian box Turtles. Photo by K. H. Switak.

only slightly webbed. The soft parts are pale yellow to white.

Up to 22 centimeters (9 inches).

Northern Vietnam, the southern Chinese coastal area, and Hainan.

Its habits are largely the same as with *C. amboinensis*, but this species is more terrestrial and feeds on land—a peculiarity among aquatic and marsh turtles. It does very well in the terrarium, with temperature and dietary requirements about the same as those of the previous species. There are no reports about breeding in captivity. Keep it outdoors only in the warm summer months.

chriskarannarum); and *C. zhoui*, Zhou's Box Turtle (including *C. pallidicephala*). All of these are from southern China, most from just north of the Vietnamese border.]

HIEREMYS
Yellow-headed Temple Turtles

Hieremys annandali
Yellow-headed Temple Turtle

The moderately arched, black carapace has a slight longitudinal keel along the midline, and the plastron also is black, only the seams are somewhat lighter in color. On each side of the

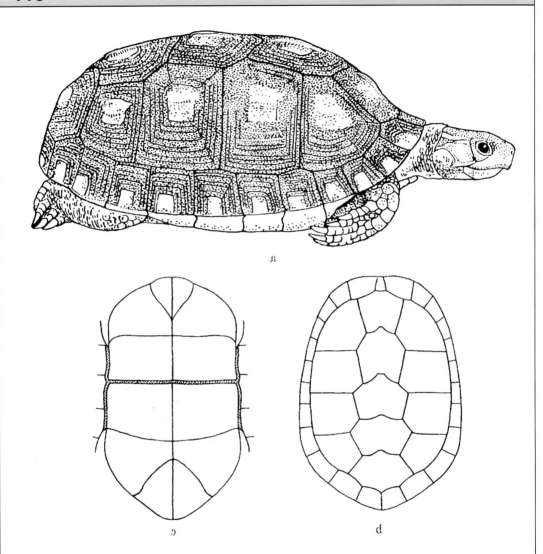

Yellow-margined Box Turtle, *Cuora flavomarginata*. Illustration: E. Bobbe in Wermuth/Mertens: Schildkröten — Krokodile — Brückenechsen.

black head there is an indistinct pale yellow stripe in the jaw area and below the tip of the snout. Another wavy stripe extends back from above the eye. The legs are black and sturdy, as are the claws. The soft parts are pale gray.

Up to 45 centimeters (18 inches). The specimens I observed and kept in captivity did not grow larger than 30 centimeters, 12 inches.

Southern Vietnam to Thailand and the Malayan peninsula.

In nature it lives in still bodies of water with abundant vegetation. Its name refers to its abundance in the ponds of Buddhist temples, particularly in Thailand. The faithful who catch one of

these turtles in the wild and bring it to the temple pond believe that in this way they have saved a life, which will bring its due reward in the hereafter.

It does well in the aquaterrarium and does not require temperatures as high as might be expected from its provenance. I routinely keep this species outdoors from April to October. It likes to stay at the surface when the sun is shining and always is one of the first in line at feeding time. I disagree with the claim in the literature that it is almost exclusively herbivorous, because my turtles are omnivorous. They take, so to speak, "whatever is put on the table." Besides leaf lettuce, dandelion, and bananas, it also takes beef heart, beef liver, snails, shrimp, earthworms, fish, and turtle aspic. There are no reports about breeding in captivity, although I do not think it would be difficult.

HARDELLA
Crowned River Turtles

Hardella thurji
Crowned River Turtle

This species is very similar in appearance to *Hieremys*. The slightly roof-like carapace is brownish black and has a hump-backed central keel. The color of the plastron is variable from yellow to dark gray to black, and there are specimens with a yellow plastron and a gray blotch in the middle of each ventral scute. A bright yellow stripe tapers back from the tip of the snout through the eye and beyond. It resembles a diadem or crown and has given the species its common name. A second yellow band runs parallel to the upper one but ends under the eye. The massive legs usually are dark gray to black and end in sturdy, sharp claws. The toes are webbed.

Females up to 50 centimeters (20 inches), males up to about 30 centimeters (12 inches).

Pakistan in the Indus basin plus northern India and Burma in the Ganges-Brahmaputra basin. The western subspecies is *H. t. indi*, the eastern one *H. t. thurji*.

It lives primarily in the river systems of the Ganges and Brahmaputra, where it usually lives in deep water. Unlike any other turtles, bony capsules formed by processes of the shell encase the lungs to protect them from water pressure. The literature usually describes it as strictly herbivorous, but it also has been reported that it takes fish, although vegetable foods predominate. Its appetite is astounding, and it is always ready to feed. It is hardy in the aquarium but is strictly aquatic and has an uncommonly peaceful disposition (even toward much smaller turtles). It never bites, although it does threaten with gaping mouth.

The required temperature range is 22 to 28°C (72 to 82°F). The pet trade rarely offers this turtle, and because of its rapid growth it is suitable only for fairly large tanks.

KACHUGA
Indian Roofed Turtles

Kachuga dhongoka
Three-striped Roofed Turtle

The only slightly arched, dark brown carapace does not do justice to the name roofed turtle. There are low bumps along the midline that represent an interrupted longitudinal keel. The plastron is grayish yellow and completely unmarked. Each side of the gray head has slightly paler blotches. The sturdy legs end in small claws and have fully webbed toes.

Up to 40 centimeters (16 inches).

From southern Nepal and northeastern India to Bangladesh through the river systems of the Ganges and Brahmaputra from Alahabad east to Assam.

In its habits and requirements, it closely resembles the *Hardella*, with which it often associates. The pet trade rarely offers it, and because of its size and rapid growth it is not a particularly good candidate for the terrarium. Furthermore, it is far less peaceful than *Hardella*.

Kachuga kachuga
Red-crowned Roofed Turtle

It resembles the previous *Kachuga* species, except that the bumps of the carapace are lower and more closely resemble a continuous longitudinal keel. There are seven conspicuous reddish longitudinal stripes on the neck. A black stripe with light-colored borders extends diagonally back from the eye and curves downward around the corner of the jaw in the form of a hook.

Up to 40 centimeters (16 inches).

Southern Nepal and northern India to Bangladesh in the Ganges River system.

Little exists in the literature about this turtle other than it basks during the warm season and lays about two dozen eggs. It is considered to be rare in nature and is protected. To my knowledge, the pet trade probably has not offered it recently.

Kachuga smithi
Brown Roofed Turtle

The moderately arched carapace of *K. smithi* is relatively flat and gray-brown in color. The bumps along the dark red-brown central keel are very low and rounded. The trailing edge is not

The Southeast Asian Box Turtle, *Cuora amboinensis* is a hardy pet if given proper care. The pet trade carries this species regularly, and it is not usually an expensive turtle. Photo by H. Reinhard.

The Chinese Three-striped Box Turtle, *Cuora trifasciata*, is a very terrestrial species, often feeding on land. They are more flattened in shape than most other *Cuora*. Photo by B. Kahl.

Eggs of the Brown Roofed Turtle, *Kachuga smithi*. Their form is completely unlike that of other turtles' eggs. Turtle eggs normally are either spherical and resemble Ping-Pong balls, or have the oval form of chicken eggs. Photo by G. Müller.

The Indian Roofed Turtle, *Kachuga tecta tecta*, is one of the most beautiful turtles. It is also a peaceful turtle, well-suited to the terrarium. Photo by G. Müller.

serrated. The plastron is brownish with light-colored seams. There is a red blotch on each side of the dark brown head behind the eye; the blotch is indistinct and usually disappears with age or becomes much paler. The neck has light and dark longitudinal lines. The legs are light gray-brown. The toes have sharp claws and full webbing.

Up to 25 centimeters (10 inches).

Pakistan and northern India eastward to Bangladesh.

In its homeland it usually lives in large rivers, often in deep water. It is an omnivore, the ratio of animal to vegetable foods about 50:50 on average. It is particularly fond of aquatic insects and young dandelion, but also takes beef heart, dog food, leaf lettuce, banana, and other sweet fruits. It requires temperatures of 24 to 28°C (75 to 82°F). This turtle can provide much enjoyment as a terrarium charge and, if given a large and deep (40 to 50 centimeters, 16 to 20 inches) swimming space, also does well in the terrarium. Recently the pet trade has carried it more regularly.

My female is at least three times as large as the male. She already has laid four (unfortunately infertile) eggs. Their unusually long, narrow form, average length 55 millimeters, width 20 millimeters (2.2 by 0.8 inches), was striking.

Kachuga sylhetensis
Assam Roofed Turtle

[This is the smallest *Kachuga* and also the most unusual. The back edge of the carapace is strongly serrated and the third vertebral scute is produced into an extremely high keel. There are 26 marginal scutes compared to only 24 or fewer in other turtles.]

Up to 20 centimeters (8 inches).

Northeastern India (Assam) and Bangladesh.

We know little about this species [other than it seems to inhabit fast-flowing hill streams and is secretive and seldom seen. A specimen took fish but not plants.]

Kachuga tecta
Indian Roofed Turtle

[This species usually is treated as two full species that occur in sympatry. They would be *Kachuga tecta*, the Indian Roofed Turtle, and

Kachuga tentoria, the Indian Tent Turtle, the latter with the subspecies *K. t. tentoria*, *K. t. circumdata*, and *K. t. flaviventer*.]

Kachuga tecta tecta
Indian Roofed Turtle

The high-domed carapace does justice to its name. It is light green in juveniles and turns gray-brown with increasing age. I cannot confirm the claim often made in the literature that it is mossy green in adult males; the pairs I have kept all have a gray-brown carapace. The first three vertebral scutes form distinct humps that are reddish with black borders. The remaining vertebral scutes have a slight longitudinal keel. The plastron usually is pinkish red or orange-red. Later it turns yellow with a slight red or pink suffusion, particularly in males. Lozenge-shaped black blotches cover the entire plastron and contrast effectively with the bright background. The top of the head is black, with a brick-red, black-bordered stripe on each side on the head. It begins under the eye at an acute angle and gradually becomes wider as it continues behind the eyes to the top of the head. A pattern of narrow black and yellow to yellow-red stripes begins on the throat and extends over the entire neck. From the upturned snout, which gives the turtle a haughty appearance, one or more reddish stripes extend down to the upper mandible. (The males have a more intense coloration than the females.) The legs have rows of reddish or reddish yellow dots on a gray ground color. The toes have sharp claws and full webbing.

Up to 20 centimeters (males are much smaller) (8 inches).

Pakistan and northern India to Bangladesh.

This roofed turtle lives in large river systems. It does not require as high temperatures as *K. smithi*, but it is just as fond of basking. My turtles immediately take advantage of every ray of sun. They rest with the neck extended and the front and hind legs spread to expose as much surface area as possible to the sun. They do extremely well in the garden pond and develop a big appetite. They are omnivores (50:50 plant and animal matter) and are very fond of finely chopped beef heart and insects. They are fond of mealworms, which I feed only occasionally, however, for obvious reasons, and also take dandelion, lettuce, sweet fruits, and banana. Until now, they have refused fish in any form; *K. t. circumdata* and *K. smithi* do not take it either. In my opinion, reports to the contrary in the literature are incorrect.

I would like to report here about an unusual experience I had: In the year 1965, I obtained a female *K. t. tecta* that took insects and vegetable foods, but never beef heart or liver. It did not grow at all in the first 30 months, but only gained some weight. Suddenly it started to take beef heart and liver avidly. Simultaneously, it started to grow and has now grown to four times its original size.

Unfortunately, I have never been able to breed this turtle, despite frequent copulations. Because the species is listed in Appendix I of CITES, captive breeding would be all the more welcome. The temperature should be from 20 to 26°C (68 to 79°F). I have not confirmed so far the need for the high required temperatures reported regularly in the literature. They are always the first to leave the garden pond in the morning—despite low outside temperatures of 8 to 10°C (46 to 50°F) —to sunbathe.

In my opinion, the much-prized water clarity stated to be necessary for kachugas is of little significance, whereas healthy water is far more important. Therefore, water splashes into all my turtle terraria and ponds to provide required oxygen. This creates positive filtration and prevents negative decomposition processes from starting. In combination with a biological filter (indoor terraria with large plants like monstera, papyrus, and the like, and outdoor installations with cattails, water lilies, reeds, and so forth), this system removes most of the nitrate as it accumulates, as long as we do not overstock the installation. I would like to apologize for this digression, but it has universal validity.

To my knowledge, since 1985 two hobbyists have bred the species regularly. Rearing the young is not difficult as long as we offer a varied diet. I particularly recommend meadow plankton with this species. In closing, I would like to mention that all turtles of the *Kachuga* group are decidedly peaceful.

Kachuga tecta circumdata
Pink-ringed Tent Turtle

This subspecies [more often treated as a subspecies of *K. tentoria*] has the same high-domed carapace as the previous species, but the color is more of a grayish olive. The red, black-bordered humps also are present on the first three vertebral scutes. Unlike *K. t. tecta*, however, there is a wide red stripe around the carapace along the seam between the marginal and costal scutes. This subspecies also has the same pattern on the plastron with lozenge-shaped black blotches and a mostly orange to pink coloration. The top of the head is olive and there is a conspicuous bright red spot on the temple on each side behind the eye. In contrast to *K. t. tecta*, the pattern of lines on the throat is indistinct. The legs are gray to gray-olive and the toes are fully webbed.

Up to 20 centimeters (8 inches).

India in the upper and central Ganges River basin.

This subspecies has the same habits as the nominate form, and I was unable to observe any difference in the specimens I kept. The requirements in the terrarium also were identical.

Kachuga tecta tentoria
Indian Tent Turtle

[Usually considered to be a full species, *K. tentoria*, with three subspecies.]

Central eastern India in the Mahanadi, Godavari, and Krishna river systems.

Kachuga trivittata
Burmese Roofed Turtle

This turtle does not do justice to the name roofed turtle, since the carapace is rather flat. Diagnostic are the three dark longitudinal bands on the carapace, of which the center one runs along a middorsal keel. The humps present in other kachugas are indistinct. The neck and legs are completely unmarked. The sturdy legs have fully webbed toes.

Up to 58 centimeters (almost 24 inches).

Burma.

This species lives in larger rivers and lakes. In contrast to the quite large females, males are relatively small. This is true of all kachugas as well as many other turtle species.

The Burmese Roofed Turtle is practically unknown in the literature and has not been studied recently. Also, to my knowledge, the pet trade has never carried it. Because of its size, it is suitable for keeping only as a juvenile, since few hobbyists would be able to keep full-grown specimens in the terrarium.

CALLAGUR
Painted Terrapins

Callagur borneoensis
Painted Terrapin

The carapace normally is brown with three keels, which, however, largely disappear with age. The carapace has black longitudinal bands and may have speckling. Klingelhoffer made the astounding observations described below with an individual of this species:

"A 14-centimeter-long specimen that came into Mertens' possession in 1937 was dirty gray-brown in color and had three longitudinal rows of indistinct black blotches on the vertebral and costal scutes. The head also was dirty gray-brown and unmarked. On January 10, 1939, I obtained the turtle. It had grown to a length of 18 centimeters and the carapace had turned nearly uniformly black. In the winter of 1940-1941 the plastron turned bright yellow and the top of the head reddish brown with small, irregular yellow dots. After about three months it became paler. In early 1942 a conspicuous orange longitudinal stripe appeared on the head from the snout across the midline of the skull. The plastron turned intense yellow. In 1943 a complete change in color occurred. Now only the rear half of the carapace was black; the front was leek green with a few conspicuous black blotches on the margin and three sharply defined longitudinal lines in the middle. The snout turned blue-gray. On the sides of the head, which had turned black, at times a very distinct light blue-gray suffusion was visible, particularly on the eyelids. The most conspicuous feature, however, was a nearly 1-centimeter-wide,

The Black-breasted Leaf Turtle, *Geoemyda spengleri*, grows to a length of only 5 inches, lives in moist forests, and is predominantly terrestrial. Photo by W. Hemmer

Geoemyda (*Heosemys*) *grandis*, the Giant Asian Pond Turtle, is highly voracious and therefore grows rapidly. Despite the name, this turtle wanders frequently on land. Photo by G. Janson.

decidedly salmon-colored to brick-red longitudinal band down the midline of the skull. The neck and the underside of the legs had turned yellowish gray, the dorsal side of the front legs light gray, and the hind legs dark gray. The plastron was whitish yellow. By now the carapace had reached a length of 30 centimeters. The red and yellow colors faded during a summer fast period in a terrific heat wave. In mid-September, 1943, the callagur began to be an active male. About this time the colors became duller again and the head turned a faint orange yellowish."

This example shows how changes in color (apparently hormonally controlled) can occur even in adult turtles.

Up to 45 centimeters (18 inches).

Malayan peninsula and Borneo, also Sumatra. This turtle, like the members of the previous genus, is a typical river turtle that lives only in deeper water. The diet, which is more highly carnivorous in juveniles, becomes predominantly herbivorous as the turtle ages. Because the Painted Terrapin is always hungry, it is not fussy about diet and takes anything it can get. In contrast to many other turtles, it does not take bites from a leaf, but swallows it whole.

It is an excellent swimmer and can make the most elegant turns. It is strictly aquatic and goes on land only to bask or to lay its eggs. P. Krefft reported, however, a specimen that always spent the night on land. It would be suitable for the terrarium only in the juvenile stage.

[This species is noted for its tolerance to full-strength sea water. The females lay their eggs on sea-front beaches where sea turtles nest. The hatchlings can live for up to two weeks in sea water, which apparently gives them time to swim to a river mouth and up the river to their feeding grounds. The nests may be many kilometers from the nearest river.]

The pet trade does not offer this turtle at all, but it would be a good candidate for large terraria with four-fifths water surface and a minimum depth of 50 centimeters (20 inches).

ORLITIA
Malaysian Giant Turtles

Orlitia borneensis
Malaysian Giant Turtle

The highly arched and bluntly keeled carapace is uniformly dark to light brown. The trailing edge is serrated only in juveniles. The plastron is mostly light in color and has dark blotches along the outer margin only in juveniles. In juveniles the head has pale blotches (never longitudinal stripes) but it turns uniformly brownish with age. Its form is oval with a very short snout. The outer margin of the upper mandible is strongly curved downward. The head, neck, and legs of adults are uniformly brownish and unmarked.

Up to 75 centimeters (30 inches).

Southern Malayan peninsula, Sumatra, and Borneo.

We know little about this very large turtle. In its habits it resembles *Callagur*, and it also occurs in the same range and biotope. The pet trade never carries it. If it did, only juveniles would be suitable candidates for the terrarium, because outside zoos no tanks of suitable size exist.

BATAGUR
River Terrapins

Batagur baska
River Terrapin

The slightly arched carapace is light gray-brown. The plastron is yellow. The head is broad and the mouth has three chewing ridges, which indicates a chiefly herbivorous diet. The legs end in sturdy claws. The front legs have only four toes.

Up to 60 centimeters (24 inches).

Coastal Southeast Asia from Burma to Cambodia, the Malayan peninsula, and Sumatra.

Like the previously discussed *Callagur* and *Orlitia*, this species lives only in larger and deeper bodies of water and also ranges into brackish water. This turtle is almost strictly herbivorous and probably feeds chiefly on aquatic plants. Information in the literature and experiences on terrarium keeping are extremely sparse.

GEOEMYDA
Forest Turtles

[As used here, *Geoemyda* includes turtles that most workers today split into four genera: *Geoemyda, Melanochelys, Heosemys,* and *Rhinoclemys*. These are treated as subgenera in this book, and admittedly they are very similar turtles differing in small details of shell structure and, in the case of the American *Rhinoclemys*, distribution. This group includes the various spiny or leaf turtles (other spiny turtles are in separate Asian genera as well) plus the so-called Neotropical wood turtles.]

The forest turtles form such a large group that a detailed discussion of each species, much less subspecies, would be beyond the scope of this book. Therefore, I will mention briefly all the species and discuss in detail only the most familiar and noteworthy ones.

Most species are terrestrial and only seek out shallow water, but forest turtles feed both in the water and on land. All are omnivores, although the preference for an animal or vegetable diet can be highly variable from species to species and with individuals of the same species. Their temperature requirements are highly variable according to the range and biotope and vary from 20 to 26°C (68 to 79°F). You can keep them outdoors, but you must protect the terrarium from wind and offer the specimens a shelter, preferably heated. The terrarium should have an aquatic section (25°C, 77°F) covering about one-third of the surface area and the remainder consisting of a moist land section. The land section should have hiding places in the form of abundant vegetation, overhanging roots, or flat rocks. The pet trade rarely offers some of these turtles, but others are bred in captivity in small numbers and are readily available; still others are imported on a sporadic basis.

Geoemyda (Geoemyda)
Leaf Turtles
Geoemyda spengleri
Black-breasted Leaf Turtle

Geoemyda spengleri spengleri
Common Black-breasted Leaf Turtle
The reddish brown, flat carapace has a longitudinal keel. The front edge of the carapace is slightly serrated and its trailing edge is strongly serrated. The plastron is black with a yellow border. The brownish head has a hooked beak and the eye has a bright yellow-white iris. The neck has fine brown and yellow longitudinal stripes with scattered red dots between them. The brownish legs have large scales.
Up to 13 centimeters (5.5 inches).
Vietnam and southeastern China.

In its range this species is primarily terrestrial and prefers moist forests, where (because it is highly light sensitive) it likes to stay hidden in the undergrowth and leaves. It occasionally lives in relatively cool, but moist, mountain regions at an altitude of up to 1200 meters. We must consider this in the terrarium. The species needs heavy shade and abundant vegetation in an enclosure with a shallow (6 centimeters, 1.5 inches) aquatic section. If abundant vegetation is not present, a few hours a day of dim lighting is sufficient.

It needs a varied diet of earthworms, insects, snails, prepared turtle food, and beef heart and liver; we also should offer fruits and lettuce, although they seldom take them. The turtle does not require high temperatures; 20 to 24°C (68 to 75°F) is adequate. *G. s. spengleri* shows absolutely no interest in basking, as is apparent when we keep it outdoors. Because of these habits, the turtles scarcely ever show themselves. The species has bred in captivity. As a rule the female lays only two eggs. The incubation period is from 74 and 110 days. Juveniles are not hard to rear because they are absolutely not fussy about diet and voraciously take everything we offer, from tubifex, chopped earthworms, and moistened prepared foods to small snails, insects (drowned meadow plankton), and, after about four months, even pinkie mice. In recent

years the pet trade has offered this species more regularly and at more reasonable prices. I must warn the beginner, however, that it is not always an easy species to keep. I consider the varied diet of insects, snails, and baby mice to be essential.

Geoemyda spengleri japonica
Okinawa Black-breasted Leaf Turtle
Up to 12 centimeters (5 inches).
Okinawa and other islands in the Ryukyus, southern Japan.

Geoemyda (Melanochelys)
Indian Black Turtles
[*Melanochelys* usually is considered a full genus.]

Geoemyda (Melanochelys) tricarinata
Tricarinate Hill Turtle
Up to 16 centimeters (6.5 inches).
Bangladesh and northeastern India.

Geoemyda (Melanochelys) trijuga
Indian Black Turtle

Geoemyda (Melanochelys) trijuga trijuga
Up to 22 centimeters (9 inches).
Peninsular India.

Geoemyda (Melanochelys) trijuga coronata
Southwestern India.

Geoemyda (Melanochelys) trijuga edeniana
Up to 28 centimeters (11.5 inches).
Burma.

Geoemyda (Melanochelys) trijuga indopeninsularis
Northern Bangladesh and northeastern India.

Geoemyda (Melanochelys) trijuga parkeri
Up to 40 centimeters (16 inches).
Arid regions on the coast and in the northern part of Sri Lanka.

In contrast to the other *G. (M.) trijuga*, *G. (M.) t. parkeri* has evolved into a purely terrestrial form. It supposedly is strictly herbivorous. All previously mentioned subspecies have highly variable habits. Some are strictly aquatic and others are exclusively terrestrial.

top: *Geoemyda* (*Heosemys*) *spinosa*. The Spiny Turtle is not easy to keep in the juvenile stage. With increasing age, the spines disappear completely.
bottom: Underside of a Spiny Turtle. Note the beautiful pattern on the plastron. Both photos by G. Janson.

Geoemyda (Melanochelys) trijuga wiroti

Western Thailand.

The most frequently imported and most familiar *G. (M.) trijuga* is the following subspecies, which I will discuss in more detail.

Geoemyda (Melanochelys) trijuga thermalis
Sri Lankan Black Turtle

The moderately arched carapace is reddish brown in juveniles and later turns completely black. It has three longitudinal keels and the trailing edge is slightly serrated in juveniles; the serrations disappear with age and the carapace becomes completely smooth. The plastron, which has a yellow margin in juveniles, also turns totally black over time. The black head has scattered reddish to yellowish blotches. The dorsal margin of the snout has a deep notch in front. The sturdy legs end in sharp-clawed toes.

Up to 25 centimeters (10 inches).

Sri Lanka, the Maldives, and southern India.

In its homeland it usually lives in moist mountainous regions. Unlike *G. (M.) t. parkeri*, it lives there in bodies of water, but also wanders on land. Some individuals supposedly are strictly terrestrial (they, however, must certainly be the exception). It lives very secretively and is quite shy, which must be considered in the terrarium. Provide hiding places both in the water and on land.

Under my care this subspecies was nearly aquatic and almost never went on land. It basked only occasionally, was not fussy about diet, and took everything I offered. Despite contradictory reports in the literature, it preferred animal food. It also took turtle and dog food. It requires temperatures of 20 to 25°C (68 to 77°F). We can keep this turtle outdoors in summer, but, because of its shyness, it will never show itself. The pet trade seldom carries it today, although it is an easy turtle to keep, even for the beginner. It has bred regularly in the past. Because it is listed on Appendix I of CITES, possession is complicated.

Geoemyda (Heosemys)
Forest Turtles

[*Heosemys* usually is considered a full genus.]

Geoemyda (Heosemys) depressa
Arakan Forest Turtle

Up to 25 centimeters (10 inches).

Supposedly Burma, but not collected in recent years.

Geoemyda (Heosemys) grandis
Giant Asian Pond Turtle

This is by far the largest of the forest turtles. The arched, brown-yellow carapace has a very pronounced longitudinal keel and a radiating pattern of dark speckles. This pattern disappears with age and changes to a dark brown to nearly black color. The plastron is yellow-brown with black, radiating markings. They still are visible even in older specimens, although the entire plastron becomes somewhat darker. Both the head and the legs have numerous small black dots and blotches on a gray-brown to gray-yellow ground color. These are very attractive, but become somewhat paler in older specimens. The sturdy legs end in sharp claws. The toes are only slightly webbed.

Up to 40 centimeters (16 inches).

Burma to southern Vietnam and the entire Malayan peninsula.

This very fast-growing turtle lives mostly in smaller bodies of water and pools in its homeland, but often goes on land often as well. It is always on the lookout, however, for something to eat. In the terrarium it soon loses its shyness and is always hungry, so it is not surprising that it grows so fast. My specimens took anything I offered: beef heart, beef liver, dried shrimp, fish (freshwater and saltwater), earthworms, snails, prepared foods of all kinds, dandelion, lettuce, banana, and so forth. It also is fond of carrion. It requires temperatures of 22 to 26°C (72 to 79°F). It likes to bask for long periods, and I recommend keeping it outdoors in the summer for that reason alone.

Geoemyda (Heosemys) leytensis
Philippine Pond Turtle

Up to 33 centimeters (13 inches).

The Philippines; known from only a few specimens.

Geoemyda (Heosemys) silvatica
Cochin Forest Cane Turtle

[This species now is placed in *Geoemyda* proper by most workers.]

Up to 12 centimeters (5 inches).

Southwestern India.

Geoemyda (Heosemys) spinosa
Spiny (Cogwheel) Turtle

When a casual observer compares a young and a full-grown specimen of this species, he or she certainly would take them for members of two different species, if not genera. On the juvenile's nut-brown carapace, each marginal scute has an outward-pointing spine that gives the turtle its name. The carapace has a hump-backed longitudinal keel along the midline, and in the middle back edge of each costal scute there is a small, rearward-pointing spine. There has been much speculation on the possible purpose of these spines. Some have proposed that they increase the turtle's buoyancy in water (but juveniles live primarily on land or in very shallow water) or that they help to anchor the juveniles in fast-flowing mountain streams. In my opinion, they are purely defensive measures against being eaten. Should a predator happen to bite down on such a spiny juvenile, it hardly could be a pleasurable experience. The spines disappear almost completely with increasing age, and in full-grown specimens only the trailing edge of the carapace is still serrated. The yellow-brown plastron has a very attractive pattern of radiating lines, but this pattern disappears in very old individuals and changes to a brown-black color. The head, neck, and legs in juveniles are a light brown ground color, and there are dark carmine blotches on the temples. The iris is bright red. The legs have conspicuous red markings that disappear with increasing age, to be replaced by an unmarked brown.

Up to 23 centimeters (9.5 inches).

Malayan peninsula, Sumatra, Borneo, and some outlying islands.

According to some of the literature it lives primarily in mountain streams, but according to other reports it also lives in rice fields. Accordingly, I do not believe the species requires high temperatures, as is often claimed in the literature. Because it lives in mountain rivers and streams, both the required water and air temperatures would have to be significantly lower. Keeping them at incorrect, too-high temperatures may be why this turtle has a reputation for being delicate in captivity. Furthermore, my experiences with keeping many tropical turtles outdoors have been overwhelmingly positive. Benefits include increased egg laying and successful rearing. This is true although the average temperatures outdoors, particularly during our summer, are significantly lower than those cited in the literature. For *Geoemyda (H.) spinosa,* I therefore consider a temperature of 20 to 24°C (68 to 75°F) to be completely adequate.

In my opinion, a day to night drop in temperature is absolutely necessary for the turtles. A hobbyist I know very well has kept a female for more than 20 years. Subsequently he acquired a male, which he has had now for eight years, yet only recently did the first copulations take place. Since then the female has laid eggs twice (two eggs on each occasion). The first clutch was infertile, but the second gives hope of success.

As juveniles they are nearly strictly terrestrial and only occasionally enter shallow water or a puddle. Adults, however, become more and more aquatic. At one time the literature often reported that these turtles were strictly herbivorous, but this is incorrect. Both the experiences of other hobbyists and my own observations have shown that the turtles are omnivorous. We must remember, however, that individual tastes are highly variable; some specimens are more carnivorous, and others more herbivorous. They are just as fond of beef heart, beef liver, earthworms, fish, and prepared foods as they are of dandelion, lettuce, and fruits (particularly bananas). They have highly variable tastes, however, and definitely are individualists. This species is not suitable for the beginner.

Geoemyda (Rhinoclemys)
Neotropical Wood Turtles

[Almost all workers today consider these American turtles to be in a genus distinct from the Asian *Geoemyda*. The genus also was known as *Callopsis* for some years.]

Geoemyda (Rhinoclemys) annulata
Brown Wood Turtle

top: *Geoemyda* (*Rhinoclemys*) *pulcherrima pulcherrima* (nominate form of the Painted Wood Turtle). With their handsome coloration, the three subspecies do justice to their name.
bottom: Plastron of the Painted Wood Turtle. Both photos by G. Müller.

Up to 20 centimeters (8 inches).

Central America and northern and western South America (Honduras to Ecuador).

Geoemyda (Rhinoclemys) areolata
Furrowed Wood Turtle

Up to 20 centimeters (8 inches).

Southeastern Mexico to northern Guatemala and Honduras.

Geoemyda (Rhinoclemys) funerea
Black Wood Turtle

Up to 23 centimeters (9.5 inches).

Central America, Caribbean Honduras to Panama.

Geoemyda (Rhinoclemys) pulcherrima
Painted Wood Turtle

Geoemyda (Rhinoclemys) pulcherrima pulcherrima
Guerrero Wood Turtle

The flat brown carapace has a pronounced longitudinal keel along the midline and has irregular yellow to orange-red blotches. The undersides of the marginal scutes are bright red with black specks. On the yellow plastron there is a wide, not sharply defined, indistinct black blotch along the medial seam. The gular and anal scutes have red markings with black specks. The top of the head is light gray and has variable red streaks. A red longitudinal stripe extends back from the snout and curves over the eye and a parallel stripe extends back from the tip of the snout across the top of the head. The iris is red. The sides of the neck are light yellow with sharply defined black longitudinal stripes. The throat and underside of the neck are pale yellow with an irregular pattern of very fine black dots. The legs have bright red scales and longitudinal lines of black dots. The toes do not have particularly well-developed webbing and end in sharp claws.

Up to 20 centimeters (8 inches).

Southwestern Mexico.

The natural habitat of this handsomely colored turtle is a type of water-meadow landscape. At times it is primarily aquatic, but it always returns to land. Various hobbyists report that this species sometimes only spends the night in the water and stays on land during the day. Later the same individuals under the same day-night rhythm reversed this behavior, now spending the night on land.

The turtles are omnivorous, and after feeding predominantly on plants for days, they often suddenly developed a voracious appetite for earthworms, chopped beef heart, or the like. I have found that they take gelatin food when nothing else is available, but they always prefer fresh beef heart or beef liver and fresh, young dandelion leaves. Juveniles always prefer live food such as bloodworms or small crustaceans to the gelatin food. Therefore, we should never feed gelatin food to the exclusion of other foods.

G. (R.) p. pulcherrima requires an average temperature of 24°C (75°F), although healthy specimens kept outdoors certainly can tolerate cooler temperatures occasionally. Temperatures below 20°C (68°F), however, will cause complications.

This species breeds regularly in captivity but the pet trade offers this turtle rather infrequently. Newcomers to the terrarium hobby should refrain from keeping this species.

Geoemyda (Rhinoclemys) pulcherrima incisa
Incised Wood Turtle

About the same as the nominate form.

Southern Mexico (Oaxaca) to Nicaragua.

Geoemyda (Rhinoclemys) pulcherrima manni
Central American Wood Turtle

As in the nominate form.

Nicaragua and Costa Rica.

[Another subspecies, *G. (R.) p. rogerbarbouri*, is recognized from northwestern Mexico.]

Geoemyda (Rhinoclemys) punctularia
Spot-legged Wood Turtle

Geoemyda (Rhinoclemys) punctularia punctularia
Spot-legged Wood Turtle

The slightly arched, dark brown carapace has a yellow-brown border and a continuous keel along the midline. The vertebral scutes sometimes have faint radiating grooved lines. The dark brown plastron is lighter in color along the midline in some specimens, but this is the exception. The top of the head has very attractive markings. There is a red or yellow blotch in front of the eye and behind it there is a longitudinal band of the same color extending to above the ear opening. A narrow bridge sometimes connects the two longitudinal bands. Some specimens have one or two pairs of blotches on the occiput. The neck and the legs have black and yellow stripes; some specimens also have reddish blotches.

Up to 20 centimeters (8 inches).

Northern South America, from northeastern Venezuela to Brazil.

This species lives in marshy areas with shallow pools and lakes. It also frequently goes on land and can feed both on land and in the water. It is a true omnivore and readily takes fruits and plants as well as animal food. In captivity this species is delicate and requires very high temperatures. Therefore, I can recommend keeping them outdoors only in midsummer in a site protected from wind. In one instance two turtles cooled down so much in a garden pond during a chilly night that one died. For this reason, I do not keep my turtles in the garden pond. This turtle and all the subspecies are unsuitable for the beginner.

[The Spot-legged Wood Turtle of the Orinoco has been described as a separate subspecies, *G. (R.) p. flammigera*.]

Geoemyda (Rhinoclemys) punctularia diademata
Maracaibo Wood Turtle
Up to 20 centimeters (8 inches).
Venezuela in the drainages of Lake Maracaibo.

The most conspicuous difference between this subspecies and the nominate form is the conspicuous large yellow mark in the form of a forward-pointing triangle on top of the black head. This subspecies supposedly requires lower temperatures than the nominate form. It is reported that some remained active in the garden pond even in cool weather.

[This form is considered a full species by many workers.]

Geoemyda (Rhinoclemys) punctularia lunata
Northeastern South America (Surinam).[This form is considered a synonym of typical *punctularia* by some workers.]
Geoemyda (Rhinoclemys) punctularia melanosterna
Colombian Wood Turtle
Northwestern South America (Colombia, Ecuador) and Panama.[This form is considered to be a full species by some workers.]

Geoemyda (Rhinoclemys) punctularia nasuta
Large-nosed Wood Turtle
Northwestern South America (Colombia and Ecuador).[Not unexpectedly, this form is considered a full species by some workers.]

Geoemyda (Rhinoclemys) rubida
Mexican Spotted Wood Turtle

Geoemyda (Rhinoclemys) rubida rubida
Oaxaca Wood Turtle
Up to 20 centimeters (8 inches).
Southern Mexico (Oaxaca and Chiapas).

Geoemyda (Rhinoclemys) rubida perixantha
Colima Wood Turtle
Southwestern Mexico (Colima and Michoacan).

FAMILY: Testudinidae
Tortoises

KINIXYS
Hinge-back Tortoises

Kinixys belliana
Bell's Hinge-back Tortoise

Kinixys belliana belliana
Eastern Hinge-back Tortoise
The olive-brown to gray-brown carapace slopes gently at the back and has black blotches and rings. The lateral margins are straight and the trailing edge is not serrated. The leading edge of the carapace does not project as far forward as in the other species. The typical joint in the carapace, which allows the rear third of the carapace to close up against the plastron for protection, is not particularly

conspicuous in this subspecies. The dark brown plastron has an irregular pale pattern and the dark head has horny scales. The legs are conspicuously robust, even massive, and scaly. The front legs have toes fused down to the base of the nails; on the hind legs they can still move somewhat freely. They have heavy claws. *K. belliana* walks on the tips of the front claws (as if on stilts), but still walks partially on the balls of the rear feet.

Up to 20 centimeters (8 inches).

Eastern Africa (Zaire to Ethiopia south to Uganda).

K. belliana is a turtle of the savanna and lives in grassy, relatively arid and slightly hilly country with scattered bushes. It is strictly herbivorous and is fussy about diet. It is very delicate in the terrarium and therefore is not suitable for the beginner. It requires high temperatures of 25 to 30°C (77 to 86°F), moderate humidity, and a shallow water basin. It does not lose its extreme shyness even after a long time in captivity.

Kinixys belliana mertensi

Up to 20 centimeters (8 inches).

Central Africa.[This form is considered a synonym of *K. b. belliana* by most workers.]

Kinixys belliana nogueyi
Western Hinge-back Tortoise

Up to 20 centimeters (8 inches).

Western Africa, Senegal to Cameroon and Central African Republic. [This subspecies has only four claws on the front feet.]

[Other subspecies recognized by most workers include *K. b. lobatsiana*, *K. b. speki*, and *K. b. zombensis*.]

Kinixys erosa
Serrated Hinge-back Tortoise

The leading edge of the tan to brown carapace is very flat and projects forward. The lateral scutes are conspicuously serrated. A brownish yellow stripe of variable width runs along the ventral half of the costal scutes around the entire carapace. The yellowish brown plastron extends even farther forward than does the carapace and is conspicuously curved upward on the sides. The head, legs, and soft parts are yellow. The legs are thick and robust.

Up to 32 centimeters (13 inches).

Western Africa from Gambia to Uganda.

Unlike the previous species, this species lives in the rainforest and requires a biotope with high humidity. Besides plants and fruits, occasionally it also takes earthworms, beef heart or liver, and possibly some fish. We must offer it a varied diet in the terrarium. A peculiarity of the *Kinixys* species is that from one day to the next they can refuse a food that they had previously been fond of, then, after some time, they will take it avidly again. They require high temperatures of 25 to 30°C (77 to 86°F). We should furnish one-third of the terrarium as a shallow water basin. To make the transition to the terrestrial section, use flat rocks to build a gradually sloping terrace. Next add a belt of coarse gravel and finally some leaf mold mixed with peat. You can plant the terrarium with monstera, staghorn fern, maranta, dracaena, and similar plants to half the height of the sides of the terrarium.

Kinixys homeana
Home's Hinge-back Tortoise

The carapace of this species is distinctly flatter than those of *K. belliana* and *K. erosa*. The fifth vertebral scute has a humped outline, and behind it the carapace slopes steeply, nearly vertically. The trailing edge is slightly upward curved and strongly serrated. The color is brownish yellow, with some individual scutes with paler margins. The leading marginal scutes are particularly flat and project well forward (like a cantilevered roof). The hinge is clearly visible at the rear third of the carapace. The plastron is brownish. The triangular head is yellowish. As in the previous species, the legs are thick and heavily scaled.

Up to 20 centimeters (8 inches).

Western Africa, Liberia to Zaire.

In its habits it mostly resembles *K. erosa* but requires even more warmth and likes temperatures of 26 to 32°C (79 to 90°F). It also needs a constant humidity of at least 70 to 80 percent. Following a drop in humidity or temperature, the tortoises immediately stop feeding. *K. homeana* probably is the most delicate of the three species.

Considering the problems involved in terrarium keeping, we should not experiment and should leave the care of this species to specialists with the necessary facilities.

Captive breedings of hinge-back tortoises are rare and most likely to happen in zoos.

[Many workers consider the Natal Hinge-back Tortoise, *K. natalensis*, to be a full species of relatively dry habitats from southern Mozambique to Natal.]

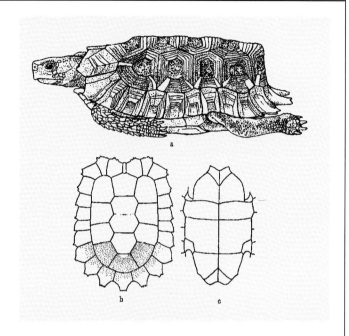

Home's Hinge-back Tortoise, *Kinixys homeana*. Illustration: E. Bobbe in Wermuth/Mertens: Schildkröten — Krokodile — Brückenechsen.

Kinixys belliana. This is Bell's Hinge-back Tortoise, which is hard to keep and fussy about diet. Therefore, the beginner should avoid it. Photo by B. Kahl.

HOMOPUS
Cape Tortoises

Homopus areolatus
Beaked Cape Tortoise

The carapace is rather flat on top and slopes steeply (nearly vertically) in the rear. The trailing edge is not serrated. The dorsal scutes are olive-green with red-brown centers (areolas) and black borders. Each dorsal scute has a sharp border of bulging, concentric margins. The plastron, head, and legs are brownish. The upper mandible ends in a down-curved beak-like tip. The legs are thick, and the front legs have large scales and just four claws each.

Up to 11 centimeters (4.5 inches).
Southern South Africa.

The Beaked Cape Tortoise lives in mountain meadows, where it forages actively for animal food. All *Homopus* species need much sun and live in southern South Africa. They are much livelier than most other tortoises and require temperatures of 22 to 28°C (72 to 82°F). Only occasional reports of captive keeping exist. Because they receive protection under Appendix II of CITES and are strictly protected under South African law, there have been few captive breedings outside South Africa.

Homopus boulengeri
Boulenger's Cape Tortoise

The carapace is chestnut-brown with pale seams; the trailing edge is not curved upward and is only slightly serrated. The plastron is light brown. The front legs have five claws. It lives in very tall granite mountains (up to 2400 meters) and is a very accomplished climber.

Up to 11 centimeters (4.5 inches).
Southern South Africa.

Homopus femoralis
Karroo Cape Tortoise

The carapace is flat on top but has a relatively highly arched outline in comparison with the other species. The dorsal scutes are uniformly olive-brown and often have narrow dark borders. Each thigh has a large, sharp tubercle. The front legs have four claws. The upper mandible

is not or is only slightly beak-like. Otherwise it is much like *H. areolatus*.

Up to 15 centimeters (6 inches).
Southern South Africa.

Homopus signatus
Speckled Cape Tortoise

The carapace is yellowish brown with a pattern of brown-black specks or radiating lines. The trailing edge is curved upward and strongly serrated. The front legs have five claws. Otherwise it is much like *H. areolatus*. [Two subspecies commonly are recognized, *H. s. signatus* and *H. s. cafer*.]

Up to 10 centimeters (4 inches).
Southwestern South Africa.

[The taxonomy of this genus remains uncertain. Many workers recognize another species, Berger's Cape Tortoise, *H. bergeri*, and there are many local forms that are being investigated for formal recognition.]

PYXIS
Spider Tortoises

Pyxis arachnoides
Common Spider Tortoise

The very highly arched, elongate-oval carapace has a dark yellow ground color. The vertebral and costal scutes have a radiating pattern of dark brown blotches and streaks that resembles (with much imagination) a spider web. The centers of the scutes are in part yellow-green. The center of each marginal scute has a large dark brown blotch or streak. The front part of the plastron is movable because of a transverse hinge. The yellowish legs have dark blotches.

Up to 10 centimeters (4 inches).
Southwestern Madagascar.

The Common Spider Tortoise lives in open, arid, scrubby grasslands. Accordingly, it requires daytime temperatures of 23 to 28°C (73 to 82°F) and a substantial nocturnal cooling of at least 10°C. This would be a problem in the terrarium, but since it is now a protected species and therefore rarely is available in the pet trade, I need not discuss this problem in detail. It is herbivorous and is one of the smallest turtles.

[This species commonly is held to have three subspecies, each with small populations: *P. a. arachnoides*, *P. a. brygooi*, and *P. a. oblonga*. A second species, the Flat-shelled Spider Tortoise, *Pyxis planicauda*, exists in western central Madagascar. This species sometimes is put into the genus *Acinixys*. The Flat-shell is seldom seen.]

MALACOCHERSUS
Pancake Tortoises

Malacochersus tornieri
African Pancake Tortoise

The unusually flat carapace has concentric growth rings on the scutes. Its ground color is yellow-brown with a pattern of radiating dark streaks. Both the carapace and plastron are thin and flexible, which is why naturalists who collected the first specimens thought they were suffering from extreme rachitis. The head is triangular and yellow-brown. The legs are the same color and end in sharp claws. The heavy scales on top of the front legs are conspicuous. The turtle cannot retract its head because of the flat shell.

Up to 15 centimeters (6 inches).

Eastern Africa (Kenya and Tanganyika).

This tortoise, which is very different from its relatives, lives in arid, rocky regions with scattered rubble mounds at an altitude of about 1000 meters. It is one of the fastest tortoises, and because its shell offers little protection when danger threatens, it tries to save itself through flight. It often escapes successfully, because it is a very accomplished climber and can hide in crevices and inflate itself. It wedges itself so firmly in crevices that it is difficult to pull it from the hiding place even with force. The Pancake Tortoise remains shy in captivity. Its diet is strictly herbivorous, and in its homeland it supposedly subsists almost exclusively on succulents. In captivity, however, it takes the usual diet for tortoises. The temperature should be about 22 to 28°C (72 to 82°F) with a distinct nocturnal cooling period. Under the proper conditions it makes a good terrarium inhabitant and occasionally is bred in captivity. Many

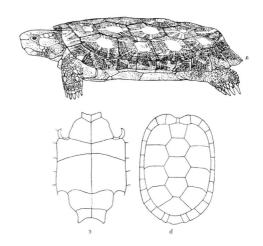

Pancake Tortoise, *Malacochersus tornieri*. Illustration: E. Bobbe in Wermuth/Mertens: Schildkröten — Krokodile — Brückenechsen.

wild specimens are imported each year, some in relatively poor condition.

TESTUDO
Mediterranean Tortoises

Testudo hermanni
Hermann's Tortoise

Testudo hermanni hermanni
Western Hermann's Tortoise

The highly arched, yellow-brown carapace has a variable black blotch with black borders in the middle of the dorsal scutes. The supracaudal scute is split (that is, two are present), a character that almost always distinguishes it from *T. graeca*, which has a single supracaudal scute. The plastron is yellow, with the dark blotches on the scutes arranged in two rows. The head, neck, and legs are olive-yellow. The top of the head has numerous small scales. The legs are thick and have sturdy, blunt claws on the toes. The tail ends in a horny, spike-like process.

Up to 20 centimeters (8 inches).

Southern and southeastern Europe, Spain to western Italy.

This tortoise lives in hilly, sometimes rocky, open landscapes with scattered shrubs or grasslands. This tortoise shuns dense thickets and needs abundant sunshine. Its diet con-

top: *Homopus areolatus*, the Beaked Cape Tortoise, in the wild of Cape Province, South Africa.
bottom: A female Karoo Cape Tortoise, *Homopus femoralis*, photographed in Karoo/Cape, South Africa. These tortoises and the others in the genus are difficult to care for and usually do not thrive in captivity. Photo by A. Schleicher.

Malacochersus tornieri. This Pancake Tortoise was photographed in its biotope in the Lift Valley, Kenya. It is the only tortoise with a naturally soft shell. When threatened it disappears into crevices, inflates itself, and becomes nearly impossible to dislodge. Photo by A. Schleicher.

Kleinman's Tortoise, *Testudo kleinmani*, is strictly protected; check that there is proper documentation on any specimens you may want to purchase. Photo by K. H. Switak.

sists of leaves, grasses, herbs, and fruits as well as animal food. Near campgrounds it supposedly also regularly eats human feces. In captivity it requires a varied diet. Many specimens have slowly but surely died in captivity because of a one-sided diet of lettuce. Instead they should receive plenty of dandelion, weeds of all kinds, grated carrot, bananas, and other fruits. Occasionally, however, feed them a meal of earthworms and chopped beef heart or liver. Many specimens are also fond of gelatin-based food. The required temperature is 20 to 30°C (68 to 86°F).

It has bred regularly in captivity. You can hear the collisions of males that are ready to breed (with some you could say "crazy to breed") from a distance as they ram with full force all other tortoises kept with them, regardless of sex. Mating usually takes place in the spring, but some males try their luck on warm days throughout the summer. Naturally, we cannot leave the eggs laid in the outdoor terrarium at our latitudes outside. Uncover them carefully and mark the top of each egg immediately (preferably with a normal, soft pencil). Then transfer them to an incubator without shaking or turning them. Except for babies, we definitely should give *Testudo h. hermanni* a winter rest period. If we give it reasonably proper care, we usually can expect offspring.

Testudo hermanni robertmertensi
Eastern Hermann's Tortoise

[This subspecies now is properly called *T. h. boettgeri*, the name *robertmertensi* being a synonym of the nominate subspecies.]

This tortoise is similar to the nominate form, except that it often has a yellow blotch under the eye. The black blotches of the plastron form a longitudinal band on either side of the midline. This subspecies often is somewhat more intensely colored than the more western form. [This is the subspecies most likely to be seen in captivity and the one most often wild-collected.]

Southeastern Europe (southern Italy to the Balkans) and western Turkey.

It does not differ from the nominate form in habits.

Testudo graeca
Spur-thighed (Greek) Tortoise

Testudo graeca graeca
Mediterranean Spur-thighed Tortoise

The coloration of the arched carapace is highly variable. Some specimens are light brown in color, others almost olive-green. Many closely resemble *T. hermanni* in coloration. The key distinguishing characters are, however, that the supracaudal scute is never split and there is no "spike" on the tip of the tail. Instead, there is a conspicuous large spur (pointed tubercle) inside the thigh on the hind leg. This spur is present in all subspecies and sometimes is so large as to resemble a small extra leg on each side. The legs are thick and stubby; the toes end in sturdy, blunt claws.

Up to 35 centimeters (14 inches).

Southeastern Europe to Iran and northern Africa.

Like *T. hermanni* in most of its needs, the required temperature (normally from 20 to 28°C, 68 to 82°F) is dependent on the provenance. Specimens from North Africa naturally need higher temperatures than those from the Balkans.

Testudo graeca ibera
Asia Minor Spurred Tortoise

Up to 30 centimeters (12 inches).

Southeastern Europe (the Balkans) through southwestern Asia to Iran.

Testudo graeca terrestris
Middle Eastern Spur-thighed Tortoise

Up to 30 centimeters (12 inches).

The Sinai, Israel, and Syria.

Testudo graeca zarudnyi
Iranian Spur-thighed Tortoise

Up to 35 centimeters (14 inches).

Eastern and southern Iran.

[The number of subspecies recognized in this species is subject to some debate. In addition to the above, some workers also recognize the subspecies *T. g. anamurensis* (Turkey) and *T. g. nikolski* (Transcaucus). Additionally, the names *whitei*, *flavominimaralis*, and *nabeulensis* are recognized as species or subspecies by a few workers. There also is a tendency to recognize most of the subspecies as full species, a move not accepted by most workers because the subspecies are difficult to define and appear to intergrade broadly where they come into contact.]

Testudo marginata
Marginated Tortoise

The Marginated Tortoise has a more elongated form than the other species of this genus. The ground color of the arched carapace is black, and at the middle of each dorsal scute is a bright yellow blotch. In older specimens the leading edge and particularly the trailing edge of the carapace are distinctly flattened and flared. The yellow plastron has various large black, usually triangular, blotches. In old age the tortoises usually are uniformly black. The gray-olive legs are stumpy, and their toes end in sturdy, blunt claws.

Up to 35 centimeters (14 inches).

Southern Greece, north to Olympus, and barely into Albania.

The Marginated Tortoise lives mainly on warm mountain slopes protected from wind and with heat-storing boulders and numerous shrubs. They bask a great deal, but hide under shade-giving bushes during the hottest part of the day. The Marginated Tortoise is the most warmth loving of the *Testudo* species. My specimens in the outdoor terrarium often did not leave their heated shelter on cooler days.

Otherwise it does well in captivity and has bred regularly. The juveniles, with their pale olive-green and dark brown coloration, are particularly striking. The dietary and keeping requirements are the same as those of *T. h. hermanni.*

German soldiers introduced the species to Sardinia during World War II. This population continues to survive. Some authors consider the Sardinian population to be of natural occurrence.

Testudo (Pseudotestudo)

[*Pseudotestudo* usually is considered to be a valid subgenus of *Testudo.*]

Testudo (Pseudotestudo) kleinmanni
Egyptian Tortoise

The tortoises have an arched carapace with a pale yellow-green to tan ground color. Each dorsal scute has a narrow black border. The pale yellow plastron has a pair of dark, approximately triangular blotches. Older specimens, particularly females, have a prominent hinge at the rear of the plastron; it is movable and allows the plastron to close against the carapace. This peculiar feature sometimes is present as well in older females of *Testudo graeca.* On top of the powerful front legs there are large, horny scales.

Up to 15 centimeters (6 inches).

Northeastern Africa to Israel.

It lives in a strictly arid biotope with stands of bushes and requires much higher temperatures than the other species of the genus *Testudo.* The Egyptian Tortoise is considered to be more delicate than the other Mediterranean tortoises in the terrarium. The temperature should not fall below 25°C (77°F); it is comfortable at temperatures up to 32°C (90°F). It also is fussy about food and needs a varied, strictly herbivorous diet and may be fond of bananas, rice, and pudding. It looks rather clumsy when feeding, is quite shy, and digs in at the slightest disturbance.

Because it is a severely threatened species, we should not keep it in the terrarium unless we can obtain captive-bred specimens. [Recently the Egyptian Tortoise has been moved to Appendix I of CITES, but some specimens still appear on the market (perhaps illegally) as Kleinmann's Tortoise. It apparently now is extinct in Egypt.]

Testudo (Geochelone)

[Almost all workers consider *Geochelone* to be a valid genus that is not especially closely related to *Testudo.* Some workers also have broken *Geochelone* into a variety of genera and subgenera, including *Manouria, Indotestudo, Megalochelys, Chelonoidis, Centrochelys, Astrochelys,* and *Stigmochelys,* with some herpetologists recognizing some and not others and variously recognizing the names at the generic and subgeneric levels.]

Testudo (Geochelone) elegans
Indian Star Tortoise

The highly arched carapace has a blackish brown to black ground color on the knobby vertebral and costal scutes. It also has radiating

top: *Testudo marginata*. The Marginated Tortoise is a protected species, but, in Greece, shepherds in particular consider it a delicacy. Captive breeding may be the only way to save this species from extinction. Photo by H. G. Zimpel.
bottom: *Testudo graeca ibera* (Asia Minor subspecies of the Spur-thighed, or Greek, Tortoise) does not differ from the nominate form in its keeping requirements. It is rare in the terrarium. Photo by H. Reinhard.

Testudo (*Geochelone*) *elegans.* Indian Star Tortoises in the act of copulation. They are delicate tortoises and are unsuitable for the beginner. Misting and frequent bathing are important in keeping them healthy. Photo by G. Janson.

yellow markings that are more orange in color in juveniles. Unlike the very similar Radiated Tortoise of Madagascar, *T. (G.) elegans* does not have even the vestige of a nuchal scute. The plastron is dark to black and has the same radiating yellow markings as the carapace. The head, neck, and thick legs have a pattern of yellow blotches on a dark ground color. Pronounced horny scales are present on the front side of the front legs.

Up to 25 centimeters (12 inches).

India and Sri Lanka, barely and questionably entering Pakistan and Bangladesh.

In their homeland these tortoises live primarily in forested regions or areas with many bushes at the base of mountains or hills. They also like to stay in tall grass. They are active only in the morning and at night, taking shelter in shady hiding places during the hottest parts of the day. Curiously, they continue to maintain this daily rhythm in captivity, although because of the relatively moderate midday temperatures at our latitudes or in the terrarium they have absolutely no reason to do so. They require relatively high temperatures of 25 to 30°C (77 to 86°F). At night the temperature can safely drop by about 6°C.

Despite being kept in the arid terrarium, they need a fairly large, shallow water bowl since they like to bathe. Spray the terrarium with water once a day, because they like a moderate level of humidity. This species is difficult to keep and it usually lives a maximum of five to six years in captivity even under good care. Beginners should not keep these tortoises. In recent years, various hobbyists have bred them successfully.

Testudo (Geochelone) pardalis
Leopard Tortoise

Testudo (Geochelone) pardalis pardalis
Western Leopard Tortoise

Western South Africa and Namibia.

Testudo (Geochelone) pardalis babcocki
Eastern Leopard Tortoise

The yellowish brown, highly arched carapace has scattered black specks and blotches. On each scute there are deep concentric grooves resembling wood carvings. The leading edge of the carapace is slightly serrated. A nuchal scute is not present, in its place being an almost rectangular notch. The trailing edge is more strongly serrated. The head, neck, and the thick and massive legs are brownish to yellow-olive. The toes have sturdy claws. There is a horny protuberance on each thigh. The front legs have shingle-like, yellowish horny plates that taper to a point in front.

Up to 68 centimeters (27 inches).

South Africa north over eastern Africa to Somalia and Ethiopia.

These handsome tortoises live mainly in the savannas of plateaus and occur only sporadically in lowlands. To find food in the arid regions they often wander widely and have been state to even cross deserts. They require very high temperatures (24 to 30°C, 75 to 86°F) and need a heated, arid terrarium in captivity. Outdoor keeping is possible only on warm days in midsummer. Then the tortoises move across the grass like lawn mowers and ignore all other food. If we give them enough warmth, they do well in captivity on the diet we feed other tortoises. *T. (G.) pardalis* is very shy, however, and does not lose this trait even after a long time in captivity. [Many keepers would strongly disagree with this characterization of the species.] During droughts and the associated meager food supply in the wild, the tortoises enter a kind of estivation. Because of the size the Leopard Tortoise can reach, it makes a suitable charge for most hobbyists only as a juvenile. It is bred regularly in captivity.

Testudo (Geochelone) sulcata
African Spurred Tortoise

The arched, yellowish carapace is rather flat in the area of the second, third, and fourth vertebral scutes, and the lateral marginal scutes slope downward nearly vertically. The leading edge of the carapace is slightly serrated, and the trailing edge is strongly serrated and slightly curved upward. The individual dorsal scutes have concentric grooves. The seams of the scutes are somewhat darker. The head and the legs are yellow. Thick, horny scales cover the dorsal side of the front legs. The thighs have large horny spurs that have given the tortoise its common name.

Up to 80 centimeters (32 inches) and weighing up to 100 kilograms (220 pounds).

Central Africa.

This species lives in arid savannas and grasslands or in semi-desert regions. In its temperature requirements, habits, and dietary requirements it is similar to the Leopard Tortoise, but may need even slightly higher temperatures (25 to 35°C, 77 to 95°F). On the other hand, it is not as shy as the other species and becomes almost confiding with time. Of course, because the tortoises grow so large, only zoos and a few hobbyists have suitable facilities for them. It has bred in captivity many times.

Testudo (Geochelone) platynota
Burmese Star Tortoise

This species has a highly arched, brownish carapace. The radiating markings resemble those of *T. (G.) elegans* except that the dorsal scutes are not as knobby. [This species is virtually unknown in either nature or captivity and has been rumored to be near extinction.]

Up to 26 centimeters (10.5 inches).

The Irrawaddy Valley of Burma.

Testudo (Acinixys)

[*Acinixys* generally is treated as either a full genus or a subgenus of *Pyxis*, not in the usual *Testudo* or *Geochelone* groups of genera.]

Testudo (Acinixys) planicauda
Flat-shelled Spider Tortoise

This very small species has particularly attractive markings. The horn-colored carapace is strongly serrated on the leading edge. The trailing edge is serrated only on the caudal scutes; the remaining scutes have rounded margins. The dorsal scutes have a pattern of irregular black blotches. Together with the light-colored borders they produce a star-like effect. The yellowish plastron has a few scattered dark blotches. Its trailing edge has a blunt-angled notch in the middle. On top of the head there are a pair of irregular pale blotches. Thick, horny scales cover the unmarked legs, particularly the front side.

Up to 12 centimeters (5 inches).

Western Madagascar.

This tortoise lives in arid regions with scattered shrubs. It requires high temperatures of 26

to 30°C (79 to 86°F) and is strictly herbivorous. Because of its small size, it would be a very good candidate for the heated, arid terrarium. Unfortunately, it is a seriously threatened (and protected) species. Outdoor keeping is a possibility only in midsummer in a protected terrarium.

Testudo (Agrionemys)

[*Agrionemys* usually is considered to be a subgenus of *Testudo* in the restricted sense.]

Testudo (Agrionemys) horsfieldi
Central Asian Tortoise

The arched, brownish olive carapace is very flat on top. It has a pattern of somewhat blurry black blotches with narrow pale edges on each scute. The plastron is black or has large black blotches. The snout of the olive head has a hook-like upper mandible. Typical of the species are the four toes always present on the front and hind feet (there are five toes on the front feet of other tortoises). The tip of the tail ends in a spike. Differences between the sexes include the male's significantly thicker tail and the presence in males of just one tubercle on the inside of the thigh while the female has three to five tubercles.

Up to 20 centimeters (8 inches).

Eastern Caspian region, Turkestan, Iran, Afghanistan, and northern Pakistan.

The Central Asian Tortoise lives on sandy or loamy grasslands with scattered shrubs. The pet trade has imported it very frequently in recent years. It requires the lowest temperatures of any tortoise, and we should try to keep it outdoors. On cool days (14 to 16°C, 57 to 60°F), when all other *Testudo* species sought out the heated shelter in my outdoor installation, this species still marched around actively and continued to feed. They are fond of dandelion, lettuce, and fruits of all kinds, especially bananas, but also take dry dog food (softened) and chopped liver and earthworms. The required temperatures are highly variable (it tolerates a range of 14 to 28°C, 57 to 82°F). In the wild they supposedly estivate (during the dry season) and observe a winter rest period. I know of hobbyists who leave the tortoises outdoor in late fall, where they dig themselves in and reappear in the spring. I do not necessarily recommend this practice. Because of the extreme fluctuations in temperature at our latitudes, there is a danger that during an extended warm period during the winter the tortoises could emerge and, with a subsequent drop in temperature, will no longer be able to dig themselves in and consequently will freeze to death. Furthermore, there is the danger that rats could discover and kill them during hibernation, since they are of course defenseless in this state. In the wild the female lays her eggs in July, but the young do not hatch until the following April. The species has bred in captivity. In the incubator the eggs need 80 to 120 days to hatch.

There are conflicting opinions about how to keep this species successfully. In my opinion it is not that hard to keep. The numerous successful breedings, even when hobbyists kept the tortoises on the balcony, show this.

Testudo (Astrochelys)

[This subgenus of *Geochelone* often is misspelled *Asterochelys*.]

Testudo (Astrochelys) radiata
Radiated Tortoise

The nearly black, highly arched carapace has an attractive radiating yellow pattern on each vertebral and costal scute. The marginal scutes also have a pattern of markings. The individual scutes normally do not have a hump-backed outline, but in exceptional cases some specimens reared in captivity develop large humps. This raises the question of whether they are suffering from rachitis. The plastron has intersecting yellow and black lines, creating a pattern of triangular to square ornaments. The leading

Testudo (Geochelone) pardalis. The Leopard Tortoise, photographed here in its biotope in Gobabis, Namibia, requires very high temperatures. Keep it outdoors only at suitably high temperatures in midsummer. Photo by A. Schleicher.

Testudo (*Asterochelys*) *radiata*. The Radiated Tortoise lives on Madagascar; it requires high temperatures but is not as delicate as *Testudo* (*Geochelone*) *elegans*. Photo by W. Hemmer.

edge of the carapace is serrated; on the trailing edge only the caudal scutes are serrated. The dorsal sides of the head, tail, and thighs are black; all remaining parts of the head, neck, and legs as well as the soft parts are uniformly light yellow.

Up to 40 centimeters (16 inches).

Southern Madagascar.

This species lives in arid regions with low shrubs and grass. It requires very high temperatures but is not as delicate as *Testudo* (*Geochelone*) *elegans*. Naturally, we must avoid extreme fluctuations in temperature. The optimum temperature probably is from 25 to 30°C (77 to 86°F).

The Radiated Tortoise is predominantly herbivorous and requires a varied diet. It is fond of sweet fruits and bananas and occasionally takes finely chopped beef heart or liver. We should provide a shelter outdoors for protection against the hot sun in midsummer. This species has lived to a considerable age in captivity: the famous "Tonga" tortoise lived to an age of at least 189 years. "Torty," which still lives today in the Alexandra Park Zoo in Bundaberg, Australia, has lived 133 years in captivity. [Caution is advisable when accepting age records for the larger tortoises because specimens often were exchanged with no change in the records.] *T. (A.) radiata* has been bred successfully in captivity.

Testudo (Astrochelys) yniphora
Angulated (Angonoka) Tortoise

T. (A.) radiata closely resembles the Radiated Tortoise in carapace form and color. The coloration and markings are somewhat indistinct, however, and the yellow rays are much wider and not as sharply defined. The most

important distinguishing character is the projecting, pointed, upward-curved gular scute of
this species. It does not differ from the Radiated
Tortoise in its biotope, habits, and its temperature and dietary requirements.

Up to 38 centimeters (15 inches).

Northwestern Madagascar.

Testudo (Chelonoidis)

[*Chelonoidis* usually is considered a subgenus of *Geochelone* and occasionally is treated as
a full genus.]

Testudo (Chelonoidis) carbonaria
Red-footed Tortoise

In the middle of each vertebral and costal
scute, the highly arched black carapace has a
yolk-yellow blotch surrounded by concentric
grooves (like the annual rings of trees). The
plastron is uniformly yellow in some specimens;
in others it is yellow with large black blotches.
The head is black with an orange-red top; some
specimens have only scattered orange-red
blotches. There are numerous bright red to orange-red horny scales on the front side of the
massive front legs as well as a few on the hind
legs. These scales contrast strongly with the
black ground color. Together with the attractive
carapace they lend the tortoise a handsome appearance.

Up to 50 centimeters (20 inches).

Tropical South America east of the Andes,
Colombia (and extreme eastern Panama) south
to Paraguay and Argentina.

This tortoise is a typical inhabitant of the
tropical rainforest and its edges (but is absent
from most of the Amazon basin) and is one of the
most beautiful species. It is omnivorous. My
specimens take an amazing variety of foods. If I
feed the aquatic turtles sardines or freshwater
fish, the Red-footed Tortoises also get their
share. When they eat fish, they devour the head,
bones, guts, and all. They are very fond of
softened dry dog food (kibble), gelatin food,
earthworms, prepared turtle food, dandelion,
lettuce, beef liver and heart, and bananas and all
sweet fruits. The more varied the diet, the more
the tortoises like it.

I obtained my specimens as juveniles with a
carapace length of 6 and 8 centimeters (about 2.5

to 3 inches). After about seven years, when the
female was 29 centimeters (11.5 inches) and the
male 26 centimeters (10.5 inches) long, I observed the first copulation attempts (the summer
of 1982). Unfortunately, the three clutches laid
yearly so far have always been infertile despite
numerous copulations. I keep my specimens in
the outdoor terrarium from May to September
and cover it on cool days. The tortoises are
inactive during the hottest part of the day, when
they withdraw into their shelter. During warm
summer showers they hurry outside to enjoy the
rain. After several consecutive hot and dry days,
as a substitute for these tropical showers I spray
them with a watering can full of lukewarm
water. There also is a shallow bathing facility in
the outdoor terrarium that the tortoises like to
use.

Wild-caught juveniles of this species supposedly are difficult to rear. This probably is true,
but only because the tortoises arrived at the pet
dealer in questionable condition.

From mid-September on I keep the tortoises
in a terrarium that is 2.50 meters (8 feet) long and
about 0.6 meter (2 feet) wide. I furnish it with a
shelter, a "sunning" place with a lamp, and a
water bowl. I also give the tortoises a lukewarm
bath once a week. I put them in water deep
enough that they can barely reach the surface. I
prefer this method to using a water basin, which
the tortoises always soil. The temperature in the
terrarium is 24 to 28°C (75 to 82°F); outdoors it
varies, depending on the weather, from 17 to
30°C (63 to 86°F). Both zoos and private keepers have bred this tortoise regularly.

Testudo (Chelonoidis) chilensis
Chaco Tortoise

The relatively flat carapace has deep, concentric grooves on the dorsal scutes. The scutes have
dark brown margins and yellow-brown centers.
The marginal scutes are strongly upward curved
and slightly serrated on the leading and trailing
edges. The massive head resembles a hawk's
because of the strong hook in the middle of the
upper mandible. The legs are thick and have
heavy tubercular scales, particularly on the thighs
of the hind legs as well as each side of the base
of the tail.

Up to 22 centimeters (9 inches).

Southern South America in Argentina and Paraguay. (Since it does not occur in Chile, its scientific name is inappropriate.)

In its homeland it lives in the transitional zone between the rainforest to grassland. It does not like too-dry conditions, but not as moist as *T. (C.) carbonaria*. Its diet is more herbivorous than that of *T. (C.) carbonaria*. In captivity it is a relatively undemanding charge that we definitely should keep outdoors during the warm season. If we keep it exclusively in the terrarium, it should be moderately moist with a dry basking place under a lamp and a shallow water basin. In the past, the pet trade rarely offered it. At our latitudes there are no reports of successful breeding in captivity, but it would certainly be possible under the right conditions. The average temperature should be 25°C (77°F). [Most authors consider this to be a species of dry, often cold, sparsely vegetated savannas, not rainforest edges. Few keepers have had much luck with this species over the course of many years.]

Testudo (Chelonoidis) denticulata
Yellow-footed Tortoise

In contrast to *T. (C.) carbonaria*, the carapace is flatter, longer, and olive-brown in color. The centers of the dorsal scutes are paler but are not as sharply defined. The blotches on the head and legs usually are yellow. The toes on the stubby and massive legs have sturdy claws. Horny yellowish scales, arranged like shingles, cover the dorsal side of the legs.

Up to 30 centimeters (12 inches).

Tropical South America east of the Andes (Colombia to southern Brazil) as well as Trinidad; introduced on several Caribbean islands.

This species also lives in the tropical rainforest and its transitional zones. Therefore, the Yellow-footed Tortoise is similar in its habits and keeping requirements to the Red-footed Tortoise, but can tolerate moister conditions.

Testudo (Chelonoidis) elephantopus
Galapagos Giant Tortoise

[Unfortunately the name of this species now is held to be *nigra* rather than *elephantopus*.]

Up to 110 centimeters (44 inches).

Restricted to the many islands of the Galapagos group west of Ecuador.

All subspecies of the Galapagos Tortoise live on the islands of the Galapagos archipelago and are difficult to tell apart. Because they are threatened with extinction and are completely protected, I will limit myself to listing the subspecies and where they live. Because of its size, this species is unsuitable in any case for the terrarium, [though captive-bred young are available at high prices. It is strictly protected and there is much red-tape required to get a permit to keep it.]

Testudo (Chelonoidis) e. abingdoni
Up to 100 centimeters (40 inches).
Abingdon Island (= Pinta) (probably extinct).

Testudo (Chelonoidis) e. chathamensis
Up to 100 centimeters (40 inches).
Chatham Island (= San Cristobal).

Testudo (Chelonoidis) e. darwini
Up to about 100 centimeters (40 inches).
James Island (= San Salvador).

Testudo (Chelonoidis) e. ephippium
Up to about 110 centimeters (44 inches).
Duncan Island (= Pinzon) (probably extinct).

Testudo (Chelonoidis) e. galapagoensis
Up to about 110 centimeters (44 inches).
Charles Island (= Floreana) (probably extinct).

Testudo (Chelonoidis) e. hoodensis
Up to about 100 centimeters (40 inches).
Hood Island (= Espanola).

Testudo (Chelonoidis) e. nigrita
Up to about 100 centimeters (40 inches).
Indefatigable Island (= Santa Cruz).

Testudo (Chelonoidis) e. phantastica
Up to about 100 centimeter (40 inches).
Narborough Island (= Fernandina).

Testudo (Chelonoidis) e. wallacei
Up to 100 centimeters (40 inches).
Jervis Island (= Rabida).

[Other subspecies are recognized by some authors, while some of those listed here are

top: *Testudo* (*Chelonoidis*) *carbonaria*. Fully grown Red-footed Tortoise with juvenile (for size comparison). It likes to bathe and when kept outdoors visibly relishes a warm rain. Simulate rain showers on dry, hot days with a watering can full of lukewarm water.
bottom: Red-footed Tortoise laying eggs. The eggs are usually spherical (like somewhat larger Ping-Pong balls), rarely oval. The incubation period is at least four months. Both photos by G. Janson.

A juvenile Chaco Tortoise, *Testudo (Chelonoidis) chilensis*. There is some debate over what types of habitat this tortoise prefers which probably has contributed to the failure of hobbyists to succeed in keeping Chaco Tortoises. Photo by B. Kahl.

treated as synonyms or unrecognizable. Few of these tortoises still exist in their natural habitats, having been transplanted by sailors and scientists to various islands over the last 150 years.]

Testudo (Chersina)

[Virtually all workers today consider *Chersina* to be a full genus related to *Pyxis, Homopus*, and *Psammobates* rather than the Mediterranean tortoises or the *Geochelone* group.]

Testudo (Chersina) angulata
Bowsprit Tortoise

The dorsal scutes of the oval and arched carapace have an approximately square dark blotch in the middle. A concentric wide yellow stripe surrounds the blotch and in turn has a black border. The marginal scutes are yellow with tapering black stripes. There is a yellow band along the line dividing the costal and marginal scutes. The nuchal scute slopes vertically downward in front and does not curve up. This species shares this feature only with *Testudo (Astrochelys) yniphora*, although it is not as conspicuous in that species. The plastron is black, occasionally with a reddish tinge. The front legs, in particular, have thick, horny scales and robust claws.

Up to about 25 centimeters (10 inches).

Southern South Africa and Namibia.

This species lives in arid grasslands with scattered shrubs. It requires average temperatures of about 25°C (77°F) and needs a heated terrarium in captivity. It is primarily herbivorous, but we should occasionally offer beef heart or beef liver. There are few reports of captive breeding.

Testudo (Indotestudo)

[The two species of this group often are considered to belong to either a full genus or more typically the subgenus *Indotestudo* of the genus *Geochelone*.]

Testudo (Indotestudo) elongata
Elongated Tortoise

The arched carapace of this species is flat on top. It has a yellowish brown to brown coloration and randomly scattered black blotches. The head and neck are yellow and the massive legs are grayish black with scattered horny scales. The

toes end in very robust claws. In juveniles of this species the carapace is uniformly light beige and completely unmarked. The rear marginal scutes are strongly serrated. The entire head is light yellow.

Up to 28 centimeters (11 inches).

Eastern India east over most of Southeast Asia.

In its homeland, this very active tortoise lives in grasslands with scattered bushes. Unlike many other tortoises, it requires moisture. Specimens may became especially active outdoors when it rains and prefer cool summer weather to high temperatures. The species is bred in captivity in small numbers.

The Elongated Tortoise is predominantly herbivorous. As a general rule, however, we should occasionally offer all tortoises something else, such as beef heart, beef liver, or dog food. The required temperature is about 25°C (77°F). I always recommend keeping the tortoises outdoors during the warm season.

Testudo (Indotestudo) forsteni
Celebes Tortoise

[Most authorities consider this to be a synonym of the Travancore Tortoise, but an older name than *travancorica*.]

The arched, brownish olive carapace has a few widely scattered black blotches. The centers of the dorsal scutes are light in color. The nuchal scute is not present, and in its place there is a notch. The plastron is yellow with a large dark blotch on each scute.

The species probably is identical to *Testudo (Indotestudo) travancorica*, which I will discuss below.

Up to 17 centimeters (7 inches).

The Celebes and Halmahera Islands of Indonesia.

Testudo (Indotestudo) travancorica
Travancore Tortoise

[Most authorities now use the name *forsteni* for this species, the Celebes Tortoise above being a synonym perhaps based on introduced populations.]

The only weakly arched carapace is brownish olive. Each vertebral and costal scute has a light-colored center and an irregular black border.

There is no nuchal scute; in its place there is a notch in the carapace. On the plastron there is a black blotch on the rear part of the bridge and on each of the humeral and femoral scutes. The head and the robust legs are brownish olive and otherwise unmarked. The front and hind legs have thick, horny scales and sturdy claws. Little is known about this species in captivity and it seldom is seen.

Up to 28 centimeters (11 inches).

Southwestern India.

[Most authorities recognize only two species of *Indotestudo*, the Elongated Tortoise and the Travancore Tortoise, *forsteni*. The latter species includes *travancorica* as a synonym and is known from two widely separated areas, India and the Celebes. How an Indian tortoise ended up in the Celebes is uncertain, but it has been suggested that it was introduced.]

Testudo (Manouria)

[Many authorities today accept *Manouria* as a full genus or a subgenus of *Geochelone*.]

Testudo (Manouria) emys
Mountain (Brown) Tortoise

The moderately arched carapace is yellowish brown to olive-brown. The dorsal scutes have pale areolas. The nuchal scute is very small, and there are two caudal scutes over the tail. The leading and trailing edges of the carapace curve upward slightly and are somewhat serrated. The plastron has a pair of gular scutes that protrude slightly forward. An important characteristic is that the pectoral scutes do not meet in the middle, but rather are widely separated. The head and legs are massive; the front legs have large, horny scales arranged like shingles and very robust claws. [These tortoises like rather cool, very humid conditions, and they especially like to feed during rain showers. The temperature should not exceed about 24°C (75°F) for long stretches. They do not like to bask in strong sunlight. A few are bred in captivity each year but they are not yet common.]

Up to 47 centimeters (19 inches).

Eastern India through Southeast Asia, Sumatra, and Borneo.

Testudo (Manouria) impressa

Impressed Tortoise

The slightly arched carapace is clearly flatter along the middle. The leading and trailing edges are strongly serrated and the trailing edge also is strongly curved upward. Because the nuchal scute is small, there is a deep notch above the head between the adjoining, significantly larger marginal scutes. The center of the vertebral and costal scutes is lighter in color, with a pattern of indistinct lines radiating from it. On the plastron, the two anal scutes have lobe-like projections to the outside, creating an angled or square notch between the two scutes. It has a robust head and massive legs with scaly, horny plates. This rare species seldom is available and apparently has not yet been bred in captivity in any numbers.

Up to 26 centimeters (10.5 inches).

Southeast Asia and southern China.

Testudo (Megalochelys)

[*Megalochelys* usually is considered a subgenus of *Geochelone*. It has been suggested that the name *Dipsochelys* should be used instead, and the name *Aldabrachelys* also has been suggested.]

Testudo (Megalochelys) gigantea
Aldabra Giant Tortoise

[Few workers today recognize subspecies in this species restricted to tiny Aldabra Island in the Seychelles group.]

Testudo (Megalochelys) gigantea gigantea

Up to 100 centimeters (40 inches).

Mahe Island, Seychelles; no longer lives in the wild.

Testudo (Megalochelys) gigantea daudini

Up to 100 centimeters (40 inches).

Southern part of Aldabra Island.

Testudo (Megalochelys) gigantea elephantina

Up to 123 centimeters (49 inches).

Northern part of Aldabra Island.

I have deliberately omitted detailed information about Aldabra Giant Tortoises because they are not suitable candidates for the private terrarium. They are commonly seen in parks and zoos, however, and are bred in small numbers each year, the young being available at high

top: *Testudo* (*Chersina*) *angulata*. Photograph of a Bowsprit Tortoise taken in southern Namibia. On rare occasions, this species has bred in captivity. Photo by A. Schleicher.
bottom: *Testudo* (*Indotestudo*) *elongata*. The Elongated Tortoise is very lively. In the wild, it is particularly active when it rains and at somewhat cooler temperatures.

Testudo (Manouria) emys, the Mountain, or Brown, Tortoise. It has a rather flat carapace and has crepuscular and nocturnal habits, making it a rather unusual tortoise. Photo by H. Reinhard.

Testudo (Psammobates) oculifera. Photograph of the Serrated Tortoise in its homeland in Gobabis, eastern Namibia. It is very delicate in captivity. Photo by A. Schleicher.

prices. There also is quite a bit of red tape to go through before purchasing one.

Testudo (Psammobates)
South African Star Tortoises

[*Psammobates* is generally considered a full genus related to *Homopus*.]

Testudo (Psammobates) geometrica
Geometric Tortoise

[*Psammobates geometricus*]

The highly arched carapace is blackish brown. It has a yellow, star-like marking on each vertebral and costal scute that radiates from a yellow center (areola) in juveniles and from a yellow circle in older specimens. The marginal scutes have a pattern of yellow stripes. The head, neck, and legs are grayish yellow in juveniles and later exhibit dark blotches. The legs have a scaly covering of horny plates. The plastron is dark. The margins of the scutes are black and often have yellow radiating lines.

Up to 18 centimeters (7.5 inches).

South Africa in southwestern Cape Province.

The species, like other South African endemic tortoises, is fully protected. It lives in flat grasslands with scattered bushes with often sandy soils. Its natural diet consists predominantly of sedges, sedum and other grasses, and irises and other bulbs. The Geometric Tortoise sometimes also lives in moist areas and likes to bathe when given the opportunity. Because of its rarity, terrarium keeping is almost out of the question, plus it is very delicate and difficult to maintain in a healthy condition for very long.

Testudo (Psammobates) oculifera
Serrated Tortoise

It shares many similarities with the Geometric Tortoise. The most important differences are the strongly up-curved leading and trailing marginal scutes that have spiny serrations and dark brown radiating lines on a yellowish ground color. The plastron also has a prominent dark brown and yellow pattern. Its biotope is arid and sandy with places to hide in the form of bushes and shrubs. It is very delicate and survives only a short time in the terrarium even under the best of conditions.

[*Psammobates oculiferus*]

Up to 14 centimeters (5.5 inches).

Namibia and Botswana plus northern South Africa.

Testudo (Psammobates) tentoria
Tent Tortoise

[*Psammobates tentorius*]

Testudo (Psammobates) tentoria tentoria

The highly arched blackish brown carapace has a pattern of yellow to reddish yellow radiating lines that extend directly from the center (not from a light-colored areola) of each dorsal scute. The marginal scutes are not as strongly curved upward and are not serrated. The plastron is dark in color without yellow radiating lines. The head has prominent yellow markings. The legs are robust, and the front legs have large horny plates.

Up to 14 centimeters (4.5 inches).

The other subspecies differ as follows:

T. (P.) t. verroxi: The dorsal scutes are not convex and the plastron has indistinct dark shading.

T. (P.) t. trimeni: The dorsal scutes are conically convex. The dark color of the plastron contrasts sharply with the carapace. The plastron also has yellow radiating lines.

South-central South Africa.

This species lives in grasslands or arid zones with scattered bushes. It is predominantly herbivorous and requires very high temperatures, averaging 28°C (82°F). I do not recommend it for the terrarium because it is very delicate and is fully protected.

Testudo (Psammobates) tentoria trimeni

Up to 12 centimeters (5 inches).

Southwestern South Africa and coastal Namibia.

Testudo (Psammobates) tentoria verroxi

Up to 14 centimeters (5.5 inches).

South Africa and interior Namibia.

GOPHERUS
Gopher Tortoises
Gopherus agassizi
Desert Tortoise

[This species and the Texas Tortoise sometimes are referred to the genus or subgenus *Xerobates*.]

Up to 34 centimeters (13.5 inches).

Southwestern United States and northwestern Mexico.

Gopherus berlandieri
Texas (Berlandier's) Tortoise

Up to 35 centimeters (14 inches).

Southern Texas and northeastern Mexico.

Gopherus flavomarginatus
Bolson Tortoise

Up to 35 centimeters (14 inches).

Northern Mexico.

Gopherus polyphemus
Gopher Tortoise

The domed carapace is brown to dark brown and the trailing edge is only slightly serrated. The head also is brown and has very small, unmarked horny scales. The thick, almost stumpy, legs also are brown. Horny scales cover the front legs, which are flattened for digging and end in sturdy claws.

The four species of gopher tortoises are rather similar to each other but differ in many aspects of shell and leg details. The Desert and Texas Tortoises are closely related, while the Gopher and Bolson Tortoises form another species pair.

Up to 35 centimeters (14 inches).

Southeastern United States from eastern Louisiana to South Carolina.

The Gopher Tortoise lives in dry, well-drained areas (especially pine hills) with warm summer daytime temperatures. During the hot hours of the day they sleep in their self-excavated burrows that often are several meters long. The young tortoises dig and subsequently enlarge these burrows. G. *polyphemus* becomes active at dusk, when it forages for food. In the wild its diet consists mainly of grasses and other coarse plants (they prefer cucumber to all other vegetable foods in captivity). Much of its water comes from its food. They need temperatures averaging about 28°C (82°F). The main difficulty in long-term keeping in captivity is that the nocturnal drop in temperature is difficult to reproduce in the normal terrarium. The tortoises require a temperature difference of at least 15°C.

FAMILY: Cheloniidae
Sea Turtles

The sea turtles all are marine and have the feet developed into large, flattened paddles, the forelegs especially long and without distinct digits. All these turtles are very large and are protected to various degrees in different countries. They are not available to the general hobbyist and make poor pets when available. I will present the individual species here only for the sake of completeness and will describe them only briefly because they would be suitable candidates for the aquarium only as juveniles.

CARETTA
Loggerhead Turtles

Caretta caretta
Loggerhead Turtle

The flat, dark olive carapace has five costal scutes. The plastron is pale yellow with three poreless inframarginal scutes on the bridge. The head is large and has a pale yellow ground color. The top and sides of the head have brown blotches but only a few are present on the underside of the head. They are good swimmers and hunters and are almost exclusively carnivorous.

Up to 100 centimeters (40 inches).

The oceans of the world from the level of northern Europe to Australia and South Africa.

Chelonia
Green Turtles

Chelonia depressa
Flatback Turtle

[This species often is placed in the separate genus *Natator*.]

Northern coasts of Australia and also southeastern New Guinea.

Chelonia mydas
Green Turtle

[The subspecies, if any, of the Green Turtle are in dispute, with several names being used by different authors. The present preferred course is to recognize a single species, *C. mydas*, which sometimes is considered to have a distinct eastern Pacific subspecies, *C. m. agassizi*. Some workers feel that *agassizi* is a full species that occurs as far west as New Guinea, but this is disputed by other workers. The name *japonica*

Testudo (Psammobates) tentoria veroxii. Photograph of a Tent Tortoise in its biotope in Poffader, in northwestern South Africa. Due to its protected status, these tortoises are never imported, which is probably best for these delicate creatures. Photo by A. Schleicher.

usually is considered to be a synonym of *C. m. mydas.*]

Chelonia mydas mydas
Common Green Turtle

The flat brownish carapace has only four costal scutes. There is only one pair of prefrontals on top of the head, and the beak is not hawk-like. Unfortunately, it provides the famous turtle soup (the common name of Green Turtle refers to the color of the fat). Juveniles are very attractive. They are dark brown on top and the vertebral keel is somewhat lighter in color. The carapace, legs, and scales of the head have white borders.

The turtles are very awkward on land and seek it out only to lay their eggs. Because they always return to the same nesting beaches and often must swim hundreds of kilometers to reach them, they lay their eggs only every two or three years.

It is interesting that *Chelonia mydas* always pushes itself forward on land with all four legs simultaneously. In contrast, *Caretta* and all other quadrupeds move by alternating the right front and left hind legs and then the left front and right hind legs.

C. m. mydas is almost exclusively carnivorous and feeds on squid, shrimp, fish, and the like.

Up to 140 centimeters (56 inches) and weighing up to 250 kilograms (550 pounds).

The Atlantic Ocean, including the Mediterranean Sea.

Chelonia mydas japonica
Indo-Pacific Green Turtle

Unlike *C. m. mydas*, the carapace usually is greenish to olive. There often is a conspicuous indentation on the trailing edge above the hind legs. Otherwise it does not differ from the nominate form.

Same as the Common Green Turtle. Pacific and Indian Oceans.

ERETMOCHELYS
Hawksbills
[Like the subspecies of Green Turtles, there is considerable controversy as to if and how many subspecies should be recognized in the Hawksbill.]

Eretmochelys imbricata
Hawksbill Turtle

Eretmochelys imbricata imbricata
Atlantic Hawksbill Turtle
In juveniles the carapace is heart-shaped and has overlapping, horn-colored scutes with a dark, radiating pattern. (These scutes provide the well-known "tortoise shell," which is why human predation always has threatened these turtles.) In old specimens the sides of the carapace are straight and parallel. The hawk-like head and the legs are predominantly hazelnut brown. There are only four costal scutes and two pairs of prefrontal scales on top of the head.

The diet is primarily carnivorous (this species even feeds on sea urchins and poisonous jellyfish) and the turtle only occasionally takes vegetable food.

Up to 90 centimeters (36 inches), weighing up to 120 kilograms (240 pounds).

Atlantic Ocean and Mediterranean Sea.

Eretmochelys imbricata bissa
Pacific Hawksbill Turtle
This subspecies differs from the nominate form in that the top of the head and particularly the front legs are nearly black. The lateral margins of the carapace are nearly heart-shaped, even in old specimens. Otherwise, it does not differ from the nominate form.

About the same size as the nominate form. Pacific and Indian Oceans.

LEPIDOCHELYS
Ridley Turtles

Lepidochelys kempi
Kemp's (Atlantic) Ridley Turtle
The habits are the same as those of *L. olivacea*, from which it differs in the following points: the carapace is dark gray with only five pairs of costal scutes, the scutes on the bridge lack pores, and the legs have five free claws each. [The species is considered to be severely threatened by shrimping and other commercial fisheries.]

Up to 75 centimeters (30 inches).

Atlantic Ocean, primarily in the Gulf of Mexico and migrating north along the American East coast to the Maritime Provinces; straying to Europe.

Lepidochelys olivacea
Olive Ridley Turtle
This is the smallest of the marine turtles. It has an olive-green, somewhat heart-shaped carapace with more than five pairs of costal scutes. Each scute on the bridge has a dark pore. There are one or two free claws on the front legs. *L. olivacea* generally lives in groups in shallow saltwater bays. It is omnivorous but predominantly carnivorous.

Up to 75 centimeters (30 inches).

Indian, Pacific, and Atlantic Oceans.

FAMILY: Dermochelyidae
Leatherback Turtles

DERMOCHELYS
Leatherback Turtles

Dermochelys coriacea
Leatherback Turtle
A brown, leathery skin covers the shell and there are no distinct scutes. The carapace has seven longitudinal keels and the plastron five. The conspicuously large, gray head has a hawk-like upper mandible. The head cannot retract into the shell. The legs are gray and have no free claws in adults.

The Leatherback feeds on any marine creatures it can catch, including invertebrates, mollusks, or fish. [The major food appears to be jellyfishes and other pelagic coelenterates.] The reproductive behavior is the same as that of the other marine turtles. It is interesting that its clutches contain a large number of small infertile eggs. We know little about the habits of this largest of all turtles. [Recently it has been studied extensively on laying beaches in South

America and the Indian Ocean and it now is fairly well known. Losses of these turtles to plastic bags floating in the water have been reported, the turtles mistaking the bags for jellyfish and dying of gastric impactions.]

Reputedly up to 200 centimeters (80 inches), weighing up to 600 kilograms (1320 pounds), but these sizes may be exaggerated.

Mediterranean Sea and the Atlantic, Pacific, and Indian Oceans.

FAMILY: Carettochelyidae
Pig-nose (New Guinea Softshell) Turtles
Carettochelys
Pig-nose Turtles
Carettochelys insculpta
Pig-nose (New Guinea Softshell) Turtle

Carettochelys is something of a connecting link between the aquatic turtles and the true softshells. They have a normal bony shell, with the full complement of bones. In place of the horny scutes, however, thick skin covers the carapace. In newly hatched young the outlines of horny scutes are still visible. The flat carapace is dark olive. The head, which is the same color, ends in a blunt snout. The eyes have a reddish iris. The front legs are nearly flipper-like with only two free claws, and those of the hind legs are paddle-like; they are dark olive. The plastron and the underside of the neck and legs are white and there is a large white blotch by the eye. The snout is distinctly elongated and pig-like.

Up to 50 centimeters (20 inches).

New Guinea and northwestern Australia.

This very agile swimmer, despite heavy predation by the native peoples, is not all uncommon in southern New Guinea. It lives there mainly in larger rivers (such as the Fly River) and is not uncommon in brackish water in river mouths. The turtles mostly stay on the bottom, where they paddle around in search of food. They come to the surface only very briefly to get air and can stay under water for a long time. Apparently they can take up oxygen from the water through the network of blood vessels in the oral cavity and the cloacal sacs. They feed primarily on invertebrates, crustaceans, and fishes and also readily take vegetable food. These turtles are scarcely suitable for keeping in the large aquarium. They can grow to a very large

size and would require correspondingly large and deep swimming spaces. A minimum tank size of at least 3 meters long, 1.5 meters wide, and 80 centimeters deep (10 feet x 5 feet x 32 inches) is absolutely necessary. Therefore, they are better candidates for zoos. [They also have a reputation for aggressive behavior.]

FAMILY: Trionychidae
Softshell Turtles

CYCLANORBINAE
Flapshell Softshells

Cyclanorbis
Sub-Saharan Flapshell Softshells Turtles

Cyclanorbis elegans
Nubian Flapshell Softshell

The flat carapace has numerous longitudinal lines of tiny bumps and large, light-colored blotches. The trailing edge lacks embedded bony plates. The plastron lacks anterior callosities (callosities are rough, bony areas that may appear in the skin of the plastron over its bony plates as the turtle ages; however, they are not always clearly visible). In addition, *C. elegans* has lateral flaps of skin on the trailing edge of the plastron that fold against the carapace to protect the hind legs when the turtle retracts them. They have fully webbed feet, with the claws protruding slightly.

Up to 60 centimeters (24 inches).

From Ghana east to the Sudan.

This softshell lives in large lakes or bodies of water and is nearly strictly carnivorous. As an animal of the tropics, it requires very high temperatures (25 to 30°C, 77 to 86°F). Because of its size, it is not suitable for the terrarium hobby and the pet trade seldom carries it.

Trionyx (*Pelodiscus*) *sinensis* is one of the smaller *Trionyx* species (up to 10 inches). It is therefore a better terrarium candidate than most of the others, but is very prone to bite. Keep it separately. Photo by H. Reinhard.

Cyclanorbis senegalensis
Senegal Flapshell Softshell

In contrast to *C. elegans*, in this species there are no large, light-colored blotches on the carapace; on the other hand, juveniles have small dark blotches. Older specimens have four or more callosities. In other respects it resembles the previous species and has similar lateral flaps of skin on the plastron.

Up to 60 centimeters (24 inches).

From Senegal east to the Sudan.

The same applies here as for *C. elegans*. Because of its size, it is unsuitable for the terrarium.

CYCLODERMA
Central African Flapshell Softshells

Cycloderma aubryi
Aubry's Flapshell Softshell

The carapace, which is reddish in juveniles, has a fine dark stripe along the midline. The central callosities are oval and the lateral callosities are close together and border the rear callosities with a broad, blunt margin. Along the edge of the dorsal side of the head there are two dark longitudinal stripes that join at the tip of the snout. There is a black longitudinal stripe along the midline of the head as well as two faint parallel stripes.

Up to 55 centimeters (22 inches).

Western Africa, mostly in the Congo system.

Its habits and requirements probably are similar to those of the species of the genus *Cyclanorbis*. There is almost no information on keeping it in the terrarium.

Cycloderma frenatum
Zambezi Flapshell Softshell

The carapace is gray in juveniles and gray-green in adults. Longitudinal stripes are not present. On the plastron there is a wide separation between the two lateral callosities and the lateral and rear callosities, or they share only a very narrow border with them. Beginning at about eye height, five dark, parallel longitudinal stripes extend over the head and top of the neck.

Up to 55 centimeters (22 inches).

Eastern Africa from Zimbabwe and Mozambique to Tanzania.

The literature reports virtually nothing about this species. Because of its size, only juveniles would be suitable candidates for the terrarium.

LISSEMYS
Indian Flapshell Softshells

Lissemys punctata
Indian Flapshell Softshell

Lissemys punctata punctata
Indian Flapshell Softshell

[The name *granosa* usually is considered to be a synonym of this subspecies.]

The olive, barely arched carapace has a leathery skin. Numerous irregular yellow blotches cover it. The plastron is pale yellow to white. It has the flaps of skin that protect the hind legs mentioned under *Cyclanorbis* and *Cycloderma*. It also is able, like the box turtle, to close the front of the plastron against the carapace to protect the retracted head and front legs. The head tapers to a short, pointed snout. The large eye has a yellow iris. The gray legs end in toes with sharp claws. They are fully webbed.

Up to 25 centimeters (10 inches).

Peninsular India and Sri Lanka.

This turtle is strictly aquatic and leaves the water only to lay its eggs. In its range it chiefly lives in large, often fast-flowing rivers. It is an agile swimmer and is, in contrast to the *Trionyx* species, a very peaceful turtle that does not bite at all.

In the aquaterrarium or aquarium it is delicate and completely unsuitable for the beginner. Moreover, because it is protected under CITES, hobbyists keep very few specimens today. There are no reports of successful breeding by amateurs. The Indian Flapshells I formerly kept were strictly carnivorous and hunted actively for guppies stocked in their aquarium, although they seldom caught one. They injured themselves frequently; the specimens formerly available in the pet trade usually had shell injuries. Accordingly, we must avoid all sharp edges and corners in the aquarium. We should only use round gravel, algae-covered wood, and very fine river sand.

Lissemys punctata andersoni
Up to 25 centimeters (10 inches).
Pakistan across northern India to western Burma.

Lissemys punctata scutata
Irrawaddy basin of Burma. [Often considered a full species.]

TRIONYCHINAE
Common Softshell Turtles

Chitra
Narrow-headed Softshells
Chitra indica
Narrow-headed Softshell Turtle
The flat, nearly circular carapace has an olive-gray ground color. Irregular hieroglyph-like pale blotches with dark borders cover it. This pattern also extends across the conspicuously long neck to the short, narrow head. The eyes are closely spaced and are placed far forward. The legs end in inconspicuous toes with very sharp claws. The feet are fully webbed.
Up to 80 centimeters (32 inches).
Pakistan, India, and Bangladesh to Thailand.
This giant softshell lives in large river systems and is strictly aquatic. Its diet consists chiefly of fishes and other aquatic animals. Because of its size, it is not a good candidate for keeping in the terrarium (moreover, it bites very readily!). The pet trade almost never offers it.

PELOCHELYS
Asian Giant Softshells

Pelochelys bibroni
Asian Giant Softshell Turtle
The olive-gray, nearly circular carapace is unusually flat and the dorsal side has indistinct pale costal markings. The plastron lacks flaps of skin, but slight vestiges of the bony plates (callosities) still are present. The nearly tubular head is short and wide, without dark longitudinal stripes or other markings. The proportionately small eyes are shifted far to the front and are rather closely spaced. The sturdy legs have very full webbing, producing almost fin-like feet. Each foot ends in three sharp claws.
Up to 130 centimeters (52 inches).

Extreme eastern India through Southeast Asia and southern China (including Hainan Island) south through Indonesia and the Philippines to New Guinea.
This species has a very wide distribution. It lives in large, deep rivers and occurs both in the brackish water of river mouths and in pure salt water. Because of its size, it is an unsuitable candidate for the terrarium and the pet trade never carries it. Unlike *Chitra*, it does not bite at all. It is strictly carnivorous but we know little about its habits and virtually nothing about reproduction.

TRIONYX
Common Softshells
[This complex genus has been split into as many as nine genera for the just 15 species in the group. The generic splits are: *Amyda, Apalone, Aspideretes, Dogania, Nilssonia, Palea, Pelodiscus, Rafetus,* and *Trionyx.* The three American softshells would be placed in *Apalone,* a genus not accepted by a good part of the recent literature.]
First, a few words about keeping these turtles in the terrarium. When you see them in the pet shop as small babies, they are only about the size of a half dollar, have dainty, pointed little snouts, are elegant swimmers, and can dig themselves into the sand in no time at all! In short, these turtles are almost irresistible! But take care! On the one hand, many of these juveniles are doomed: They have been torn from their normal surroundings and weakened during shipment. They have a hard time acclimating to these changes or are unable to do so at all. On the other hand, you soon will discover that with good care the turtles grow very fast. The older they get, the more they bite, particularly their tankmates. Therefore, we must keep them singly. Because they grow to a considerable size (many species grow larger than 40 centimeters, 16 inches), they soon outgrow the tank. In any case, a large swimming space is essential for these turtles. A 40-centimeter specimen, for example, needs a tank at least 2 meters (80 inches) long. Mind you, that is for just one turtle! Furthermore, fully grown specimens have a long, flexible neck that enables them to

easily bite the careless keeper. This makes them hard to handle and dangerous to treat when they are sick.

Therefore, I advise the beginner against keeping any *Trionyx* species, and I advise the specialist to choose softshells only when he can provide the optimal conditions. I will present all the species below, but I will discuss in detail only the more familiar species.

Trionyx [Apalone] ater
Black Spiny Softshell Turtle

Because of its very limited range, this species never reaches the pet trade. [It is a relict of more southerly distribution of the Spiny Softshell, restricted to a series of small springs and canals. Its behavior is much like that of the Spiny Softshell.] The hind part of the nearly black carapace has longitudinal folds and is otherwise unmarked. The leading edge is smooth and lacks tubercles. There is a ridge in each nostril extending from the nasal septum. [Recently this turtle has been considered an isolated subspecies of *Trionyx spiniferus*.]

Up to 40 centimeters (16 inches).

Northern Mexico, restricted to springs in the Cuatro Cienegas system of Coahuila.

Trionyx [Amyda] cartilagineus
Asiatic Softshell Turtle

The carapace is flat, with numerous small, interrupted, elongated grooves distributed over the entire surface. The plastron is white and unmarked. The head is olive with yellow blotches that do not have dark borders. The snout tapers very sharply and is slightly curved upward. The legs are robust, fully webbed, and have three sturdy claws.

Up to 70 centimeters (28 inches).

Southeast Asia to Indonesia and Borneo.

A pair of Spiny Softshells, *Trionyx spiniferus*. The female is the smaller of the two. Note the different markings. Photo by W. Hemmer.

top: The Spiny Softshell, *Trionyx spiniferus*, occurs in six subspecies, which, unlike the other *Trionyx* species, usually do not bite. Photo by W. Hemmer.
bottom: *Trionyx suplanus*, the Malayan Softshell. Klingelhöffer describes it as peaceful, but the author disagrees. His specimens were aggressive as juveniles and had to be separated. Photo by H. Reinhard.

Like many other large softshells, this species lives in large bodies of water and lives down-river as far as the river mouth in brackish water; it supposedly also lives in bays in pure salt water. The pet trade has offered it regularly, but because of its size it is hard to keep.

It is strictly carnivorous (fishes, mollusks, crustaceans, and the like) and requires an average temperature of 25°C (77°F). I strongly recommend single keeping, because it is very prone to bite.

Trionyx [Rafetus] euphraticus
Euphrates Softshell Turtle

The carapace is flat and nearly circular. It has a dark olive-green ground color with numerous small, pale yellow dots that also cover the head, neck, and legs. Numerous longitudinal rows of small dots also are present on the carapace. The neck is long and the head tapers to a rather blunt snout.

The Near East from eastern Turkey to Iran.

The Euphrates Softshell lives in fairly large bodies of water with a muddy bottom. It waits for prey while buried in the mud and is able to catch fishes simply by suddenly thrusting out its head.

In captivity it takes all sorts of animal foods, including fish, beef heart and liver, snails (small ones with shell and all), dry food, and dried shrimp. It can stay under water a long time without coming up for air. (Softshells can meet 70 percent of their oxygen requirement through the leathery skin of the carapace and plastron as well as the short, finger-shaped villi inside the throat that function as gills. They meet only 30 percent of their oxygen requirement by breathing air.) I also recommend single keeping with this species, because it is aggressive not only toward its conspecifics, but toward turtles of other genera as well. It requires a temperature of 25°C (77°F). The turtle never sunbathes. The substrate should consist of fine sand.

Trionyx [Apalone] ferox
Florida Softshell Turtle

The carapace is flat and oval. It is brownish, without a dark border, but with irregular dark blotches. A few small tubercles are present only on the leading edge. The plastron is whitish. The neck is long and the head has a long, pointed snout and fleshy lips. Beginning between the eyes and extending to the tip of the snout is a Y-shaped yellow band. Yellowish longitudinal stripes also are present on the sides of the head and the neck. The legs are robust with lobe-like webbing and three sharp claws.

Up to 45 centimeters (18 inches).

Florida north to South Carolina.

The Florida Softshell lives in slow-flowing large rivers with a muddy bottom. In its habits, diet, and other requirements it is similar to other softshells. The required temperature is about 22°C (72°F) on average. Because this species also lives in brackish water, I usually add some salt to the water (2 grams per liter) with softshells to guard against fungus to which these turtles, particularly as juveniles, are susceptible. You can use normal table salt or the sea salt available in the pet trade for this purpose.

Trionyx [Nilssonia] formosus
Burmese Peacock Softshell Turtle

The flat olive-green carapace has four conspicuous eyespots that usually become paler with age and sometimes disappear entirely. The whole carapace also has irregularly distributed indistinct wide dark streaks. The plastron is white. The head, neck, and legs have light and dark mottling. The snout is relatively short, the lips fleshy, and the area around the eyes slightly swollen. The legs are robust and fully webbed; they have three claws.

Up to 40 centimeters (16 inches).

The Irrawaddy basin of Burma.

In habits this softshell does not differ from the previously discussed *Trionyx* species. It requires the same temperature as *T. cartilagineus.*

Trionyx [Aspideretes] gangeticus
Indian Softshell Turtle

This very large species lives in the river systems of the Indus, the Ganges, and the Mahanadi. The carapace is similar to that of *T. formosus* but usually has more than four eyespots. The head and legs have diagonal stripes. It is scarcely suitable for the terrarium. The habits are the same as those of the previously described species, except that we must consider its size. It also is very prone to biting and aggressive toward conspecifics.

Up to 70 centimeters (28 inches).

Pakistan across northern India to Bangladesh.

Trionyx [Aspideretes] hurum
Indian Peacock Softshell Turtle

This rather large species is found in the lower course of the Ganges and the Brahmaputra Rivers. Its four eyespots on the carapace are very conspicuous and attractive. The carapace also has wide pale rings. Large, irregular, pale blotches cover the rest of the carapace. It has a yellow blotch on the top of the head and another large yellow blotch extends across the snout. The snout is rather blunt in contrast to the other species. Its habits are similar to those of the other large *Trionyx* species.

Up to 60 centimeters (24 inches).

Eastern India and Bangladesh.

Trionyx [Aspideretes] leithi
Leith's Softshell Turtle

This species also has two pairs of eyespots, but the remaining blotches are absent. The top of the head has a continuous dark longitudinal stripe between the eyes. To the side of the eyes it has dark longitudinal lines that diverge to the rear. The habits are the same as those of the previously described species.

Up to 50 centimeters (20 inches).

Northern and central India.

Trionyx [Apalone] muticus
Smooth Softshell

Trionyx muticus muticus
Midland Smooth Softshell

The completely smooth olive-brown carapace has pale yellow blotches and dots. A dark marking is present on top of the head. Extending from the snout, and continuing at eye height, is a yellow, unbordered temporal stripe. In *T. m. calvatus* this stripe has a thick black border and the turtle also lacks the dark marking on top of the head. The snout is very long. This species has the same robust legs, fully webbed feet, and sharp claws as the previously described species. It also exhibits a similar behavior. It is very prone to bite, so that I recommend single keeping. It requires an average temperature of 25°C (77°F).

Up to 35 centimeters (14 inches).

Central and southern United States except in the Gulf Coast drainages.

Trionyx muticus calvatus
Gulf Coast Smooth Softshell

Up to 35 centimeters (14 inches).

Southern United States in rivers draining into the Gulf of Mexico.

Trionyx [Aspideretes] nigricans
Black Softshell Turtle

This protected species is extraordinarily rare. It is easy to distinguish from the other species because the carapace and plastron, as well as all soft parts, are dark brown to black. The head is unmarked. Its habits are poorly known but probably do not differ from those of the other Indian species.

Up to 40 centimeters (16 inches).

A shrine pond near Chittagong, Bangladesh.

Trionyx [Pelodiscus] sinensis
Chinese Softshell Turtle

In juveniles, a pattern of fine pale and dark squiggles covers the flat olive carapace. The plastron is yellowish and sometimes has dark blotches in juveniles. A dark longitudinal stripe begins behind the eye and extends to the rear. The head has pale blotches that become paler or even disappear with age. The legs are olive, very robust, fully webbed, and have three very sturdy, sharp claws.

Up to 25 centimeters (10 inches).

Eastern Asia from Siberia south through Korea and eastern China to Vietnam, including Japan and Taiwan; introduced into Hawaii.

This species has a very large range for a softshell. It lives primarily in slow-flowing rivers with sandy or muddy inlets as well as in fairly large lakes. Because of its small size for a *Trionyx* species, it is a particularly good candidate for keeping in large aquaterraria (5:1 water to land ratio). Fully grown specimens swim elegantly through the tank. They are extremely exciting to watch as they chase and catch a food fish. It is interesting to observe how the turtle always turns the captured fish so that it can swallow it head-first. They are able to swallow whole surprisingly large fish. For example, one of my turtles with a carapace length of about 20 centimeters (8 inches) swallowed whole sardines that were 10 and 12 centimeters (4 to 5 inches) long and sometimes ate three or four in succession. After that, the turtle often fasted for a week. These softshells also are very fond of all other animal foods, such as beetles, aquatic snails, and large cockroaches, as well as beef heart, beef liver, and gelatin food. I advise keeping this species singly, because it is very prone to bite. In this connection let me point out that injuries such as scrapes, bites, and cuts can be very dangerous in all softshells because they are susceptible to infections that are slow to heal. Softshells also injure themselves much more readily than do typical turtles with a tougher shell.

It requires an average temperature of 26°C (79°F). Outdoor keeping is feasible but not necessary because the turtles never go on land to bask. In my experience a softshell that goes on land and spends much time there usually is sick.

Trionyx [Apalone] spiniferus
Spiny Softshell Turtle
Trionyx spiniferus spiniferus
Eastern Spiny Softshell

This wide-ranging and common species resembles *T. ferox* in body form and shares part of the same range with that species. The main distinguishing color characters from *T. ferox* are the presence of one or more lines around the shell's margin and the absence of numerous squarish blotches. The numerous (about six) subspecies differ in adult size, presence or absence of yellow pustules on the shell, and the presence of one or two (or more) narrow dark lines around part of the carapace. They are very difficult to distinguish in life.

Up to 45 centimeters (18 inches).

The species ranges over the central United States from the Canadian border (with a few Canadian records) to the Gulf of Mexico (except the East Coast and Florida) and west to the Arizona-California border and Montana, plus northeastern Mexico. This subspecies occurs from the Great Lakes over the eastern central United States south to northern Mississippi.

In habits it does not differ from *T. ferox*, except that it tolerates lower temperatures averaging about 23°C (73°F). Unlike the other *Trionyx* species, *T. spiniferus* does not bite. Therefore, you can keep it in groups. This makes the species easier to breed. The spherical eggs were 25 millimeters (1 inch) in diameter. The incubation period was 110 days. [Many keepers would not agree that this species does not bite and would say that it is just as vicious as any other softshell, inflicting bites on other tank inhabitants and also the keeper if it gets a chance. Caution is advised.]

Trionyx spiniferus asperus
Gulf Coast Spiny Softshell
　　Up to 45 centimeters (18 inches).
　　North Carolina to Mississippi.

Trionyx spiniferus emoryi
Texas Spiny Softshell
　　Up to 37 centimeters (15 inches).
　　The Rio Grande basin of Texas and adjoining northern and northeastern Mexico.

Trionyx spiniferus guadalupensis
Guadalupe Spiny Softshell
　　To about 35 centimeters (14 inches).
　　Central Texas.

Trionyx spiniferus hartwegi
Western Spiny Softshell
　　Up to 40 centimeters (16 inches).
　　The Great Plains to Montana and New Mexico.

Trionyx spiniferus pallidus
Pallid Spiny Softshell
　　To about 35 centimeters (14 inches).
　　Southern Oklahoma and eastern Texas through Louisiana.

Trionyx [Palea] steindachneri
Wattle-necked Softshell Turtle
　　The flat dark olive carapace has a slight keel and a few large black blotches. The plastron is white with numerous indistinct dark blotches. On both sides of the back of the head there is a wide yellow-white dark-bordered band that runs downward and to the rear. On each side of the nape, as well as on the trailing edge of the carapace, there is a group of large tubercles.
　　Up to 24 centimeters (9.5 inches).
　　Southern China including Hainan Island.

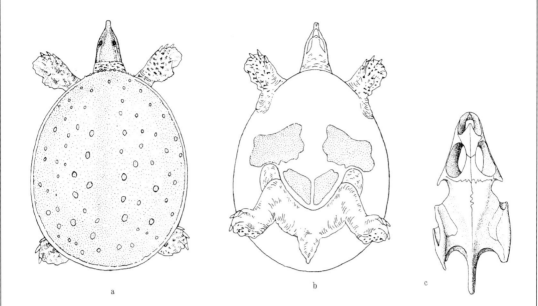

Eastern Spiny Softshell, *Trionyx spiniferus spiniferus*. Illustration: E. Bobbe in Wermuth/Mertens: Schildkröten — Krokodile — Brückenechsen.

This species likes slow-flowing bodies of water with a muddy bottom. Its habits are similar to those of the other *Trionyx* species, particularly *T. sinensis*.

Because of its small size for a softshell, it would make a particularly well-suited terrarium charge. Furthermore, unlike most other *Trionyx* species, it supposedly does not bite at all. This is another plus and also would make it easier to breed. Unfortunately, the pet trade rarely offers it.

Trionyx [Dogania] subplanus
Malayan Softshell Turtle

The gray-brown carapace is rather flat and has longitudinal grooves on the surface. The dark longitudinal stripe on the midline and four dark spots described in the literature were not present in my specimens. Unlike other softshells, the neck is quite short and thick. The large head ends in a sharp snout. On its top is a fine dark pattern that begins as a triangle between the eyes and extends backward in three dark parallel lines. The red blotch also described in the literature was not present in my specimens, although they were still juveniles when I acquired them. The plastron is white. The legs are robust and the toes are fully webbed with sharp claws.

Up to 25 centimeters (10 inches).

Southern Southeast Asia into Indonesia and Borneo.

This species usually lives in waters with abundant vegetation and a muddy bottom in which it likes to bury itself. In the aquarium, we should offer the turtles a substrate of fine river sand at least 10 centimeters (4 inches) deep. It is remarkable how quickly this turtle can dig itself in. When it thinks it has dug deep enough, it shakes itself briefly to distribute the sand over any exposed body parts. After several minutes, when everything seems quiet above, it thrusts the tip of the snout upward, but only far enough that the snout barely protrudes from the sand.

My specimens were strictly carnivorous. I noticed that they preferred food with a red color. Juveniles liked tubifex worms and bloodworms. Later they took finely chopped beef heart and earthworms, which they, like most aquatic turtles, were particularly fond of. They also readily took small, freshly killed freshwater fishes or pieces of saltwater fishes. Occasionally they even took well-soaked dried shrimp.

I cannot concur with the claims of some authors that this species is very peaceful. My specimens were very prone to bite and were quarrelsome with one another. Therefore, single keeping is absolutely advisable. When we breed the adults, we must keep them in very large tanks with plenty of hiding places where they can establish territories. This species has bred in captivity and is easier to breed because it does not reach the size of most other *Trionyx* species. The adults, which are fully grown at 20 to 25 centimeters (8 to 10 inches), do not need too large a breeding facility.

Trionyx [Trionyx] triunguis
African Softshell Turtle

The flat, nearly black carapace is almost circular and has numerous small pale dots. The plastron is light in color. Light-colored spots are present on top of the broad olive head and become more line-like on the sides. The neck and legs also have dark dots. The snout is very long. The legs are robust and paddle-like, fully webbed, and have three sharp claws.

Up to 90 centimeters (36 inches).

Central Africa north along the Nile to the eastern Mediterranean in Israel and Turkey.

This large species lives in large rivers, where it spends most of its time in the muddy inlets. It requires a temperature of about 26°C (79°F) and is strictly carnivorous. I do not recommend it for the terrarium because the juveniles grow very rapidly and soon become difficult to keep. Furthermore, it is very prone to bite.

FAMILY: Pelomedusidae
African and American Side-necked Turtles

The species of this family are not true sidenecks like the Australian species because they first retract the head slightly and only then turn the head to the side.

PELOMEDUSA
Helmeted Turtles

Pelomedusa subrufa
Helmeted Turtle

The relatively flat dark gray to dark brown carapace has conspicuous growth rings. The edges are not serrated. In juveniles the carapace has a yellowish border that later disappears. The plastron varies from a yellowish color with a large, dark, somewhat blurry

blotch along the margin and the seams to completely black. The top of the head usually is dark olive and often is completely unmarked. The throat and underside of the neck contrast sharply with the olive head. The olive, robust legs all have five claws. This is an important character that distinguishes *Pelomedusa* and *Pelusios* from the genus *Podocnemis* and its relatives. Another important feature is the rigid plastron of this species as opposed to the movable plastron of the *Pelusios* species.

Up to 25 centimeters (10 inches).

All of Africa but the northern deserts, plus Madagascar and the southwestern tip of the Arabian peninsula.

In its range it lives in almost every slowflowing body of water, lake, or pond with a muddy bottom. During the hottest season, hence the dry period, when many of these waters dry up completely, it stays dug in or dried in the mud in a kind of estivation. It reawakens when the rainy season arrives and the pools and ponds fill with water again.

This species also wanders extensively on land and thus does not necessarily appear to be site-faithful. It is a quite hardy terrarium charge. Do not keep it with smaller conspecifics, because it often is quite prone to bite. Its dietary needs are modest, and it eats all kinds of animal foods, as well as gelatin food, and sometimes (although rarely) vegetable food. It needs rather high temperatures averaging about 26°C (79°F), so I advise keeping it outdoors only in midsummer. It is not fond of basking and usually lives secretively in the aquaterrarium. It has bred successfully in the terrarium.

PELUSIOS
African Hinged Terrapins

[The taxonomy of this genus has become quite confused of late, with most former subspecies being elevated to specific rank on the basis of very small distinctions. Some authors recognize 16 to 20 (or more) species, though the species all look very much alike. The following treatment is quite conservative, but most hobbyists would find even these few species difficult to recognize.]

Pelusios adansoni
Adanson's Mud Turtle

Pelusios adansoni adansoni
The slightly arched carapace is yellowish to pale brown with radiating brown lines and blotches. The edge is not serrated. The plastron is yellowish and usually unmarked. The seam along the midline between the humeral scutes is at least three times as long as the seam between the pectoral scutes. The transverse plastral hinge (typical of the genus), which allows the front of the plastron to close against the carapace to protect the front part of the head and front legs, runs straight across the middle of the plastron. The joint has limited flexibility, however, and becomes noticeably more rigid with age. The yellow top of the head has brown mottling or squiggles. The legs are robust, with webbing between the toes of the hind feet.

Up to 15 centimeters (6 inches).

Western and central Africa.

It lives in about the same biotope as *Pelomedusa subrufa* and likes shallow pools and other waters with abundant vegetation and numerous hiding places. Like all *Pelusios* species, it likes to live secretively and is crepuscular in habits. It does not bask at all and is predominantly aquatic. It takes all sorts of animal foods, whether living or dead, as well as gelatin food. As the smallest *Pelusios* species, it is a good candidate for the aquaterrarium (3:1 ratio of water to land). The species requires a temperature of about 26°C (79°F) so outdoor keeping is possible in summer but is not absolutely necessary because of its habits. I am unaware of any captive breeding, but it certainly must be possible and may already have happened.

Pelusios adansoni nanus
Western Africa (Angola, Congo, Zaire).

Pelusios carinatus
Western and central Africa (Republic of the Congo and Zaire).

Pelusios castaneus
From western Africa across central Africa to Zanzibar, plus Madagascar and the Seychelles. [This range includes the form or species *castanoides*, which occurs in eastern Africa while the typical *castaneus* occurs in western Africa.]

Pelusios gabonensis
African Forest Turtle
The dark brown, flat carapace has a dark stripe along the midline. It is distinctly narrower in front than in the rear. The edges are not serrated. The plastron is almost completely black with light-colored seams between the scutes, and the medial seam between the humeral scutes is at most twice as long as the seam between the pectoral scutes. The transverse hinge of the plastron forms a blunt angle that is open to the front. On top of the yellow-brown head there is a black Y-shaped marking. The legs are robust with sturdy claws.

Up to 25 centimeters (10 inches).

Western and central Africa.

In its habits, diet, and temperature requirements it does not differ from the previously described species.

Pelusios niger
West African Black Turtle
The rather flat carapace is black and not serrated, growth rings are clearly visible, and the plastron also is black. The head is broad, nearly triangular, and sometimes has light-colored dots. Adults have a hooked upper mandible. The legs are robust and end in toes with sturdy claws. Webbing is present only on the hind legs.

Up to 25 centimeters (10 inches).

Western Africa from Sierra Leone to Gabon.

In habits it does not differ from *Pelusios adansoni*.

Pelusios sinuatus
East African Serrated Mud Turtle
The somewhat arched carapace is olive-green in juveniles and turns gray-brown to blackish brown as the turtle ages. The trailing edge of the carapace is distinctly serrated and the posterior edges of the vertebral scutes have keel-like serrations but later become flat. The pale plastron has a distinct black border. The legs are very robust, appearing thick, and have sturdy claws. Only the hind legs are webbed.

Up to 45 centimeters (18 inches).

Eastern and southeastern Africa.

This largest of the *Pelusios* species very closely resembles the previously described species though a peculiarity has been reported for this species: the turtles nearly went wild over somewhat rotten lettuce leaves, which they did not bite off in pieces but rather swallowed whole. On this topic I would like to note that in my experience aquatic turtles of all kinds should always be offered plants in some form occasionally. Turtles that have taken a strictly carnivorous diet all year often suddenly develop a taste for some sort of fruit or lettuce. Naturally, the reverse also can be true. Because of its size and tendency to bite, *P. sinuatus* is a poor candidate for normal terrarium keeping.

Pelusios subniger
East African Black Mud Turtle

The flat black carapace has large brownish blotches. The trailing edge is not serrated and is rounded. The plastron usually is yellow with dark patches. The gular scute is narrower in front and the hind part of the plastron is narrower and has a distinct indentation. The top of the head is olive-gray with black dots and streaks. On the underside of the throat there is a pair of small barbels. The legs are very robust, with webbing between the toes of the hind legs.

Up to 40 centimeters (16 inches).

Southeastern Africa as well as Madagascar, Mauritius (introduced), and the Seychelles.

Because of its range in a heavily collected area, the pet trade carries it somewhat regularly. Because it grows very large, however, it is suitable for terrarium keeping only as a juvenile, and anyone who wants to acquire a turtle of this species should consider what will be done with it after it has increased ten-fold in size. Few hobbyists can offer turtles with a carapace length exceeding 30 centimeters (12 inches) a terrarium of the proper size.

Concerning the habits, diet, temperature, and keeping requirements, it does not differ from the previously discussed species.

Pelusios williamsi
Williams' Mud Turtle
Pelusios williamsi williamsi

Pelusios subniger, the African Black Mud Turtle, is a relatively regular offering in the pet trade, but in the full-grown state of 16 inches it is suitable only for large enclosures. Photo by H. Reinhard.

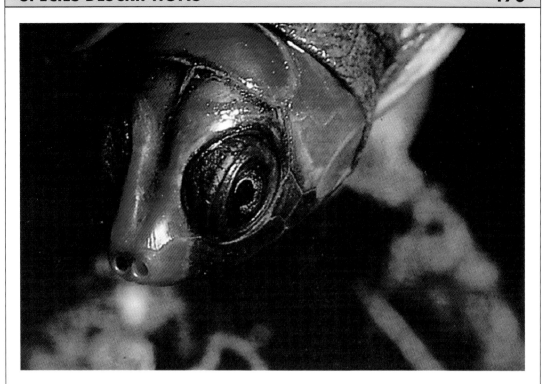

top: *Podocnemis erythrocephala* (formerly *cayennensis*), the Red-headed River Turtle, is certainly the most beautiful member of its genus. Photo by W. Hemmer.
bottom: The Arrau River Turtle, *Podocnemis expansa*, grows to a length of 80 centimeters and therefore is the largest river turtle. It requires enormous enclosures. Photo by H. Reinhard.

Southeastern Africa in the Lake Victoria region.

Pelusios williamsi lutescens

Southeastern Africa in the vicinity of Lakes Albert and Edward and their tributaries as well as the Semliki River.

PODOCNEMIS
River Turtles

Podocnemis dumeriliana
Big-headed River Turtle

[This species usually is placed in the genus *Peltocephalus* and differs from the other American *Podocnemis* by having a hooked upper jaw and lacking a deep groove between the eyes.]

The slightly arched carapace is smooth and dark gray and still has a distinct keel even in old age. The plastron is grayish yellow. The infragular scute separates completely the gular scutes and the seam between the femoral scutes is longer than the one between the anal scutes. The sturdy legs are gray and are fully webbed between the toes. The front legs have five robust, sharp claws, and the hind legs have four. This is true of all *Podocnemis* species.

Up to 48 centimeters (19 inches).

Northeastern South America, the Guianas, Orinoco, and Amazon.

This species lives mostly in the inlets of rivers. It is strictly aquatic and goes on land only to bask or to lay its eggs.

I am not aware of any information about keeping in captivity. Because of its size, however, it is not suitable for the normal terrarium. In its dietary, temperature, and keeping requirements, it does not differ from the familiar *Podocnemis* species.

Podocnemis erythrocephala
Red-headed River Turtle

The slightly arched carapace is brown only in babies and later turns gray-black to black. It is not serrated. The outermost margin is bright red in juveniles but later becomes somewhat paler. The plastron is beige to light gray. A bright red blotch begins below the nostrils and extends upward between the eyes, where it splits and then ends. At some distance

behind the eye there is a red blotch on each side. In some specimens the two blotches extend across the top of the head and meet at the midline. The margin of the upper mandible has a sharply angled indentation at the tip of the snout that extends upward between the nostrils to about the middle of the head. The legs are gray-black to black and have full webbing. Sharp claws are present.

Up to 27 centimeters (11 inches).

Northern South America in the middle Amazon and the Orinoco and their tributaries.

It lives in the river systems of its range but is more abundant in the tributaries. It is strictly aquatic and comes on land only to lay its eggs or to bask on a protruding log or boulder from which it drops back into the water at the slightest disturbance. I have observed this behavior in all the *Podocnemis* species I have kept. They remain somewhat shy even after many years in captivity. The dietary requirements change with the growth of the turtles. Young turtles and growing specimens are predominantly carnivorous. I have fed juveniles a diet of bloodworms, tubifex, small crustaceans, meadow plankton, finely chopped beef heart or liver, small-grained turtle food, dried shrimp, small aquatic snails, and fish of all kinds, as well as some lettuce, dandelion, and bananas. When the turtles are older, they become predominantly herbivorous and their diet consists of lettuce, dandelion, all kinds of fruits (they are particularly fond of strawberries), as well as dog food, fish, and beef heart. They require an average temperature of 26°C (79°F). In my experience, the *Podocnemis* species require rather high temperatures and do not tolerate low temperatures. Therefore, I keep my specimens in the outdoor pond at most in midsummer and bring them inside immediately when there is a sudden drop in temperature. You should be careful with ultraviolet rays because the eyes of all *Podocnemis* are very sensitive to an irradiation period of more than 15 minutes (from a distance of one meter).

Podocnemis expansa
Arrau River Turtle

The only slightly arched carapace is light brown in juveniles and later turns gray-brown. The plastron is yellow to grayish yellow. On top of the head there is a deep longitudinal furrow between the eyes. The upper mandible has a rounded, unnotched front margin. On the underside of the head there are two barbels on the chin. The head has yellow blotches in juveniles. The intergular plate is much narrower in front than the greatest length of the gular plate. The neck and legs are gray. The toes are fully webbed; the front legs have five sharp claws, the hind legs four.

Up to 80 centimeters (32 inches).

Northern South America.

This, the largest of all river turtles, lives exclusively in the drainage areas of the Orinoco and the Amazon. It is almost strictly aquatic. Carnivorous as a juvenile, it later prefers a vegetarian diet. Because of its size and its growth, it is at most a suitable charge for zoos or show terraria. Its average required temperature, like that of *P. erythrocephala*, is about 26°C (79°F).

Podocnemis lewyana
Magdalena River Turtle

The dark, somewhat strongly arched carapace is only slightly serrated on the trailing edge and has a sharply angled notch between the two supracaudal scutes. The plastron is light gray to grayish yellow. The intergular scute is just as wide in front as the greatest length of the gular scutes. The upper mandible has a rounded, unnotched front margin. On the top of the head there is a longitudinal furrow between the eyes. The head does not have yellow blotches. The robust legs are strongly webbed between the toes. In other particulars it is similar to the previous species.

Up to 40 centimeters (16 inches).

The Rio Magdalena basin of Colombia.

This species lives in the Rio Magdalena region and perhaps in adjacent river systems of Venezuela. It does not differ in its requirements regarding diet, temperature, and so forth from the previously mentioned species. There is virtually no information about terrarium keeping in the literature.

Podocnemis madagascariensis
Madagascan Big-headed Turtle

[This, the only Old World river turtle, usually is put into a distinct genus, *Erymnochelys*, that differs from the American species in the short intergular scute of the plastron that fails to separate the gular scutes.]

The only slightly arched, dark carapace has a slight keel in old age and is not serrated. On the plastron the gular scutes meet in the middle behind the small intergular scute. The seam between the femoral scutes is shorter than the one between the anal scutes. On the head the cranial plates form a common medial seam behind the tapering intercranial scute. The legs are also robust. The toes have sturdy claws and are strongly webbed.

Up to 35 centimeters (14 inches).

Madagascar.

This is the only species of river turtle that does not come from South America, an unusual distribution that indicates that the river turtles probably once were far more widely distributed than they are today. Despite the great distance separating them, this species does not differ in its habits or its temperature and dietary requirements from the other species. It also grows relatively large. There is little information about keeping it in the terrarium.

Podocnemis sextuberculata
Six-tubercled River Turtle

The dark gray, slightly arched carapace has a distinct dorsal keel that forms a conspicuous hump on the second vertebral scute. The plastron is grayish yellow. Juveniles have a tubercle on each of the (paired) pectoral, abdominal, and femoral scutes. On top of the gray-black head, which is unmarked, there is a deep groove between the eyes. The neck and legs are gray. The feet are very strongly webbed, the front legs with five claws, the hind legs four.

Up to 30 centimeters (12 inches).

The Amazon basin of South America.

This quite rare turtle lives mainly in the Amazon region of northern Brazil. In its habits and other requirements it does not differ in any way from the previously discussed species. It does well in an aquaterrarium with a water to land ratio of 7:1. Because it is so rare, however, there are scarcely any instances of captive keeping. It would be a good charge because it does not grow too large.

Above: The Yellow-spotted River Turtle, *Podocnemis unifilis,* was, at one time, a regular import to the pet trade. Now, however, it is a protected species that is never imported. Photo by B. Kahl.

Right: Six-tubercled River Turtle, *Podocnemis sextuberculata.* Illustration: M. Bechtle in Wermuth/ Mertens: Schildkröten — Krokodile — Brückenechsen.

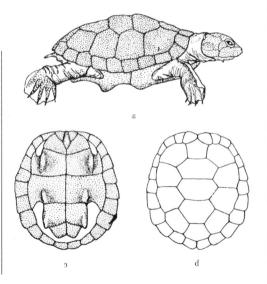

Podocnemis unifilis
Yellow-spotted River Turtle

The slightly arched carapace is black and has a keel along the midline. It has a deep notch in front and is significantly wider in the rear than in the front. The plastron is light gray and unmarked. The head, which tapers strongly toward the snout, is black and has an irregular pattern of bright yellow blotches both on top and on the side. This color becomes paler and paler with age. Only males retain the color. The neck and legs are slate gray. Between the toes there is well-developed webbing. The front legs have five sturdy and sharp claws, the hind legs four.

Up to 45 centimeters (18 inches).

Northern South America.

This probably is the most abundant *Podocnemis* species. It lives in large rivers and is also almost exclusively aquatic, but is quite fond of basking. Until it became protected, the pet trade offered it regularly. Juveniles are not hard to rear if they are given a varied diet. Juveniles are primarily carnivorous, and it is noteworthy that they prefer food with a red color. They always prefer chopped beef heart, bloodworms, tubifex, and daphnia. I also offer small crustaceans, dry foods of all kinds, gelatin food, and in particular meadow plankton. Meadow plankton is particularly important for rearing young turtles because it includes a wide variety of animals and thus a diversity of nutriments. Unfortunately, the Yellow-spotted River Turtle quickly grows to a very large size, so the largest aquaterraria then are necessary to house it. It needs a relatively high average temperature of 26°C (79°F). At this temperature *P. unifilis* is a grateful and hardy charge. In 1985 a turtle keeper I know was the first to breed it in captivity. Of the 21 hatchlings, in 1986 there were 19 juveniles still alive. In the meantime, they have grown significantly. The Frankfurt Zoo and others also have bred this turtle.

Podocnemis vogli
Savanna River Turtle

The moderately arched, dark carapace has a paler area on the trailing edge of each dorsal scute, covering about a third of the surface. The carapace has a slight keel or no keel and a slight indentation on the leading edge and is not wider in the rear than in front. The plastron is grayish yellow. The head is rather blunt and has irregular pale blotches. The sturdy legs are strongly webbed between the toes and end in sharp claws.

Up to 28 centimeters (11 inches).

Northeastern South America in Colombia and Venezuela.

This relatively small river turtle lives primarily in the Orinoco River system in Venezuela. It does not differ from the previously discussed species in its requirements. The pet trade virtually never offers this turtle, so there are few reports on terrarium keeping.

Chelodina longicollis longicollis, the Common Snake-necked Turtle. It is notably peaceful towards all other inhabitants of the terrarium. Photo by Photo by L. Trutnau.

FAMILY: Chelidae
True Side-necks

CHELODINA
Australasian Snake-necks

Chelodina expansa
Giant Snake-necked Turtle

The flat, olive-brown to gray-brown carapace is not serrated. It is distinctly wider toward the rear. The plastron is uniformly whitish and the seams do not show any dark color. The head and neck are brownish above and yellowish below. The neck is very long, its length, fully extended, corresponding to about 65 percent of the carapace length. The brownish legs are very robust; the toes are webbed and end in sharp claws.

Up to 48 centimeters (19 inches).

Southeastern Australia.

This familiar snake-neck lives mainly in large rivers and lakes. Like all chelodinas, it is an agile swimmer. Because of its maneuverability and its long neck, which it can thrust forward like a snake, it has no trouble catching fish. Because of its size (it grows very fast), *C. expansa* is a poor choice for the terrarium. It is strictly carnivorous. Temporarily cooler temperatures do not bother this species. The species has been bred several times and usually lays a total of about 40 eggs (their average weight about 24 grams) usually twice a year. The incubation period sometimes lasts more than six months, but in my opinion the determining factor is the temperature of the substrate in which the eggs mature. John Cann reports in *Tortoises of Australia* that when one of his females laid 18 eggs outdoors, he left half outside and put the other half in an incubator. The eggs in the incubator had a developmental period of 154 days. The eggs remaining in the original nest needed about a year to develop. He reports further that he knew of a case in which a nest was opened after 664 days and living babies emerged!

Chelodina longicollis, the Common Snake-necked Turtle. Illustration: E. Bobbe in Wermuth/Mertens: Schildkröten — Krokodile — Brückenechsen.

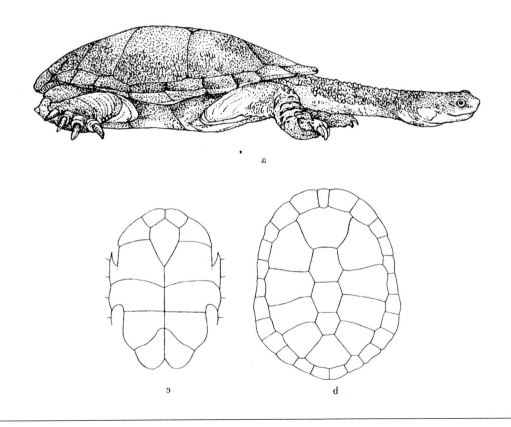

$\mathfrak{b}$

$\mathfrak{c}$ d

Chelodina longicollis
Common Snake-necked Turtle

The rather flat, dark brown carapace widens significantly toward the rear and is not serrated. The plastron is yellowish, the seams between the individual ventral scutes with dark borders. The two gular scutes displace the intergular scute to the rear. The combined length of the head and neck makes up 65 percent of the carapace length (I have consistently obtained this result in measurements of my own specimens). On the upper side of the dark gray neck are numerous small tubercles. The legs are dark gray, very robust, and end in toes with well-developed webbing and sharp claws.

Up to 30 centimeters (12 inches) but usually stays smaller, particularly in captivity.

Eastern Australia from southeastern Queensland south.

C. l. longicollis lives in pools, ponds, and slow-flowing bodies of water with shallow inlets in Queensland, New South Wales, and Victoria. It feeds on all kinds of aquatic animals, including mollusks and fishes. Like all snakenecks, it is very agile when hunting fish. In an aquaterrarium that held, among other species, *C. l. longicollis*, I kept various guppies, red and green swordtails, and platies, and never imagined that the turtles could catch the agile fishes. This was true for *Podocnemis, Pseudemys, Chrysemys, Clemmys*, and *Mauremys*. The chelodinas, however, caught one fish after another. It also is worth mentioning that they first hunted all the red-colored fishes and only after they ate all of them also took notice of the differently colored ones. All chelodinas are strictly carnivorous. When I feed bananas, many emyduras (which otherwise also are strictly carnivorous) "give in" and take the fruits, but *C. l. longicollis* refuses bananas. I have held out pieces of strawberry and tomato to the constantly begging specimens of this genus and they avidly snapped them up, but they always spit the tidbits out again. I therefore am very skeptical of the reports that repeatedly show up in the literature claiming that chelodinas take vegetable foods. *C. l. longicollis* is one of the most highly recommended turtles for the aquaterrarium. It is almost insensitive to low temperatures. I put all my chelodinas and emyduras in the outdoor pond in April, and they stay there until late September or early October, depending on the weather. In the unusual summer weather of 1992 the pond temperature, despite the heater, fell to 18°C (65°F) and on one particularly cool night even to 16°C (60°F). These circumstances did not affect the condition of the chelodinas (and emyduras) at all; despite the low temperatures, the chelodinas begged for food. The species breeds regularly in captivity. With the strict ban on the export of these turtles from Australia, the babies offered today are almost exclusively captive-bred specimens.

Chelodina longicollis sulcifera

According to the most recent findings this name is not a subspecies, but rather at most a "variety." It is said to be a juvenile of *Chelodina longicollis* before the first molt of the horny scutes.

The carapace is almost exactly the same as that of the nominate form, the only difference being that the dorsal scutes have concentric grooves. Otherwise there are no differences. For a long time, experts classified it as a separate subspecies, but it now is considered a synonym. In habits and terrarium keeping it does not differ from *C. l. longicollis*. It is also a very commendable charge, but seldom is offered in the pet trade.

Up to 20 centimeters (8 inches).
Southeastern Australia.

Chelodina novaeguineae
New Guinea Snake-necked Turtle

This species has a flat, dark olive-brown carapace that is nearly oval in outline, slightly wider in the rear. The plastron and the entire underside are yellowish, only some of the seams between the ventral scutes having dark borders. The upper side of the head, neck, and legs is gray-brown to nearly black, the undersides as well as the soft parts whitish. At the end of the legs are well-developed toes with extensive webbing and long, sharp claws.

Up to 18 centimeters (7 inches).

Southeastern New Guinea, Roti island west of New Guinea, and northeastern Australia in Queensland and the adjacent Northern Territory.

Like its relatives, it lives in ponds, pools, and slow-flowing streams or rivers. It also is strictly carnivorous and in other respects is similar to the previously discussed species. Because of its small size, it is of course a particularly good candidate for the terrarium. It is very hardy and insensitive to cooler temperatures. Each year between December and March, my two females laid usually 10 to 12 elongate-oval eggs that always were infertile, although a sexually mature male shared the aquarium with them. By chance I read the following tip in the journal *Die Schildkrote* (issue 2, year 3, July 1983): "*Chelodina novaeguineae* copulated successfully only after the water level had been lowered so far that the males could barely reach the water's surface with the tip of the snout when they mounted the females." I would like to mention an observation that I have made with ready-to-lay female snake-necks: After they excavated the nest cavity, they always stuck their head in the hole. They often abandoned this hole to dig a new hole in a different location (sometimes not until the following day), and under certain circumstances they repeated this procedure several times until they finally laid their eggs. I suspect that the turtle checks the nest temperature with its head, and only when it is satisfactory begins with egg laying. In most cases it also uses the same site for subsequent clutches.

Chelodina oblonga
Narrow-breasted Snake-necked Turtle

The flat, dark olive-brown to black carapace becomes wider toward the rear and is not serrated. The plastron is ivory colored and is concave in males. The head and neck are dark grayish olive and are lighter in color below. The side and underside of the head have faint pale mottling. The head and neck together are longer than the carapace in adults, so the turtle is unable to hide the head completely under the shell. The legs are robust, with well-developed webbing and sharp claws.

Up to 23 centimeters (9 inches).
Southwestern Western Australia.

This chelodina lives in about the same habitats as the previously discussed species. It is strictly carnivorous and also predominantly aquatic. Some keepers describe it as extremely delicate and advise against keeping it in the terrarium, but others present it as a very highly recommended charge that is completely without problems about diet. Keep in mind, however, that those who recommend it tend to live in Australia and thus the turtles do not have to face the difficulty of acclimating to a different climate and different environmental conditions. A few keepers have succeeded in breeding them. Females lay their eggs in the months of October and November. The eggs mature in about 200 days.

Chelodina parkeri
Parker's Snake-necked Turtle

Up to 25 centimeters (10 inches).
South-central New Guinea.

Chelodina rugosa
Northern Australian Snake-necked Turtle

The flat, brown carapace is lighter in color toward the margin. The plastron is pale yellow. The head and neck are very long and are brownish gray in color with scattered small red dots, especially on the neck. The robust legs are brownish gray with webbing and end in sharp claws.

Up to 40 centimeters (16 inches).
Northern Australia.

It too lives in slow-flowing bodies of water, ponds, and lakes and is carnivorous, with a diet consisting of aquatic insects, crustaceans, and fish. In captivity it is a candidate for outdoor keeping during the warm season. It is not common in its relatively small range, therefore exports are extremely rare, particularly since Australia has a general ban on the export of animals. In Australia it has bred successfully in the terrarium. The female laid 14 eggs with an average size of 35 X 25 centimeters (1.4 x 1 inches). I have no information about the incubation period.

Chelodina siebenrocki
Siebenrock's Snake-necked Turtle

The reddish brown carapace is flat and significantly wider in the rear than in the front. Some specimens have a nearly black carapace. The plastron usually is grayish yellow to yellow, and the head and neck are brownish gray and

Chelodina parkeri, Parker's Side-necked Turtle, a native of New Guinea, has been bred on a few occasions by German hobbyists. It is very rare in the pet trade. Photo by M. Mohr.

nearly as long as the carapace. The legs are robust with well-developed webbing on the toes.

Up to 30 centimeters (12 inches).

South-central New Guinea and offshore islands.

Like the other chelodinas, it lives mainly in bodies of water within marshy regions and supposedly spends more time outside the water. When threatened it does not seek out the water, but rather stays half-hidden in the mud with retracted head, neck, and legs, at least according to some observers. Other keepers, however, have not observed this behavior, instead reporting that the turtles were strictly aquatic even when they had the opportunity to go on land. It has been described as more warmth-loving than the other chelodinas. This species has been bred in captivity. The babies had an average length of 4 centimeters (1.6 inches) and weighed about 12.5 grams (0.45 ounce). The female always chose particularly warm places to lay the eggs, which had an average weight of 24 grams (0.8 ounce). The maturation period was about six months. The hatching period sometimes extended over two or three weeks, thus much longer than with other turtles. The females lay twice a year, with about 20 eggs per clutch. The young need a rather varied diet because otherwise they are susceptible to collapsed bellies that later often do not grow normally.

Besides the fairly high temperature (about 24°C, 75°F) it requires, it is similar to the other chelodinas regarding the remaining keeping requirements and the strictly carnivorous habits. It seldom is available in the pet trade.

Chelodina steindachneri
Steindachner's Snake-necked Turtle

The brownish carapace is flat and nearly circular. Along the middle of the second, third, and fourth vertebral scutes there is an indentation in the form of a furrow. The plastron is pale yellow, the seams of the ventral scutes with black borders. The head and neck are smaller, more slender, and shorter than they are in other chelodinas. They are grayish brown in color and whitish to pale yellow on the underside. The legs are the same color, but are not as robust as in the other species. The toes have well-developed webbing and end in sharp claws.

Up to 22 centimeters (9 inches).

Western Australia.

C. steindachneri lives in a relatively small area but supposedly is abundant there. It is very rare in captivity and the pet trade never imports it. It lives in small ponds and pools and even in water holes. The average temperature in its range is very high; a temperature of 45°C (114°F) certainly is not unusual in the summer. Furthermore, the tremendous heat often dries up the bodies of water completely. That does not bother this species, because it can survive a fairly long time without water by storing water in the bladder. It survives this dry period by digging into the mud and estivating. Accordingly, it requires high temperatures with a large nocturnal temperature drop (a difference of at least 10°C). It feeds on aquatic animals, mollusks, and fish.

This species probably would be difficult to keep in the aquaterrarium, but the experienced hobbyist could manage it, particularly since this snake-neck is of a reasonable size.

Chelodina reimanni

[The poorly known *Chelodina reimanni*, described only in 1990, usually is considered a full species. It is known from southeastern Irian Jaya, New Guinea.]

CHELUS
Matamatas

Chelus fimbriatus
Matamata

The relatively flat, dark brown carapace has pyramidal vertebral and costal scutes with the points facing to the rear. They have the effect of three humped longitudinal keels. The individual scutes have radiating grooves. The leading marginal scutes are slightly curved upward. The yellowish to brownish plastron is comparatively small and has a dark radiating pattern on the scutes. The brownish head is completely flat on top and because of the horizontal folds of skin on the sides of the head looks triangular. At its tip there is a thin, snorkel-like snout. The tiny, forward-placed eyes are barely visible; their size is completely out of proportion to the entire body size. On the brownish neck and the underside of the head there is a fringe-like fold of skin that

gives the turtle a grotesque appearance. The head and neck are nearly as long as the carapace. The brown legs are thick and the toes are webbed. The front legs have five sturdy, sharp claws and the hind legs have four. Juveniles have a pale reddish brown carapace, and the head, legs, and plastron also are reddish. They also have a pattern of dark stripes.

Up to 40 centimeters (16 inches).

Northern and central South America, from Venezuela and the Guianas to southern Brazil.

This bizarre turtle lives in lakes, ponds, and slow-flowing bodies of water with a muddy bottom. It stays on the bottom, hidden in the mud. Because the lobes of skin erase all the outlines, the turtle is practically invisible. When a fish swims by, the turtle opens its very large mouth with a sudden movement, creating a vortex that pulls the fish into the mouth. Then the turtle closes its mouth and swallows the fish whole. The silvery scales of the fish appear to trigger this "suction snapping." The turtles have swallowed floating mercury thermometers but never those with red ethyl alcohol.

I disagree with the claim reported widely in the literature that the Matamata takes only live fish. My specimens took both live and dead fish as well as strips of beef heart and large earthworms without further ceremony.

This is a very quiet charge, and we should not expect much activity from it. Turtles that have eaten their fill (a 30-centimeter, 12-inch, specimen easily eats five or six fish each 8 to 10 centimeters, 3 to 4 inches, long one after another) rest for several days, if not a week.

Keep the Matamata only with others of its kind. At most keep it with very peaceful, quiet, and likewise crepuscular turtle species. These rather large turtles need an aquaterrarium of appropriate dimensions and with an aquatic section covering about 80 percent of the floor. Cover the bottom of the aquatic section with fine sand. For the transition to the terrestrial section, use decorative cork or resinous bog roots to prevent injury to the turtles. Do not plant the terrestrial section or put the plants out of the turtles' reach. An average temperature of 23°C (73°F) is adequate. It is claimed that the Matamata continues to feed and digest even at 17°C (63°F). This should not be the rule, of course, but I have noticed repeatedly that many hobbyists keep their turtles too warm. This only serves to coddle them unnecessarily. In my experience there are very few species that truly require high temperatures. All in all, the Matamata, apart from its size, does well in captivity and is a commendable charge. The turtle has bred regularly in captivity.

ELSEYA
Australian Snapping Turtles

Elseya dentata
Northern Australian Snapping Turtle

The flat, dark brown to nearly black carapace is strongly serrated on the trailing edge. In juveniles, the last third of each vertebral and costal scute has a dark or black spot on a brown or olive carapace; the spot disappears completely with age. The plastron normally is yellowish, although it is not unusual for parts of the plastron or even all of it to be black. A plate covers the top of the head; the snout protrudes conspicuously. Small round tubercles, which are significantly larger in the nape region, cover the neck and there is a large barbel on the chin. The legs are dark brown; the toes end in sharp claws and have well-developed webbing.

Commonly up to 30 centimeters (12 inches).

Northern and northeastern Australia.

E. dentata lives in rivers that enter into the ocean, and some specimens survive in brackish water in the river mouths. The name snapping turtle for these side-necks is deserved because they bite immediately when given the opportunity. Supposedly this species once bit off a child's finger.

Its appearance varies so much that some authorities believe that several valid subspecies exist. Females grow significantly larger than males. Imports of E. dentata are extremely rare, but it does well in captivity. I highly recommend keeping the turtle outdoors during the warm season. The only known captive breedings are from Australia. The eggs, with dimensions of 5.6 X 3.1 centimeters (about 2 x 1 inches), are very large in proportion to the length of the carapace (average length 27 centimeters, 11 inches).

Cann reports that in his collection he once had a specimen collected from the brackish water of the Raglan River. It had a carapace length of 36.5 centimeters (14.5 inches) and a width of 35.5 centimeters (14 inches). It took various aquatic plants and fruit that had fallen into the water, but also readily took any sort of animal food.

Elseya latisternum
Serrated Snapping Turtle

The carapace is bright orange to brown with dark blotches on the scutes. Its trailing edge is distinctly serrated. Juveniles have a distinct longitudinal keel that disappears with age. The plastron is yellowish and the scutes have dark borders. The head is brownish orange on the upper side, otherwise brownish or olive and the relatively short neck is the same color. Erect, pointed tubercles thickly cover the upper side of the neck. The legs are brown. The toes have sharp claws and well-developed webbing.

Up to 28 centimeters (11 inches).

Coastal Queensland and northern New South Wales, Australia.

This species lives in lakes, streams, and marshes as well as lagoons to an altitude of as much as 1000 meters. It is not fussy in the least about diet and takes all offered animal foods, but supposedly also takes vegetable foods. It is an extremely hardy terrarium charge. Females lay their clutch of 9 to 17 eggs in the months of September and October. I have no information about the incubation period. As I can report from my own experience, males are quite quarrelsome toward one another, but are peaceful toward other species. I unfortunately have no females, so I have nothing to report about behavior between the sexes.

Elseya novaeguineae
New Guinea Snapping Turtle

Juveniles have a flat brown to light brown carapace with a distinct longitudinal keel. Each vertebral and costal scute has a black blotch. In adults the carapace usually turns dark brown to nearly black so the black blotches are nearly invisible. In adults the keel is indistinct or no longer visible at all. The plastron is yellowish to reddish and unmarked. The head and neck are dark gray above and whitish below. In addition,

top: *Chelus fimbriatus.* Juvenile Matamata. Before deciding to care for this species, keep in mind that it can grow to a length of 16 inches.
bottom: *Chelus fimbriatus.* Plastron of the juveniles. The red coloration later disappears completely, as the photograph of the adult on the following page shows. Both photos by R. Müller.

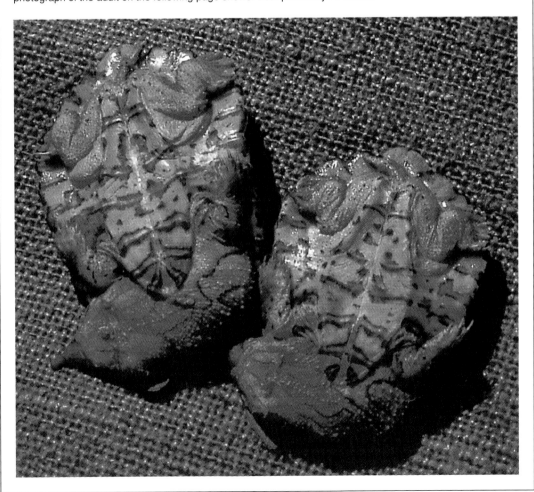

top: A fully grown specimen of *Chelus fimbriatus*. Woe to the fish that gets too close to this lurking turtle! Like a flash, it falls prey to the "suction snapper." Photo by H. G. Zimpel.
bottom: *Elseya novaeguineae*, the New Guinea Snapping Turtle. These are extremely shy turtles, even after years in captivity. They are not prone to biting. Photo by G. Müller

there is a dark plate on top of the head. Two barbels are present on the underside of the head. The legs are dark gray, the toes fully webbed and ending in sharp claws.

Up to 22 centimeters (9 inches).

The whole island of New Guinea.

E. novaeguineae lives in lakes, ponds, and pools with abundant vegetation. It is very shy and likes to hide. When it basks together with emyduras and chelodinas, it is always the first one to plunge into the water at the slightest sign of danger. It is strictly carnivorous. My specimens have never taken any plants, not even banana.

I own a pair of this species. For the last four years my female regularly has laid seven to nine eggs at intervals of three to four weeks five or six times a year. I leave the eggs in the ground and protect them with wire mesh. The incubation period is about 75 days, and the hatching rate is 95 percent. The rearing of the young is without problems. They eat all sorts of animal foods but ignore plants. The hatchlings are significantly larger than, for example, young *Emydura albertisi*. The turtles never lose their strong flight reaction in captivity. Contrary to other reports, my two specimens do not bite at all. The male does not even bite during courtship and copulation. On the other hand, hatchlings often bite turtles of their own or other species if they do not have a roomy tank with many hiding places for rearing. In any case, they are very commendable charges for the terrarium, but the pet trade seldom offers them.

EMYDURA
Short-necked Turtles

Emydura albertisi
Red-banded Short-necked Turtle

The dark brown to black carapace is flat and not serrated. In freshly hatched specimens it usually is entirely black except for a reddish to red band on the outermost margin. The plastron including the bridge is red in babies with a gray blotch in the center. In half-grown specimens and adult females it becomes paler and turns reddish yellow or pale orange. In males it turns bright red just before the onset of sexual maturity and the outer margin of the carapace also

turns red again. Only in the middle does the plastron become somewhat paler. Sometimes an irregular band along the bridge remains light gray with a few red speckles. A triangle on top of the head is black. Small, pointed tubercles thickly cover the adjoining dorsal side of the black neck. Beginning behind the temple and extending forward through the eye to the tip of the snout are two wide yellow stripes. The chin has an approximately horseshoe-shaped bright red band and the two small barbels usually are reddish or red. The underside of the neck and the legs as well as the tail are dark gray with scattered red markings (spots or streaks, sometimes faint, sometimes prominent). The robust legs are fully webbed and have extremely sturdy and sharp claws.

Up to 24 centimeters (9.5 inches).

New Guinea.

In its homeland it lives in lakes, ponds, and other bodies of water. It is a very active turtle that never loses a certain shyness in captivity. The males and juveniles are particularly handsome with their black-red-yellow markings. It is one of the best suited turtles for keeping in captivity. Also, it is not at all fussy in its dietary requirements, but the assertion in the literature that emyduras are fond of vegetable foods is, in my opinion, incorrect. All species of *Emydura* that I have kept and fed were strictly carnivorous, disregarding the very rare cases when they took the odd piece of banana out of jealousy. I never saw them take lettuce, dandelion, and the like. My *E. albertisi*, as well as the other species, live on dried shrimp as the basic food because it also supplies roughage. Once a week they also receive beef heart or fish and whatever else is on hand, such as slugs and small snails, earthworms, and prepared fish food.

The required temperature is not too high; about 22°C (72°F) is sufficient. This turtle is therefore a very good candidate for keeping in the outdoor pond from May to September or early October, depending on the fall weather. When the daytime temperature in the pond falls below 20°C (68°F) despite supplemental heating and the water temperature at night falls to only 17°C (63°F), it is time to put the turtles indoors in the large aquaterrarium.

For many years I have obtained offspring regularly from my sexually mature females. They start their laying activity in October (often a few days after I bring them inside) and lay the last eggs in late February or early March. Each female normally lays five clutches. They do not always use the same site. This behavior affects the incubation period, because the temperature of the substrate of the terrestrial section is highly variable (25 to 31°C, 77 to 88°F). Therefore, the incubation period of the individual clutches varies from 49 to 78 days. The average size of the eggs is 32 X 20 millimeters (1.3 X 0.8 inch). The number of young varies from six to ten per clutch. The young have an average weight of 4 grams (0.14 ounce) at birth, an average carapace length of 28 millimeters (1.1 inches), and an average carapace width of 24 millimeters (almost 1 inch). Only a few specimens have a yolk sac the size of a lentil. It disappears after a week at the latest and usually after two to three days. The normal hatching rate is from 95 to 100 percent. I leave the eggs in the substrate (mixture of sand, peat, and soil) and protect them with wire mesh. The hatching rates are significantly higher in this case than when I transfer them to an incubator. I feed the young turtles a varied diet of midge larvae, meadow plankton, prepared pellets, shaved beef heart, and finely pulverized shrimp. They usually take their first food after three to four days.

After the turtles hatch, I put them in a small tank with about 6 centimeters (2.4 inches) of water for about a half hour and clean them. Then I move them to a fairly large aquarium (with a capacity of about 100 liters, 26 gallons) with a cork island and a water level of about 30 centimeters (12 inches). The water's depth forces the juveniles to swim a great deal, which promotes muscular development, stimulates the appetite, and contributes to good health and normal growth. This is no problem for any juvenile aquatic turtles with webbed toes. I disagree with the rule of thumb often recommended for young turtles, that the water depth should equal the width of the carapace. No small turtle has ever drowned in my aquarium because of the water depth. In isolated cases, turtles have gotten stuck under water and could not come to the surface for air.

This experience teaches us that we should avoid such sources of danger in the furnishing of the aquarium.

Until a carapace length of 8 to 10 centimeters (about 3 to 4 inches), the juveniles grow very fast, but growth slows after that. The turtles are sexually mature in six to seven years. In my opinion, seasonal outdoor keeping accelerates the maturation process. I have discussed the species *E. albertisi* in such detail because the same keeping and rearing conditions apply to all other species of the genus *Emydura*. By the way, in my opinion the name *Emydura australis subglobosa* is unjustified and incorrect for this turtle. [Though the taxonomy of the short-necked turtles is greatly confused, it would appear that the proper name for *E. albertisi* is *E. subglobosa*, an older name.]

Emydura australis
Australian Big-headed Turtle

In juveniles the carapace is light brown with a longitudinal keel. The trailing edge is slightly serrated. In adults the longitudinal keel and serrations disappear and the color turns dark brown to olive. The plastron is light gray with a reddish suffusion. The dark brown head has a reddish yellow temporal stripe; the tip of the snout also is reddish yellow. Parallel to the temporal stripe, an indistinct reddish yellow stripe extends back from the corner of the mouth. On the brown neck there is a pattern of red, slightly raised spots. The legs are brownish with webbed toes and sharp claws.

Up to 25 centimeters (10 inches).

Northern Australia (northern Queensland to Northern Territory).

This species lives in slow-flowing bodies rivers, ponds, and lakes. In behavior and habits it largely corresponds to the previously discussed *E. albertisi*. Importations have been virtually nonexistent so far, and few reports exist on terrarium keeping and breeding, but there is no reason to suspect that it would differ from *E. albertisi*. It requires an average temperature of about 24°C (75°F). The species is reported to be highly variable in coloration and markings, and several Australian workers feel that a revision and possible division into subspecies would be welcome.

Emydura albertisi, Red-banded Short-necked Turtle. Youngster about one week old. Captive breedings of this species are relatively common today. It is a good candidate for the terrarium. Photo by B. Kahl.

Emydura branderhorsti
Green Short-necked Turtle

Up to 38 centimeters (15 inches).

Southern New Guinea. This turtle is supposedly identical with *Elseya novaeguineae*, but I disagree. I have kept and bred many *Elseya novaeguineae*, but not one specimen was similar to the *branderhorsti* I've seen. Moreover, *E. novaeguineae* never reaches the size of *branderhorsti*.

Emydura kreffti
Krefft's River Turtle

This turtle closely resembles *Emydura albertisi*, but it lacks any red coloration. The carapace is flat and olive to dark brown or even black. The plastron is yellowish. The head is dark brown. Beginning behind the eye, a wide yellow or pale grayish green temporal stripe extends back to the ear. The ventral half of the head, including the throat, is light in color. The nape has numerous small circular tubercles. The legs are dark brown and quite robust, with well-developed webbing between the toes. The claws are very sharp.

Up to 25 centimeters (10 inches).

Northeastern coastal rivers of Australia.

It lives in approximately the same biotope as the previously discussed species. Formerly it was a regular import, but it is fairly rare in captivity today. The turtle has bred in captivity, but little detailed information exists. It usually is very hardy and does not require particularly high temperatures, thus it is a good candidate for outdoor keeping during the warm season. My specimens are almost exclusively carnivorous, although they cannot resist bananas, and they also are fond of dry dog food. Of course, they also take fish and dried shrimp. Unfortunately, my turtles have not bred so far. *E. kreffti* is a very commendable charge.

top: *Emydura albertisi*. This is a male Red-banded Short-necked Turtle captive-bred by the author. Though common in the European hobby, it is rarely seen in the U. S.
bottom: Plastron of the same specimen. Note the rich red color of the plastron. Normally only the males retain the color or develop the color again at the onset of sexual maturity. Females become paler with increasing age. Both photos by G. Müller.

Emydura macquarri
Murray River Turtle

Emydura macquarri macquarri
Murray River Turtle

The flat brown to olive-brown carapace is not serrated. The plastron is pale yellow with several large gray-green zones. The head, neck, and legs are uniformly slate gray above, uniformly light gray below. On the side of the head, extending back from the corner of the mouth and ending in the middle of the stretched-out neck, there is a yellow to white stripe. It is wide in front, but gradually becomes narrower, and finally disappears. The legs are robust, with extensive webbing and large, sharp claws. Juveniles have a light olive to light brown carapace with a distinct longitudinal keel. The turtles normally have five (one of my juveniles had six) slightly humped vertebral scutes. In the middle of the trailing edge of each costal scute there is a short, backward-pointing spine. The rear half of the carapace is slightly serrated. All of these juvenile characters disappear completely with age.

Up to 27 centimeters.

New Guinea and Australia.

In its homeland it lives mainly in the smaller, shallower river systems. It has the same dietary, temperature, and other requirements as *Emydura albertisi.* I have kept the two species together for many years without problems, since both are very peaceful. I never have observed fighting among the emyduras. Only at feeding time will one turtle occasionally seizes a neighbor's food while snapping at a piece of food. In any case, this never leads to injury. Also, this never leads to fighting, as would be the case with other genera, such as *Kinosternon* or even *Chelydra.*

I have bred *E. macquarri macquarri* regularly. The female usually lays two clutches a year at an interval of several weeks. The clutch consists of six to ten eggs that require 55 to 60 days on average to hatch. Rearing is unproblematic and is the same as was described with *E. albertisi.* The juveniles grow very slowly.

Unfortunately, this Australian species appears only rarely in the pet trade and at a correspondingly high price. It has been called a "wonder of hardiness" because it continues to feed at 7°C (45°F). I have not tested this, although my specimens were completely unaffected by falls in temperature that caused the temperature of the pond (despite supplemental heating) to drop to 17°C (63°F). Even after many years in captivity, *E. m. macquarri* never completely loses a certain shyness, and as soon as I put it in the outdoor pond in the spring it behaves like a wild animal again.

Emydura macquarri signata
Brisbane Short-necked Turtle

Up to 25 centimeters (10 inches).

Eastern Australia in southeastern Queensland and New South Wales along the coast.[This form often is considered a full species because its distribution does not overlap that of *E. m. macquarri.*]

Emydura subglobosa
Round Short-necked Turtle

Up to 26 centimeters (10.5 inches).

New Guinea. A separate description is unnecessary because I think this species is identical to *Emydura albertisi.* When you compare descriptions given by Cann in his book *Tortoises of Australia,* there is absolutely no difference between it and *E. albertisi.* The color photographs strengthen this thesis. A comparison of the illustrations of both species in Wermuth & Mertens reveals that the only difference is that the nuchal scute is slightly longer in *E. albertisi.* Such small differences often are present in turtles of the same species. [Most workers agree that the names *subglobosa* and *albertisi* refer to the same species. However, *subglobosa* was described by Krefft in 1876 and *albertisi* by Boulenger in 1888, so the name *subglobosa* should be used.]

In closing, I would like to make the following general observation about *Emydura*: To my knowledge this genus has more undetermined species than any other. When you read in Cann how he designates all of these "unknowns" with *Emydura* species number 1 to 4 or simply lists them as unknown species, it seems to be urgently necessary to perform a general revision here. Some of these species probably are just hybrids, but surely not all.

HYDROMEDUSA
South American Snake-necked Turtles

Hydromedusa maximiliani
Brazilian Snake-necked Turtle

The flat carapace is smooth and dark brown in adults. In juveniles it is more yellowish, with erect dorsal scutes and a keel along the midline. The color of the plastron supposedly depends on the growth of algae and varies from yellowish white through yellow-brown to dark brown. The color is darker where the alga is growing. The head, neck, and legs are dark gray (more light gray in juveniles) above, whereas the underside of the extremities is whitish. Very conspicuous folds of skin are present at the corner of the mouth.

Between the four toes on each of the front and hind legs there is well-developed webbing. The claws are sharp. The shape of the carapace, and particularly that of the plastron, distinguishes the sexes. Females always have a narrower plastron than males; this character is less distinct with the upper carapace.

Up to 22 centimeters (9 inches).
Southeastern Brazil.

This snake-neck usually lives in large and small bodies of water in forests near the coast. It is almost strictly aquatic and feeds on fish, crustaceans, and aquatic insects, taking scarcely any vegetable foods. It is not hard to keep in the aquaterrarium with a small terrestrial section. Importations, however, are rare. *H. maximiliani* is chiefly crepuscular and nocturnal and hides during the day. Therefore, the aquaterrarium should have a hiding place in the form of an easily accessible underwater cave without any angles, corners, or other projections. I once lost a turtle because it could not find its way out of the cave and drowned the first night. So, in this case "easily accessible" means "easily left" as well as "easily entered." The peacefulness is highly variable. Apparently some specimens are very aggressive and others are completely peaceful. In any case, with this species do not keep individuals of very different sizes together.

I have no information on captive breeding, but it surely must be in the realm of possibility.

Hydromedusa maximiliana, Brazilian Snake-necked Turtle. Illustration: E. Bobbe in Wermuth/Mertens: Schildkröten — Krokodile — Brückenechsen.

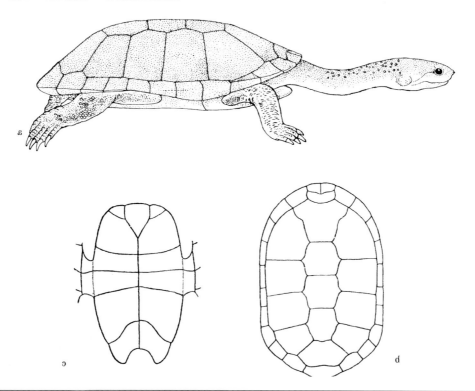

top: *Emydura branderhorsti*, the Green Short-necked Turtle, head portrait.
bottom: *Emydura branderhorsti.* Fully grown specimen. There is virtually no information about this rare turtle. Probably best kept like *E. albertisi.* Both photos by G. Müller.

It needs a high average temperature of about 26°C (79°F).

Hydromedusa tectifera
Argentine Snake-necked Turtle

The dark brown carapace is flat in adults, but in juveniles the carapace has strongly raised scutes forming a longitudinal keel along the vertebral scutes and the costal scutes end in weak spines. The turtles lose all these characters with increasing age, so that in adults the dorsal scutes are smooth and the longitudinal keel disappears. This species also has a highly variable plastron coloration that varies from reddish brown with irregular dark brown blotches to yellowish with brown to light brown blotches. Some specimens even have a yellowish plastron that is darker toward the midline and nearly blackish brown in the middle. Females have a conspicuously narrower plastron than do the males. The head and legs are dark gray or gray-brown. On each side of the head and neck there is a light yellow to orange or white longitudinal band. It extends back horizontally from the tip of the snout and sometimes also has dark borders. Medium-sized tubercles cover the neck. The underside of the extremities is whitish. The legs are relatively short. The toes have well-developed webbing and sharp claws on the tips.

Up to 25 centimeters (10 inches).

Southeastern South America, in particular Paraguay, southeastern Brazil, Uruguay, and Argentina.

This snake-neck usually lives in fairly shallow pools, ponds, or lakes within marshy regions and avoids deeper water. Unlike *H. maximiliani*, it likes to bask occasionally. It requires a temperature of about 25°C (77°F). Its diet is largely the same as that of *H. maximiliani*. My specimens are strictly carnivorous. Even after a fairly long time in captivity, they never lost their shyness. Unfortunately, they were rather prone to bite, and since I keep many species as well as smaller specimens together, this caused problems, so I traded them for another species. Other hobbyists, on the other hand, have told me that their *H. tectifera* were completely peaceful.

This species is crepuscular or nocturnal and therefore spends the day in hiding. I have no information on captive breeding.

PHRYNOPS
Toad-headed Turtles

I must mention beforehand that the genus *Phrynops* today contains the formerly independent genera *Mesoclemmys* and *Batrachemys*, which are treated as subgenera.

Phrynops geoffroanus
Geoffroy's Side-necked Turtle

Phrynops geoffroanus geoffroanus

The flat, dark brown carapace has a thin orange-yellow stripe on the outermost margin. In juveniles, the keeled carapace is black and has gray-green speckling and a reddish mark on the outermost edge of each marginal scute. In adults, the plastron is reddish yellow with irregular black spots. In babies, on the other hand, it is red with many sharply defined black streaks and squiggles. The relatively flat head in juveniles is yellowish on the sides and below and has a pattern of black lines and blotches. The conspicuous pattern and coloration, however, disappear with age. The head, neck, and legs turn uniformly blackish brown to dark olive. Only the broad yellow-white stripe, which begins on the snout, becomes narrower under the eyes, and then becomes wider again before ending at the eardrum, is still present. The legs are robust. Webbing is present.

Up to 35 centimeters (14 inches).

Central and southern South America.

It usually lives in fairly large, often fast-flowing bodies of water. In my experience it is strictly carnivorous. My specimens never took any vegetable food, even slices of banana, which often is the only plant many other carnivorous species take. They usually hide during the day and—except when there is something to eat—become active only in the evening.

I keep this species only in pairs of the same size or one male with two females. My specimens were very prone to bite and were dangerous for smaller turtles, particularly at feeding time. If a smaller turtle seizes a piece of food and the *Phrynops* snaps at it, there is the danger that the *Phrynops* could grab the other turtle's head by accident, causing a serious injury.

One of my females laid eggs that were precisely spherical and the size of ping-pong balls.

top: The author reared this female Murray River Turtle, *Emydura macquarri*, from the time it was small and obtained offspring from it.
bottom: Breeding pair of *Emydura macquarri*, male on the left and female on the right. This species can develop unbelievable climbing skills. Both photos by G. Müller

Phrynops rufipes, the Red Side-necked Turtle. It is a real treasure among turtles, but is also a delicate charge in captivity. Photo by H. G. Zimpel.

Unfortunately, they were infertile, the male apparently being still too young. I observed attempts at copulation, but no true union. Because of their tendency to bite, I subsequently gave the turtles away. On the other hand, other hobbyists have told me that their *Phrynops* did not bite at all. Apparently my turtles had individual sympathies and antipathies. I have observed similar behavior in other species that were aggressive only toward conspecifics or certain other species.

It requires an average temperature of 25°C (77°F). I recommend keeping them outdoors in summer. This species has been bred in captivity.

Phrynops geoffroanus tuberosus

This subspecies differs from the nominate form in having three longitudinal keels and long, spiny tubercles on the neck and the hind part of the trunk, which give the subspecies its name. Otherwise it has the same habits and keeping requirements as described for the nominate form. [Some workers consider this to be a synonym of *geoffroanus*.]

Up to 25 centimeters (10 inches).

Northeastern and eastern South America (Guyana and eastern Brazil, south to Bahia).

Phrynops (Mesoclemmys) gibbus
Gibba Turtle

The flat carapace is dark brown to black. It has a conspicuous longitudinal keel that very old specimens no longer exhibit. The plastron is dark brown to blackish with a yellowish border. The trailing edge has a deep notch. The gular scutes are yellowish, the intergular scute dark. The bridge and the underside of the marginal scutes also are yellowish. The short, broad head has yellow and brown mottling above to the level of the margin of the lower jaw, with the brown color predominating. The throat is yellow with a few scattered small dark blotches and two chin barbels in front. On the dark gray neck there are numerous small tubercles above and on the side. The tail is very short. The legs are dark gray to black above, light in color below. The legs are robust, with well-developed webbing between the toes and sturdy, sharp claws.

Up to 23 centimeters (9 inches).

Northeastern and central South America, Trinidad and the Guianas through northern and central Brazil.

It lives in muddy pools and ponds as well as in small forest streams, black-water streams, and rivers with a muddy bottom. It is strictly aquatic and leaves the water only to lay its eggs. During the day it usually hides, becoming active particularly at twilight and at night. It reaches the pet trade rarely, so we know little about its behavior in captivity. A recently collected female laid eggs in captivity, but this was not a true captive breeding because fertilization had occurred in the wild. In another case, eggs from a wild turtle hatched in captivity.

I kept a female that was simple to keep. It was strictly carnivorous, very shy, and virtually never made an appearance in the outdoor pond. Because I was unable to find a mate, I traded the turtle to another hobbyist.

Phrynops hilari
Hilaire's Side-necked Turtle

The flat carapace is dark gray to black. Only juveniles have a longitudinal keel. The outermost margin of the carapace has a narrow, light yellowish red border. The plastron, including the bridge and the underside of the marginal scutes, is reddish yellow with numerous irregular, medium-sized black blotches. The head, neck, and legs are dark gray only above, the undersides and the soft parts whitish with numerous scattered large and small blotches and streaks. The underside of the very broad head has two fairly large, light-colored barbels. A narrow deep black band extends from the tip of the snout horizontally through the eye along the neck and separates the dark dorsal surface from the

pale ventral surface. The legs are robust, the toes fully webbed and with sturdy claws.

Up to 40 centimeters (16 inches).

Southeastern South America, southernmost Brazil to Uruguay and Argentina.

Its temperature, dietary, and keeping requirements are the same as those of *P. geoffroanus*. It is a rather rare turtle in the pet trade. Many specimens are prone to bite, which the hobbyist must consider when keeping it with other turtles. I have no information on captive breeding, but it must have succeeded by now. It needs a spacious installation, however, because it is the largest of the *Phrynops* species.

Phrynops hogei
Hoge's Side-necked Turtle

The narrow, low, and unkeeled carapace is dark brown and oval in outline. The first vertebral scute is very long, the second nearly a fourth shorter and arched slightly to the inside. The plastron is yellowish beige with dark pigment along the sides, the bridge, and the underside of the marginal scutes. It is wider in front than in back. The medial seam between the abdominal scutes is twice as long as the seam between the humeral and anal scutes. The head is small in comparison to other *Phrynops* species. The skin is smooth and scales are present only in the temporal region. The dorsal side of the head is approximately triangular with a rather pointed snout. The barbels on the chin are very small.

Up to 35 centimeters (14 inches).

Southern Brazil.

Phrynops hogei still is largely unknown. Mertens first described it in 1967, when he obtained a 34-centimeter (14.5 inches) female supposedly from the Rio Pequena near Sao Paulo. Little has been reported on its natural history, and it apparently does not occur at the reported type locality.

Phrynops (Batrachemys) nasutus
Common Toad-headed Turtle

Phrynops (Batrachemys) nasutus nasutus
Guianan Toad-headed Turtle

The carapace is flat, unkeeled, and dark brown to grayish brown. It is considerably wider behind than in front. Only younger specimens have radiating grooves on the dorsal scutes. The plastron and bridge are yellowish with a strong, completely random black pigmentation. The trailing edge has a blunt notch. The dorsal surfaces of the pointed head and the neck are dark gray. Small tubercles cover the neck. The head itself is conspicuously wide. The tip of the snout is light in color, with dark dots above the very broad mouth. On each side of the head, from the lower jaw up to and including the eardrums, the color turns a paler grayish yellow. The chin has two barbels. The robust legs are gray and slightly lighter in color below. The toes have full webbing and end in sturdy, sharp claws.

Up to 30 centimeters (12 inches) but generally remains smaller.

The subspecies *P. nasutus dahli* differs from the nominate form mainly in that the entire lower temporal region is a contrasting lighter color, the plastron is narrower, and the notch behind the anal scutes is much more sharply angled.

P. nasutus wermuthi differs from the other two subspecies in that it has a broad yellow stripe extending back from the mouth to behind the ear. On the forehead there is a dark marking in the form of two successive V's open to the rear. The soft parts also are yellow, and all other body parts, including the head, neck, carapace, plastron, and legs, are uniformly blackish brown to black.

The nominate subspecies is restricted to the eastern Guianas and possibly adjacent Brazil.

It lives in lakes, ponds, and pools as well as slow-flowing bodies of water. It almost never goes on land. In my outdoor pond I have never seen this species outside the water, even to sun itself. It hides during the day—except at feeding time—and is mainly active at dusk. My turtles never bit; to the contrary, other, often much smaller, species were more likely to intimidate them at feeding time. Other hobbyists, on the other hand, have reported that their specimens were prone to bite. My specimens have never taken any vegetable foods, but they are fond of all animal foods, including earthworms, insects, snails, dried shrimp, beef heart or liver, fish of all kinds, and so forth. I am unaware of any reports of breeding with this species. It requires a temperature of about 24°C (75°F) but continued to feed voraciously even when the temperature in

the outdoor pond dropped to only 18°C (65°F) because of a fall in temperature in the summer. On the basis of my experiences, I must say that this is a very persistent, relatively robust, and quite undemanding turtle that I recommend for the terrarium.

Phrynops (Batrachemys) nasutus dahli
Colombian Toad-headed Turtle

Up to 30 centimeters (12 inches), but generally smaller.

Known only from a few localities in Colombia.

Phrynops (Batrachemys) nasutus wermuthi
Amazon Toad-headed Turtle

Up to 30 centimeters (12 inches), but generally smaller.

Northern central South America in the Amazon and Orinoco basins.

[The three subspecies of *P. nasutus* usually are treated today as three distinct species with non-overlapping (or nearly so) ranges. Additionally, the name *wermuthi* has been replaced by the older *raniceps* for the Amazon Toad-head.]

Phrynops rufipes
Red Side-necked Turtle

The keeled, dark brown carapace is not completely flat. The plastron is uniformly yellow and unmarked. It has a sharply angled notch in the trailing edge. The dorsal surfaces of the head, neck, and legs are grayish brown and unmarked. The underside of all extremities and the soft parts is reddish. The legs are robust, with well-developed webbing between the toes. They end in sharp claws.

Up to 22 centimeters (9 inches).

Central South America in the central and western Amazon basin.

It lives almost exclusively in black water (small rivers or streams), is strictly nocturnal, and preys on anything it can catch, whether fish, amphibians, or insects. It is hard to keep in captivity; in most cases the hobbyist cannot obtain black water of the right quality, which is essential for success. Furthermore, adults are aggressive toward one another, which leads to constant fighting. Keep the turtles singly except

The Amazon Toad-headed Turtle, *Phrynops* (*Batrachemys*) *nasutus wermuthi*, occasionally is found in pet stores. They are not difficult to breed; the females lay about a dozen eggs. Photo by K. H. Switak.

for breeding, when you can keep them in pairs. In its native range, the native peoples are threatening the survival of this species, because it is an important source of protein for them. Therefore, it would be desirable to breed the specimens currently in captivity. I ask all other hobbyists who keep this species to share their experiences with other hobbyists. If necessary, I also ask that they trade or give away their specimens in the interests of breeding.

Phrynops (Batrachemys) tuberculatus
Tuberculate Toad-headed Turtle

Phrynops tuberculatus tuberculatus

The flat, blackish carapace is oval in outline. The relatively large plastron is grayish yellow and more or less strongly blotched with brown. The head, neck, and legs are gray above, yellowish below, with scattered gray blotches. Conspicuous long, spiny tubercles, which give the turtle its name, are present on the neck and the rear of the body. The legs are robust, with pronounced webbing and sharp claws.

Up to 25 centimeters (10 inches).

Eastern Brazil.

This predominantly aquatic species lives in lakes and ponds as well as slow-flowing bodies of water. It is active only at dusk and at night and avoids light, particularly sunlight. It likes to hide during the day, so install easily accessible, dark hiding places in the aquatic section. The diet consists of fish, carrion, insects, earthworms, and snails. *P. tuberculatus* is extremely aggressive. In the aquaterrarium (one-fifth land, four-fifths water) it is advisable to keep it only with specimens of the same size in large tanks with numerous hiding places. It needs a very high average temperature of 26°C (79°F). For this reason outdoor keeping would be possible only in the warmest season. In any case, it almost never turns up in the pet trade.

Phrynops tuberculatus vanderhaegei

Unlike the nominate form, this turtle lacks tubercles on the neck and the carapace is brownish, not black. It is even rarer, however, than the nominate form. Captive keeping is extremely rare or nonexistent. [Recently many authorities

has suggested that this is a full species, *P. vanderhaegei*.]

Up to 25 centimeters (10 inches).

Southern Brazil, Paraguay, and northern Argentina.

Phrynops williamsi
William's Side-necked Turtle

Southern Brazil to Argentina.

Phrynops (Batrachemys) zuliae
Zulia Toad-headed Turtle

It lives primarily in marshy areas and digs itself into the mud during droughts. It may be fairly terrestrial, but more detailed information is lacking. A freshly caught specimen excreted the remnants of a waterbug, but, like all *Phrynops* species, it appears to take a varied diet.

These turtles are extremely rare. At present, mostly a few zoos are keeping some specimens.

To about 28 centimeters (11 inches).

The southwestern Maracaibo basin of Venezuela.

PLATEMYS
Twist-necked Turtles

[Recently this genus has been split, with *Acanthochelys* recognized for four species: *pallidipectoris, spixi, radiolata,* and *macrocephala*.]

Platemys [Acantochelys] macrocephala
Pantanal Swamp Turtle

Bolivia and southwestern Brazil.

Platemys [Acanthochelys] pallidipectoris
Chaco Side-necked Turtle

The flat and broad carapace is olive-brown and has black seams between the scutes. There is a faint dorsal furrow; longitudinal keels are not present. The dark color of the plastron has scattered pale patches. The two anal scutes have a slightly curved, but not tapered, trailing edge. The intergular scute is displaced forward so that, in contrast to all other species, the gular scutes meet in the middle. The head, neck, and the dorsal surfaces of the legs are grayish brown, the covered soft parts whitish. The dorsal side of the neck and the hind part of the thigh have numerous humped tubercles. Two of the tubercles on the thigh are significantly larger, and one projects forward as a long spine. The legs have heavy scales, webbing, and short claws.

Up to 20 centimeters (8 inches).

Argentina and Paraguay.

This side-neck lives primarily in shallow bodies of water, which it leaves only occasionally to make short excursions on land. Sometimes it does not feel at home in the community tank and hides on land. When put with quieter tankmates in another tank it may stay in the water and spend only the night on land. It requires an average temperature of 22°C (72°F). Primarily carnivorous and requiring a varied diet, it is rather voracious.

Platemys platycephala
Twist-necked Turtle

The very flat, brown carapace has a black, occasionally cross-shaped, blotch. Between the two longitudinal keels a deep furrow extends from the second to the fourth vertebral scute. The plastron is uniformly black with a yellow border. The bridge has a black longitudinal band and the underside of the marginal scutes is yellow with scattered black blotches. The dorsal side of the head is orange-red to yellow and slightly darker in the middle. The underside is black and sharply defined. The dorsal surface of the neck (which has scattered tubercles) and the very scaly legs are black. The soft parts are light gray to yellow. A conspicuous character on the inside of the lower leg consists of two distinctly enlarged, spur-like scales with yellow tips. The legs are slender, and the well-developed toes have slight webbing and short, blunt claws.

Up to 16 centimeters (6.5 inches).

Central South America from the Guianas to Peru and southern Brazil.

It prefers shallow bodies of water but is a fairly good swimmer. In my experience it is strictly carnivorous, taking tubifex worms, bloodworms, and small crustaceans as well as finely chopped beef heart, beef liver, fish, and occasionally mealworms. Antibiotics, vitamins, and the like are particularly easy to administer with mealworms. Offer the pre-

pared worm first to the hungry turtle at feeding time. In my experience, the turtle always swallows the mealworm immediately, so I know that the remedy has ended up in the turtle's stomach. (Of course, you can use the same technique with other turtle species.) *P. platycephala* often lives aquatically and usually leaves the water during showers or soon after it stops raining. Sometimes it also stays for days in the moist leaves of the riparian region, where it lays its eggs. My specimens also like to go on land after the daily spraying. They may take their food there but primarily feed in the water.

Females lay their eggs in any season. The female lays four to six eggs, often rather far from the water. It requires an average temperature of about 26°C (79°F). One specimen was kept for more than 30 years. The turtle becomes tame very quickly and after a short acclimation period takes food from the hand. It is doubtless a very good terrarium charge. Recently it has become available in increased numbers, at reasonable prices.

[Two subspecies are recognized by some workers, *P. p. platycephala* from most of the range, and *P. p. melanonota* from the upper Amazon of Peru and Ecuador.]

Platemys [Acanthochelys] radiolata
Radiolated Swamp Turtle

The flat, dark brown carapace is virtually unfurrowed and unkeeled. The vertebral scutes of the carapace have sculpted, radiating lines. The plastron is yellow-brown with a large dark brown blotch on each scute. The head, neck, and legs are black. The tubercles on the neck are blunt. Otherwise, it resembles *P. platycephala*.

Up to 20 centimeters (8 inches).

Coastal southeastern Brazil.

It lives in lakes, ponds, and pools with a muddy bottom. The dietary and temperature requirements are the same as those of the previously described species. Some specimens reportedly were so shy that they fed only in cloudy water and basked only rarely. They were fond of live fish, which they caught with great skill and ate with gurgling noises. It is very uncommon in captivity and the pet trade almost never carries it.

In all other respects it is the same as the previously discussed species.

Platemys [Acanthochelys] spixi
Spiny-necked Turtle

The very flat carapace is blackish brown to black and unmarked and the plastron is completely black. The head and extremities are lead-colored. The common name refers to the numerous large, conical tubercles on the dorsal side of the neck. In other respects it resembles the previously discussed species.

Up to 16 centimeters (6.5 inches).

Northern Argentina and Uruguay to southern Brazil.

This species resembles the other *Platemys* species regarding its habitat as well as the dietary, temperature, and keeping requirements. It is reported to be timid and seldom loses its innate shyness. Swimming is not its strength, so it swims little and instead crawls along the bottom of the aquatic section in search of food. It would doubtless be a keepable if somewhat problematic charge, but the pet trade almost never carries it. Usually, the females at most lay infertile eggs. In my opinion the turtles of the genus *Platemys* are better than their reputation and I do not find them at all boring. They merit more attention.

PSEUDEMYDURA
Western Swamp Turtles

Pseudemydura umbrina
Western Swamp Turtle

The color of the flat and broad carapace varies from yellowish brown to nearly black. The extremely large plastron is yellowish brown with dark-bordered seams. In some specimens there is a black blotch on each ventral scute. The intergular scute is conspicuously large, whereas the gular scutes are very small. The brown head is very broad and flat, the snout quite short and rounded. The sides of the head and the throat are very light in color. On the dorsal side of the gray-brown neck there are numerous large horny tubercles. The chin has two small barbels. The legs are gray-brown to gray-olive. The toes have sharp claws and well-developed webbing.

Up to 15 centimeters (6 inches).

Southwestern Australia near Perth.

This is by far the smallest of all Australian turtles, and it has a very small range. Scientists considered it to be extinct until a boy found it again in 1953. The boy brought his freshly caught turtle, whose short neck attracted his attention, to the West Australian Museum to have the turtle identified. At first the scientists thought that they had a new species, but later they established its true identity. After many difficulties, the government declared the locality (and a second one with a separate population of the turtles) a nature reserve. These two separate regions have a total area of 226 hectares. Today about 200 turtles live there.

The pools the turtles live in usually dry up for six months in the summer. During this time the turtles bury themselves under leaves, twigs, or in holes in the ground and estivate until the pools fill with water again in the winter rainy season. They are strictly carnivorous and must make up for the months of fasting, because they only feed under water. The turtles, of course, grow only when they are actively feeding. They reach sexual maturity very late, at about ten years of age. Females lay their three to five eggs in November or early December and the young turtles hatch in May or June. There is always the danger that they will die in the egg if the dry period lasts longer than six months (in recent years the droughts often have lasted eight or even nine months). Only its extreme toughness has saved this species from extinction so far.

[Two other Australian side-necks, both described rather recently, should be mentioned for completion. The Fitzroy River Turtle, *Rheodytes leukops*, was described in 1980 and is known from a few localities in the Fitzroy River drainage of eastern Queensland. It has large cloacal bursae that allow it to breathe underwater. The Mary River Turtle, *Elusor macrurus*, was described in 1994. It has a dark eye and a vertically compressed, high tail that in the adult male is as long as the head and neck. Neither species is available to hobbyists because they are protected by Australian laws.]

Index

Page numbers in bold represent illustrations.